THE
SYMBOLIST MOVEMENT
IN LITERATURE

THE
SYMBOLIST MOVEMENT
IN LITERATURE

BY

ARTHUR SYMONS

AUTHOR OF

*"Cities of Italy," "Plays, Acting and Music," "The Romantic
Movement in English Literature," "Studies in Seven
Arts," "Colour Studies in Paris," etc.*

REVISED AND ENLARGED EDITION

NEW YORK

E. P. DUTTON & COMPANY

681 FIFTH AVENUE

150528

Printed in the United States of America

CONTENTS

v

THE
SYMBOLIST MOVEMENT
IN LITERATURE

THE SYMBOLIST MOVEMENT

INTRODUCTION

"It is in and through Symbols that man, consciously or unconsciously, lives, works, and has his being: those ages, moreover, are accounted the noblest which can the best recognise symbolical worth, and prize it highest."

CARLYLE

WITHOUT symbolism there can be no literature; indeed, not even language. What are words themselves but symbols, almost as arbitrary as the letters which compose them, mere sounds of the voice to which we have agreed to give certain significations, as we have agreed to translate these sounds by those combinations of letters? Symbolism began with the first words uttered by the first man, as he named every living thing; or before them, in heaven, when God named the world into being. And we see, in these beginnings, precisely what Symbolism in literature really is: a form of expression, at the best but approximate, essentially but arbitrary, until it has obtained the force of a convention, for an unseen reality apprehended by the consciousness. It is sometimes permitted to us to hope that our convention is indeed the reflection rather than merely the sign of that unseen reality. We have done much if we have found a recognisable sign.

"A symbol," says Comte Goblet d'Alviella, in his book on *The Migration of Symbols*, "might be defined as a representation which does not aim at being a reproduction." Originally, as he points out, used by the Greeks to denote "the two halves of the tablet they divided between themselves as a pledge of hospitality," it came to be used of every sign, formula, or rite by which those initiated in any mystery made themselves secretly known to one another. Gradually the word extended its meaning, until it came to denote every conventional representation of idea by form, of the unseen by the visible. "In a Symbol," says Carlyle, "there is concealment and yet revelation: hence, therefore, by Silence and by Speech acting together, comes a double significance." And, in that fine chapter of

Sartor Resartus, he goes further, vindicating for the word its full value: "In the Symbol proper, what we can call a Symbol, there is ever, more or less distinctly and directly, some embodiment and revelation of the Infinite; the Infinite is made to blend itself with the Finite, to stand visible, and as it were, attainable there."

It is in such a sense as this that the word Symbolism has been used to describe a movement which, during the last generation, has profoundly influenced the course of French literature. All such words, used of anything so living, variable, and irresponsible as literature, are, as symbols themselves must so often be, mere compromises, mere indications. Symbolism, as seen in the writers of our day, would have no value if it were not seen also, under one disguise or another, in every great imaginative writer. What distinguishes the Symbolism of our day from the Symbolism of the past is that it has now become conscious of itself, in a sense in which it was unconscious even in Gérard de Nerval, to whom I trace the particular origin of the literature which I call Symbolist. The forces which mould the thought of

men change, or men's resistance to them slack-
ens; with the change of men's thought comes
a change of literature, alike in its inmost
essence and in its outward form: after the
world has starved its soul long enough in the
contemplation and the re-arrangement of material things, comes the turn of the soul; and
with it comes the literature of which I write in
this volume, a literature in which the visible
world is no longer a reality, and the unseen
world no longer a dream.

The great epoch in French literature which
preceded this epoch was that of the offshoot
of Romanticism which produced Baudelaire,
Flaubert, the Goncourts, Taine, Zola, Leconte
de Lisle. Taine was the philosopher both
of what had gone before him and of what
came immediately after; so that he seems to
explain at once Flaubert and Zola. It was
the age of Science, the age of material things;
and words, with that facile elasticity which
there is in them, did miracles in the exact
representation of everything that visibly existed, exactly as it existed. Even Baudelaire,
in whom the spirit is always an uneasy guest
at the orgie of life, had a certain theory of

Realism which tortures many of his poems into strange, metallic shapes, and fills them with imitative odours, and disturbs them with a too deliberate rhetoric of the flesh. Flaubert, the one impeccable novelist who has ever lived, was resolute to be the novelist of a world in which art, formal art, was the only escape from the burden of reality, and in which the soul was of use mainly as the agent of fine literature. The Goncourts caught at Impressionism to render the fugitive aspects of a world which existed only as a thing of flat spaces, and angles, and coloured movement, in which sun and shadow were the artists; as moods, no less flitting, were the artists of the merely receptive consciousnesses of men and women. Zola has tried to build in brick and mortar inside the covers of a book; he is quite sure that the soul is a nervous fluid, which he is quite sure some man of science is about to catch for us, as a man of science has bottled the air, a pretty, blue liquid. Leconte de Lisle turned the world to stone, but saw, beyond the world, only a pause from misery in a Nirvana never subtilised to the Eastern ecstasy. And, with all these writers, form aimed above all things at being precise, at saying rather than suggesting, at saying what they had to say so completely that nothing remained over, which it might be the business of the reader to divine. And so they have expressed, finally, a certain aspect of the world; and some of them have carried style to a point beyond which the style that says, rather than suggests, cannot go. The whole of that movement comes to a splendid funeral in M. de Heredia's sonnets, in which the literature of form says its last word, and dies.

Meanwhile, something which is vaguely called Decadence had come into being. That name, rarely used with any precise meaning, was usually either hurled as a reproach or hurled back as a defiance. It pleased some young men in various countries to call themselves Decadents, with all the thrill of unsatisfied virtue masquerading as uncomprehended vice. As a matter of fact, the term is in its place only when applied to style; to that ingenious deformation of the language, in Mallarmé for instance, which can be compared with what we are accustomed to call the Greek and Latin of the Decadence. No doubt perversity of form and perversity of matter are often found together, and, among the lesser men especially, experiment was carried far, not only in the direction of style. But a movement which in this sense might be called Decadent could but have been a straying aside from the main road of literature. Nothing, not even conventional virtue, is so provincial as conventional vice; and the desire to "bewilder the middle-classes" is itself middle-class. The interlude, half a mock-interlude, of Decadence, diverted the attention of the critics while something more serious was in preparation. That something more serious has crystallised, for the time, under the form of Symbolism, in which art returns to the one pathway, leading through beautiful things to the eternal beauty.

In most of the writers whom I have dealt with as summing up in themselves all that is best in Symbolism, it will be noticed that the form is very carefully elaborated, and seems to count for at least as much as in those writers of whose over-possession by form I have complained. Here, however, all this elaboration comes from a very different motive

and leads to other ends. There is such a
thing as perfecting form that form may be
annihilated. All the art of Verlaine is in
bringing verse to a bird's song, the art of
Mallarmé in bringing verse to the song of an
orchestra. In Villiers de l'Isle-Adam drama
becomes an embodiment of spiritual forces,
in Maeterlinck not even their embodiment,
but the remote sound of their voices. It
is all an attempt to spiritualise literature, to
evade the old bondage of rhetoric, the old
bondage of exteriority. Description is banished that beautiful things may be evoked,
magically; the regular beat of verse is broken
in order that words may fly, upon subtler
wings. Mystery is no longer feared, as the
great mystery in whose midst we are islanded
was feared by those to whom that unknown
sea was only a great void. We are coming
closer to nature, as we seem to shrink from it
with something of horror, disdaining to catalogue the trees of the forest. And as we brush
aside the accidents of daily life, in which
men and women imagine that they are
alone touching reality, we come closer to
humanity, to everything in humanity that

may have begun before the world and may outlast it.

Here, then, in this revolt against exteriority, against rhetoric, against a materialistic tradition; in this endeavour to disengage the ultimate essence, the soul, of whatever exists and can be realized by the consciousness; in this dutiful waiting upon every symbol by which the soul of things can be made visible; literature, bowed down by so many burdens, may at last attain liberty, and its authentic speech. In attaining this liberty, it accepts a heavier burden; for in speaking to us so intimately, so solemnly, as only religion had hitherto spoken to us, it becomes itself a kind of religion, with all the duties and responsibilities of the sacred ritual.

BALZAC

1

THE first man who has completely understood Balzac is Rodin, and it has taken Rodin ten years to realise his own conception. France has refused the statue in which a novelist is represented as a dreamer, to whom Paris is not so much Paris as Patmos: "the most Parisian of our novelists," Frenchmen assure you. It is more than a hundred years since Balzac was born: a hundred years is a long time in which to be misunderstood with admiration.

In choosing the name of the *Human Comedy* for a series of novels in which, as he says, there is at once "the history and the criticism of society, the analysis of its evils, and the discussion of its principles," Balzac proposed to do for the modern world what Dante, in his *Divine Comedy*, had done for the world of the Middle Ages. Condemned to write in prose, and finding his opportunity in that restriction, he created for himself a form which is perhaps the nearest equivalent for the epic or the poetic drama, and the only form in which, at all events, the epic is now possible. The world of Dante was materially simple compared with the world of the nineteenth century; the "visible world" had not yet begun to "exist," in its tyrannical modern sense; the complications of the soul interested only the Schoolmen, and were a part of theology; poetry could still represent an age and yet be poetry. But to-day poetry can no longer represent more than the soul of things; it had taken refuge from the terrible improvements of civilisation in a divine seclusion, where it sings, disregarding the many voices of the street. Prose comes offering its infinite capacity for detail; and it is by the infinity of its detail that the novel, as Balzac created it, has become the modern epic.

There had been great novels, indeed, before Balzac, but no great novelist; and the novels themselves are scarcely what we should to-day call by that name. The interminable *Astrée* and its companions form a link between the *fabliaux* and the novel, and from them developed the characteristic eighteenth-century *conte*, in narrative, letters, or dialogue, as we see it in Marivaux, Laclos, Crebillon *fils*. Crebillon's longer works, including *Le Sopha*, with their conventional paraphernalia of Eastern fable, are extremely tedious; but in two short pieces, *La Nuit et le Moment* and *Le Hasard du Coin du Feu*, he created a model of witty, naughty, deplorably natural comedy, which to this day is one of the most characteristic French forms of fiction. Properly, however, it is a form of the drama rather than of the novel. Laclos, in *Les Liaisons Dangereuses*, a masterpiece which scandalised the society that adored Crebillon, because its naked human truth left no room for sentimental excuses, comes much nearer to prefiguring the novel (as Stendhal, for instance, is afterward to conceive it), but still preserves the awkward traditional form of letters. Mairvaux had indeed already seemed to suggest the novel of analysis, but in a style which has christened a whole manner of writing that precisely which is least suited to the writing of fiction. Voltaire's *contes*, *La Religieuse* of

Diderot, are tracts or satires in which the story is only an excuse for the purpose. Rousseau, too, has his purpose, even in *La Nouvelle Héloise*, but it is a humanising purpose; and with that book the novel of passion comes into existence, and along with it the descriptive novel. Yet with Rousseau this result is an accident of genius; we cannot call him a novelist; and we find him abandoning the form he has found, for another, more closely personal, which suits him better. Restif de la Bretonne, who followed Rousseau at a distance, not altogether wisely, developed the form of half-imaginary autobiography in *Monsieur Nicolas*, a book of which the most significant part may be compared with Hazlitt's *Liber Amoris*. Morbid and even mawkish as it is, it has a certain uneasy, unwholesome humanity in its confessions, which may seem to have set a fashion only too scrupulously followed by modern French novelists. Meanwhile, the Abbé Prévost's one great story, *Manon Lescaut*, had brought for once a purely objective study, of an incomparable simplicity, into the midst of these analyses of difficult souls; and then we return to the confession,

in the works of others not novelists: Benjamin
Constant, Mme. de Staël, Chateaubriand, in
Adolphe, Corinne, René. At once we are in
the Romantic movement, a movement which
begins lyrically among poets, and at first with
a curious disregard of the more human part of
humanity.

Balzac worked contemporaneously with the
Romantic movement, but he worked outside it,
and its influence upon him is felt only in an
occasional pseudo-romanticism, like the episode
of the pirate in *La Femme de Trente Ans.* His
vision of humanity was essentially a poetic
vision, but he was a poet whose dreams were
facts. Knowing that, as Mme. Necker has
said, "the novel should be the better world,"
he knew also that "the novel would be nothing
if, in that august lie, it were not true in details." And in the *Human Comedy* he proposed to himself to do for society more than
Buffon had done for the animal world.

"There is but one animal," he declares, in
his *Avant-Propos,* with a confidence which
Darwin has not yet come to justify. But
"there exists, there will always exist, social
species, as there are zoological species."

"Thus the work to be done will have a triple form: men, women, and things; that is to say, human beings and the material representation which they give to their thought; in short, man and life." And, studying after nature, "French society will be the historian, I shall need to be no more than the secretary." Thus will be written "the history forgotten by so many historians, the history of manners." But that is not all, for "passion is the whole of humanity." "In realizing clearly the drift of the composition, it will be seen that I assign to facts, constant, daily, open, or secret, to the acts of individual life, to their causes and principles, as much importance as historians had formerly attached to the events of the public life of nations." "Facts gathered together and painted as they are, with passion for element," is one of his definitions of the task he has undertaken. And in a letter to Mme. de Hanska, he summarises every detail of his scheme.

"The *Études des Mœurs* will represent social effects, without a single situation of life, or a physiognomy, or a character of man or woman, or a manner of life, or a profession,

or a social zone, or a district of France, or
anything pertaining to childhood, old age, or
maturity, politics, justice, or war, having
been forgotten.

"That laid down, the history of the human
heart traced link by link, the history of society
made in all its details, we have the base. . . .

"Then, the second stage is the *Études philosophiques*, for after the *effects* come the *causes*.
In the *Études des Mœurs* I shall have painted
the sentiments and their action, life and the
fashion of life. In the *Études philosophiques*
I shall say *why the sentiments, on what the
life. . . .*

"Then, after the *effects* and the *causes*,
come the *Études analytiques*, to which the
Physiologie du mariage belongs, for, after the
effects and the *causes*, one should seek the
principles. . . .

"After having done the poetry, the demon-
stration, of a whole system, I shall do the
science in the *Essai sur les forces humaines*.
And, on the bases of this palace I shall have
traced the immense arabesque of the *Cent
Contes drolatiques!*"

Quite all that, as we know, was not carried

out; but there, in its intention, is the plan; and after twenty years' work the main part of it, certainly, was carried out. Stated with this precise detail, it has something of a scientific air, as of a too deliberate attempt upon the sources of life by one of those systematic French minds which are so much more logical than facts. But there is one little phrase to be noted: "La passion est toute l'humanité." All Balzac is in that phrase.

Another French novelist, following, as he thought, the example of the *Human Comedy*, has endeavoured to build up a history of his own time with even greater minuteness. But *Les Rougon-Macquart* is no more than system; Zola has never understood that detail without life is the wardrobe without the man. Trying to outdo Balzac on his own ground, he has made the fatal mistake of taking him only on his systematic side, which in Balzac is subordinate to a great creative intellect, an incessant, burning thought about men and women, a passionate human curiosity for which even his own system has no limits. "The misfortunes of the *Birotteaus*, the priest and the perfumer," he says, in his

Avant-Propos, taking an example at random, "are, for me, those of humanity." To Balzac manners are but the vestment of life; it is life that he seeks; and life, to him (it is his own word) is but the vestment of thought. Thought is at the root of all his work, a whole system of thought, in which philosophy is but another form of poetry; and it is from this root of idea that the *Human Comedy* springs.

2

The two books into which Balzac has put his deepest thought, the two books which he himself cared for the most, are *Séraphita* and *Louis Lambert*. Of *Louis Lambert* he said: "I write it for myself and a few others"; of *Séraphita*: "My life is in it." "One could write *Goriot* any day," he adds; " *Séraphita* only once in a lifetime." I have never been able to feel that *Séraphita* is altogether a success. It lacks the breadth of life; it is glacial. True, he aimed at producing very much such an effect; and it is, indeed, full of a strange, glittering beauty,

the beauty of its own snows. But I find in
it at the same time something a little factitious, a sort of romanesque, not altogether
unlike the sentimental romanesque of Novalis;
it has not done the impossible, in humanising abstract speculation, in fusing mysticism
and the novel. But for the student of Balzac
it has extraordinary interest; for it is at once
the base and the summit of the *Human Comedy*. In a letter to Mme. de Hanska, written
in 1837, four years after *Séraphita* had been
begun, he writes: "I am not orthodox, and I
do not believe in the Roman Church. Swe-
denborgianism, which is but a repetition, in
the Christian sense, of ancient ideas, is my
religion, with this addition: that I believe in
the incomprehensibility of God." *Séraphita* is a prose poem in which the most
abstract part of that mystical system, which
Swedenborg perhaps materialised too crudely,
is presented in a white light, under a single,
superhuman image. In *Louis Lambert* the
same fundamental conceptions are worked
out in the study of a perfectly human intellect, "an intelligent gulf," as he truly calls
it; a sober and concise history of ideas in their

devouring action upon a feeble physical nature. In these two books we see directly, and not through the coloured veil of human life, the mind in the abstract of a thinker whose power over humanity was the power of abstract thought. They show this novelist, who has invented the description of society, by whom the visible world has been more powerfully felt than by any other novelist, striving to penetrate the correspondences which exist between the human and the celestial existence. He would pursue the soul to its last resting-place before it takes flight from the body; further, on its disembodied flight; he would find out God, as he comes nearer and nearer to finding out the secret of life. And realising, as he does so profoundly, that there is but one substance, but one ever-changing principle of life, "one vegetable, one animal, but a continual intercourse," the world is alive with meaning for him, a more intimate meaning than it has for others. "The least flower is a thought, a life which corresponds to some lineaments of the great whole, of which he has the constant intuition." And so, in his concerns with the world, he will find spirit everywhere; nothing for him will be inert matter, everything will have its particle of the universal life. One of those divine spies, for whom the world has no secrets, he will be neither pessimist nor optimist; he will accept the world as a man accepts the woman whom he loves, as much for her defects as for her virtues. Loving the world for its own sake, he will find it always beautiful, equally beautiful in all its parts. Now let us look at the programme which he traced for the *Human Comedy*, let us realise it in the light of this philosophy, and we are at the beginning of a conception of what the *Human Comedy* really is.

3

This visionary, then, who had apprehended for himself an idea of God, set himself to interpret human life more elaborately than any one else. He has been praised for his patient observation; people have thought they praised him in calling him a realist; it has been discussed how far his imitation of life was the literal truth of the photograph.

But to Balzac the word realism was an insult. Writing his novels at the rate of eighteen hours a day, in a feverish solitude, he never had the time to observe patiently. It is humanity seen in a mirror, the humanity which comes to the great dreamers, the great poets, humanity as Shakespeare saw it. And so in him, as in all the great artists, there is something more than nature, a divine excess. This something more than nature should be the aim of the artist, not merely the accident which happens to him against his will. We require of him a world like our own, but a world infinitely more vigorous, interesting, profound; more beautiful with that kind of beauty which nature finds of itself for art. It is the quality of great creative art to give us so much life that we are almost overpowered by it, as by an air almost too vigorous to breathe: the exuberance of creation which makes the Sibyl of Michelangelo something more than human, which makes Lear something more than human, in one kind or another of divinity.

Balzac's novels are full of strange problems and great passions. He turned aside from nothing which presented itself in nature; and his mind was always turbulent with the magnificent contrasts and caprices of fate. A devouring passion of thought burned on all the situations by which humanity expresses itself, in its flight from the horror of immobility. To say that the situations which he chose are often romantic is but to say that he followed the soul and the senses faithfully on their strangest errands. Our probable novelists of to-day are afraid of whatever emotion might be misinterpreted in a gentleman. Believing, as we do now, in nerves and a fatalistic heredity, we have left but little room for the dignity and disturbance of violent emotion. To Balzac, humanity had not changed since the days when Œdipus was blind and Philoctetes cried in the cave; and equally great miseries were still possible to mortals, though they were French and of the nineteenth century.

And thus he creates, like the poets, a humanity more logical than average life; more typical, more sub-divided among the passions, and having in its veins an energy almost more than human. He realised, as the Greeks did, that human life is made up of elemental passions and necessity; but he was the first to realise that in the modern world the pseudonym of necessity is money. Money and the passions rule the world of his *Human Comedy*.

And, at the root of the passions, determining their action, he saw "those nervous fluids, or that unknown substance which, in default of another term, we must call the will." No word returns oftener to his pen. For him the problem is invariable. Man has a given quantity of energy; each man a different quantity: how will he spend it? A novel is the determination in action of that problem. And he is equally interested in every form of energy, in every egoism, so long as it is fiercely itself. This pre-occupation with the force, rather than with any of its manifestations, gives him his singular impartiality, his absolute lack of prejudice; for it gives him the advantage of an abstract point of view, the unchanging fulcrum for a lever which turns in every direction; and as nothing once set vividly in motion by any form of human activity is without interest for him, he makes every point of his vast chronicle of human affairs equally interesting to his readers.

Baudelaire has observed profoundly that

every character in the *Human Comedy* has
something of Balzac, has genius. To himself, his own genius was entirely expressed in
that word "will." It recurs constantly in his
letters. "Men of will are rare!" he cries.
And, at a time when he had turned night into
day for his labour: "I rise every night with a
keener will than that of yesterday." "Nothing wearies me," he says, "neither waiting nor
happiness." He exhausts the printers, whose
fingers can hardly keep pace with his brain;
they call him, he reports proudly, "a man-
slayer." And he tries to express himself: "I
have always had in me something, I know not
what, which made me do differently from
others; and, with me, fidelity is perhaps no
more than pride. Having only myself to rely
upon, I have had to strengthen, to build up
that self." There is a scene in *La Cousine
Bette* which gives precisely Balzac's own sentiment of the supreme value of energy. The
Baron Hulot, ruined on every side, and by
his own fault, goes to Josépha, a mistress who
had cast him off in the time of his prosperity, and
asks her to lodge him for a few days in a garret.
She laughs, pities, and then questions him.

"'Est-ce vrai, vieux,' reprit-elle, 'que tu as tué ton frère et ton oncle, ruiné ta famille, surhypothéqué la maison de tes enfants et mangé la grenouille du gouvernement en Afrique avec la princesse?'

"Le Baron inclina tristement la tête.

"'Eh bien, j'aime cela!' s'écria Josépha, qui se leva pleine d'enthousiasme. 'C'est un *brûlage* général! c'est sardanapale! c'est grand! c'est complet! On est une canaille, mais on a du cœur.'"

The cry is Balzac's, and it is a characteristic part of his genius to have given it that ironical force by uttering it through the mouth of a Josépha. The joy of the human organism at its highest point of activity: that is what interests him supremely. How passionate, how moving he becomes whenever he has to speak of a real passion, a mania, whether of a lover for his mistress, of a philosopher for his idea, of a miser for his gold, of a Jew dealer for masterpieces! His style clarifies, his words become flesh and blood; he is the lyric poet. And for him every idealism is equal: the gourmandise of Pons is not less serious, nor less sympathetic, not less perfectly realised, than the search of Claës after the Absolute. "The great and terrible clamour of egoism" is the voice to which he is always attentive; "those eloquent faces, proclaiming a soul abandoned to an idea as to a remorse," are the faces with whose history he concerns himself. He drags to light the hidden joys of the *amateur*, and with especial delight those that are hidden deepest, under the most deceptive coverings. He deifies them for their energy, he fashions the world of his *Human Comedy* in their service, as the real world exists, all but passive, to be the pasture of these supreme egoists.

4

In all that he writes of life, Balzac seeks the soul, but it is the soul as nervous fluid, the executive soul, not the contemplative soul, that, with rare exceptions, he seeks. He would surprise the motive force of life: that is his *recherche de l'Absolu;* he figures it to himself as almost a substance, and he is the alchemist on its track. "Can man by thinking find out God?" Or life, he would have added; and he would have answered the question with at least a Perhaps.

And of this visionary, this abstract thinker, it must be said that his thought translates itself always into terms of life. Pose before him a purely mental problem, and he will resolve it by a scene in which the problem literally works itself out. It is the quality proper to the novelist, but no novelist ever employed this quality with such persistent activity, and at the same time subordinated action so constantly to the idea. With him action has always a mental basis, is never suffered to intrude for its own sake. He prefers that an episode should seem in itself tedious rather than it should have an illogical interest.

It may be, for he is a Frenchman, that his episodes are sometimes too logical. There are moments when he becomes unreal because he wishes to be too systematic, that is, to be real by measure. He would never have understood the method of Tolstoi, a very stealthy method of surprising life. To Tolstoi life is always the cunning enemy whom one must lull asleep, or noose by an unexpected lasso. He brings in little detail after little detail, seeming

to insist on the insignificance of each, in order
that it may pass almost unobserved, and
be realised only after it has passed. It is his
way of disarming the suspiciousness of life.

But Balzac will make no circuit, aims at an
open and an unconditional triumph over
nature. Thus, when he triumphs, he triumphs
signally; and action, in his books, is perpetually crystallising into some phrase, like the
single lines of Dante, or some brief scene, in
which a whole entanglement comes sharply
and suddenly to a luminous point. I will give
no instance, for I should have to quote from
every volume. I wish rather to remind myself
that there are times when the last fine shade of
a situation seems to have escaped. Even
then, the failure is often more apparent than
real, a slight bungling in the machinery of
illusion. Look through the phrase, and you
will find the truth there, perfectly explicit on
the other side of it.

For it cannot be denied, Balzac's style, as
style, is imperfect. It has life, and it has an
idea, and it has variety; there are moments
when it attains a rare and perfectly individual beauty; as when, in *Le Cousin Pons*, we

read of "cette prédisposition aux recherches
qui fait faire à un savant germanique cent
lieues dans ses guêtres pour trouver une
vérité qui le regard en riant, assise à la marge
du puits, sous le jasmin de la cour." But I
am far less sure that a student of Balzac would
recognise him in this sentence than that he
would recognise the writer of this other: "Des
larmes de pudeur, qui roulèrent entre les beaux
cils de Madame Hulot, arrêtèrent net le garde
national." It is in such passages that the
failure in style is equivalent to a failure in
psychology. That his style should lack sym-
metry, subordination, the formal virtues of
form, is, in my eyes, a less serious fault. I
have often considered whether, in the novel,
perfect form is a good, or even a possible thing,
if the novel is to be what Balzac made it, history added to poetry. A novelist with style
will not look at life with an entirely naked
vision. He sees through coloured glasses.
Human life and human manners are too various,
too moving, to be brought into the fixity of a
quite formal order. There will come a moment, constantly, when style must suffer, or
the closeness and clearness of narration must

be sacrificed, some minute exception of action or psychology must lose its natural place, or its full emphasis. Balzac, with his rapid and accumulating mind, without the patience of selection, and without the desire to select where selection means leaving out something good in itself, if not good in its place, never hesitates, and his parenthesis comes in. And often it is into these parentheses that he puts the profoundest part of his thought.

Yet, ready as Balzac is to neglect the story for the philosophy, whenever it seems to him necessary to do so, he would never have admitted that a form of the novel is possible in which the story shall be no more than an excuse for the philosophy. That was because he was a great creator, and not merely a philosophical thinker; because he dealt in flesh and blood, and knew that the passions in action can teach more to the philosopher, and can justify the artist more fully, than all the unacting intellect in the world. He knew that though life without thought was no more than the portion of a dog, yet thoughtful life was more than lifeless thought, and the dramatist more than the commentator. And

I cannot help feeling assured that the latest
novelists without a story, whatever other
merits they certainly have, are lacking in the
power to create characters, to express a philosophy in action; and that the form which they
have found, however valuable it may be, is
the result of this failure, and not either a
great refusal or a new vision.

5

The novel as Balzac conceived it has created
the modern novel, but no modern novelist
has followed, for none has been able to follow,
Balzac on his own lines.   Even those who have
tried to follow him most closely have, sooner
or later, branched off in one direction or
another, most in the direction indicated by
Stendhal. Stendhal has written one book
which is a masterpiece, unique in its kind,
Le Rouge et le Noir; a second, which is
full of admirable things, *Le Chartreuse de
Parme;* a book of profound criticism, *Racine
et Shakspeare;* and a cold and penetrating
study of the physiology of love, *De l'Amour,*
by the side of which Balzac's *Physiologie du*

Mariage is a mere *jeu d'esprit*. He discovered for himself, and for others after him, a method of unemotional, minute, slightly ironical analysis, which has fascinated modern minds, partly because it has seemed to dispense with those difficulties of creation, of creation in the block, which the triumphs of Balzac have only accentuated. Goriot, Valérie Marneffe, Pons, Grandet, Madame de Mortsauf even, are called up before us after the same manner as Othello or Don Quixote; their actions express them so significantly that they seem to be independent of their creator; Balzac stakes all upon each creation, and leaves us no choice but to accept or reject each as a whole, precisely as we should a human being. We do not know all the secrets of their consciousness, any more than we know all the secrets of the consciousness of our friends. But we have only so say "Valérie!" and the woman is before us. Stendhal, on the contrary, undresses Julien's soul in public with a deliberate and fascinating effrontery. There is not a vein of which he does not trace the course, not a wrinkle to which he does not point, not a nerve which he does not touch to

the quick. We know everything that passed
through his mind, to result probably in some
significant inaction. And at the end of the
book we know as much about that particular
intelligence as the anatomist knows about
the body which he has dissected. But meanwhile the life has gone out of the body; and
have we, after all, captured a living
soul?

I should be the last to say that Julien Sorel
is not a creation, but he is not a creation after
the order of Balzac; it is a difference of kind;
and if we look carefully at Frédéric Moreau,
and Madame Gervaisais, and the Abbé Mouret,
we shall see that these also, profoundly different as Flaubert and Goncourt and Zola are
from Stendhal, are yet more profoundly, more
radically, different from the creations of Balzac. Balzac takes a primary passion, puts
it into a human body, and sets it to work
itself out in visible action. But since Stendhal,
novelists have persuaded themselves that the
primary passions are a little common, or noisy,
or a little heavy to handle, and they have
concerned themselves with passions tempered
by reflection, and the sensations of elaborate

brains. It was Stendhal who substituted the brain for the heart, as the battle-place of the novel; not the brain as Balzac conceived it, a motive-force of action, the mainspring of passion, the force by which a nature directs its accumulated energy; but a sterile sort of brain, set at a great distance from the heart, whose rhythm is too faint to disturb it. We have been intellectualising upon Stendhal ever since, until the persons of the modern novel have come to resemble those diaphanous jelly-fish, with balloon-like heads and the merest tufts of bodies, which float up and down in the Aquarium at Naples.

Thus, coming closer, as it seems, to what is called reality, in this banishment of great emotions, and this attention upon the sensations, modern analytic novelists are really getting further and further from that life which is the one certain thing in the world. Balzac employs all his detail to call up a tangible world about his men and women, not, perhaps, understanding the full power of detail as psychology, as Flaubert is to understand it; but, after all, his detail is only the background of the picture; and there, step-

ping out of the canvas, as the sombre people
of Velazquez step out of their canvases at the
Prado, is the living figure, looking into your
eyes with eyes that respond to you like a
mirror.

The novels of Balzac are full of electric fluid.
To take up one of them is to feel the shock
of life, as one feels it on touching certain magnetic hands. To turn over volume after volume is like wandering through the streets of a
great city, at that hour of the night when
human activity is at its full. There is a particular kind of excitement inherent in the very
aspect of a modern city, of London or Paris;
in the mere sensation of being in its midst,
in the sight of all those active and fatigued
faces which pass so rapidly; of those long and
endless streets, full of houses, each of which is
like the body of a multiform soul, looking out
through the eyes of many windows. There
is something intoxicating in the lights, the
movement of shadows under the lights, the
vast and billowy sound of that shadowy
movement. And there is something more than
this mere unconscious action upon the nerves.
Every step in a great city is a step into an

unknown world. A new future is possible at every street corner. I never know, when I go out into one of those crowded streets, but that the whole course of my life may be changed before I return to the house I have quitted.

I am writing these lines in Madrid, to which I have come suddenly, after a long quiet in Andalusia; and I feel already a new pulse in my blood, a keener consciousness of life, and a sharper human curiosity. Even in Seville I knew that I should see to-morrow, in the same streets, hardly changed since the Middle Ages, the same people that I had seen to-day. But here there are new possibilities, all the exciting accidents of the modern world, of a population always changing, of a city into which civilisation has brought all its unrest. And as I walk in these broad, windy streets and see these people, whom I hardly recognise for Spaniards, so awake and so hybrid are they, I have felt the sense of Balzac coming back into my veins. At Cordova he was unthinkable; at Cadiz I could realise only his large, universal outlines, vague as the murmur of the sea; here I feel him, he speaks the language I am talking, he sums up the life in whose midst I find myself.

For Balzac is the equivalent of great cities. He is bad reading for solitude, for he fills the mind with the nostalgia of cities. When a man speaks to me familiarly of Balzac I know already something of the man with whom I have to do. "The physiognomy of women does not begin before the age of thirty," he has said; and perhaps before that age no one can really understand Balzac. Few young people care for him, for there is nothing in him that appeals to the senses except through the intellect. Not many women care for him supremely, for it is part of his method to express sentiments through facts, and not facts through sentiments. But it is natural that he should be the favourite reading of men of the world, of those men of the world who have the distinction of their kind; for he supplies the key of the enigma which they are studying.

6

The life of Balzac was one long labour, in which time, money, and circumstances were all against him. In 1835 he writes: "I have lately spent twenty-six days in my study without leaving it. I took the air only at that window which dominates Paris, which I mean to dominate." And he exults in the labour: "If there is any glory in that, I alone could accomplish such a feat." He symbolises the course of his life in comparing it to the sea beating against a rock: "To-day one flood, to-morrow another, bears me along with it. I am dashed against a rock, I recover myself and go on to another reef." "Sometimes it seems to me that my brain is on fire. I shall die in the trenches of the intellect."

Balzac, like Scott, died under the weight of his debts; and it would seem, if one took him at his word, that the whole of the *Human Comedy* was written for money. In the modern world, as he himself realised more clearly than any one, money is more often a symbol than an entity, and it can be the symbol of every desire. For Balzac money was the

key of his earthly paradise. It meant leisure
to visit the woman whom he loved, and at the
end it meant the possibility of marrying her.

There were only two women in Balzac's life:
one, a woman much older than himself, of
whom he wrote, on her death, to the other:
"She was a mother, a friend, a family, a companion, a counsel, she made the writer, she
consoled the young man, she formed his taste,
she wept like a sister, she laughed, she came
every day, like a healing slumber, to put sorrow
to sleep." The other was Mme. de Hanska,
whom he married in 1850, three months before
his death. He had loved her for twenty years;
she was married, and lived in Poland; it was
only at rare intervals that he was able to see
her, and then very briefly; but his letters to
her, published since his death, are a simple,
perfectly individual, daily record of a great
passion. For twenty years he existed on a
divine certainty without a future, and almost
without a present. But we see the force of
that sentiment passing into his work; *Séraphita* is its ecstasy, everywhere is its human
shadow; it refines his strength, it gives him
surprising intuitions, it gives him all that was

wanting to his genius. Mme. de Hanska is
the heroine of the *Human Comedy*, as
Beatrice is the heroine of the *Divine Comedy*.

A great lover, to whom love, as well as
every other passion and the whole visible
world, was an idea, a flaming spiritual perception, Balzac enjoyed the vast happiness of the
idealist. Contentedly, joyously, he sacrificed
every petty enjoyment to the idea of love, the
idea of fame, and to that need of the organism
to exercise its forces, which is the only definition of genius. I do not know, among the
lives of men of letters, a life better filled, or
more appropriate. A young man who, for a
short time, was his secretary, declared: "I
would not live your life for the fame of Napoleon and of Byron combined!" The Comte
de Gramont did not realise, as the world in
general does not realise, that, to the man of
creative energy, creation is at once a necessity
and a joy, and to the lover, hope in absence is
the elixir of life. Balzac tasted more than all
earthly pleasures as he sat there in his attic,
creating the world over again, that he might
lay it at the feet of a woman. Certainly to

him there was no tedium in life, for there was
no hour without its vivid employment, and no
moment in which to perceive the most desolate
of all certainties, that hope is in the past.   His
death was as fortunate as his life; he died at
the height of his powers, at the height of his
fame, at the moment of the fulfilment of his
happiness, and perhaps of the too sudden relief
of that delicate burden.

1899.

PROSPER MÉRIMÉE

1

Stendhal has left us a picture of Mérimée
as "a young man in a grey frock-coat, very
ugly, and with a turned-up nose. . . . This
young man had something insolent and extremely unpleasant about him. His eyes,
small and without expression, had always the
same look, and this look was ill-natured. . . .
Such was my first impression of the best of my
present friends. I am not too sure of his heart,
but I am sure of his talents. It is M. le Comte
Gazul, now so well known; a letter from him,
which came to me last week, made me happy
for two days. His mother has a good deal of
French wit and a superior intelligence. Like
her son, it seems to me that she might give
way to emotion once a year." There, painted
by a clear-sighted and disinterested friend, is a
picture of Mérimée almost from his own point

of view, or at least as he would himself have
painted the picture. How far is it, in its insistence on the *attendrissement une fois par an*,
on the subordination of natural feelings to a
somewhat disdainful aloofness, the real Mérimée?

Early in life, Mérimée adopted his theory,
fixed his attitude, and to the end of his life
he seemed, to those about him, to have walked
along the path he had chosen, almost without
a deviation. He went to England at the age
of twenty-three, to Spain four years later, and
might seem to have been drawn naturally to
those two countries, to which he was to return
so often, by natural affinities of temper and
manner. It was the English manner that he
liked, that came naturally to him; the correct,
unmoved exterior, which is a kind of positive
strength, not to be broken by any onslaught
of events or emotions; and in Spain he found
an equally positive animal acceptance of things
as they are, which satisfied his profound, re-
strained, really Pagan senusality, Pagan in the
hard, eighteenth-century sense. From the
beginning he was a student, of art, of history,
of human nature, and we find him enjoying, in

his deliberate, keen way, the studied diversions
of the student; body and soul each kept exactly
in its place, each provided for without par-
tiality. He entered upon literature by a mystification, *Le Théâtre de Clara Gazul,* a book
of plays supposed to be translated from a
living Spanish dramatist; and he followed it by
La Guzla, another mystification, a book of
prose ballads supposed to be translated from
the Illyrian. And these mystifications, like the
forgeries of Chatterton, contain perhaps the
most sincere, the most undisguised emotion
which he ever permitted himself to express;
so secure did he feel of the heart behind the
pearl necklace of the *décolletée* Spanish actress,
who travesties his own face in the frontispiece
to the one, and so remote from himself did he
feel the bearded gentleman to be, who sits
cross-legged on the ground, holding his lyre or
guzla, in the frontispiece to the other. Then
came a historical novel, the *Chronique du
Règne de Charles IX.,* before he discovered,
as if by accident, precisely what it was he was
meant to do: the short story. Then he drifted
into history, became Inspector of Ancient
Monuments, and helped to save Vézelay,

among other good deeds toward art, done in
his cold, systematic, after all satisfactory manner. He travelled at almost regular intervals,
not only in Spain and England, but in Corsica,
in Greece and Asia Minor, in Italy, in Hun-
gary, in Bohemia, usually with a definite,
scholarly object, and always with an alert
attention to everything that came in his way,
to the manners of people, their national characters, their differences from one another.
An intimate friend of the Countess de Montijo,
the mother of the Empress Eugénie, he was a
friend, not a courtier, at the court of the Third
Empire. He was elected to the Academy,
mainly for his *Études sur l'Histoire Romaine*, a piece of dry history, and immediately
scandalised his supporters by publishing a
story, *Arsène Guillot*, which was taken for a
veiled attack on religion and on morals. Soon
after, his imagination seemed to flag; he
abandoned himself, perhaps a little wearily,
more and more to facts, to the facts of history
and learning; learned Russian, and translated Poushkin and Tourguenieff; and died in
1870, at Cannes, perhaps less satisfied with
himself than most men who have done, in their

lives, far less exactly what they have intended
to do.

"I have theories about the very smallest
things—gloves, boots, and the like," says
Mérimée in one of his letters; *des idées très-
arrêtées*, as he adds with emphasis in another.
Precise opinions lead easily to prejudices, and
Mérimée, who prided himself on the really
very logical quality of his mind, put himself
somewhat deliberately into the hands of his
prejudices. Thus he hated religion, distrusted
priests, would not let himself be carried away
by any instinct of admiration, would not let
himself do the things which he had the power
to do, because his other, critical self came
mockingly behind him, suggesting that very
few things were altogether worth doing.
"There is nothing that I despise and even
detest so much as humanity in general," he
confesses in a letter; and it is with a certain
self-complacency that he defines the only kind
of society in which he found himself at home:
"(1) With unpretentious people whom I have
known a long time; (2) in a Spanish *venta*,
with muleteers and peasant women of Andalusia." One day, as he finds himself in a pen-

sive mood, dreaming of a woman, he translates for her some lines of Sophocles, into verse,
"English verse, you understand, for I abhor
French verse." The carefulness with which
he avoids received opinions shows a certain
consciousness of those opinions, which in a
more imaginatively independent mind would
scarcely have found a place. It is not only
for an effect, but more and more genuinely,
that he sets his acquirements as a scholar
above his accomplishments as an artist. Clearing away, as it seemed to him, every illusion
from before his eyes, he forgot the last illusion
of positive people: the possibility that one's
eyes may be short-sighted.

Mérimée realises a type which we are accustomed to associate almost exclusively with the
eighteenth century, but of which our own time
can offer us many obscure examples. It is
the type of the *esprit fort:* the learned man,
the choice, narrow artist, who is at the same
time the cultivated sensualist. To such a
man the pursuit of women is part of his constant pursuit of human experience, and of the
document, which is the summing up of human
experience. To Mérimée history itself was a

matter of detail. "In history, I care only for
anecdotes," he says in the preface to the
Chronique du Règne de Charles IX. And
he adds: "It is not a very noble taste; but I
confess to my shame, I would willingly give
Thucydides for the authentic memoirs of
Aspasia or of a slave of Pericles; for only
memoirs, which are the familiar talk of an
author with his reader, afford those portraits
of *man* which amuse and interest me." This
curiosity of mankind above all things, and of
mankind at home, or in private actions, not
necessarily of any import to the general course
of the world, leads the curious searcher naturally to the more privately interesting and the
less publicly important half of mankind.
Not scrupulous in arriving at any end by the
most adaptable means, not disturbed by any
illusions as to the physical facts of the universe, a sincere and grateful lover of variety,
doubtless an amusing companion with those
who amused him, Mérimée found much of
his entertainments and instruction, at all
events in his younger years, in that "half
world" which he tells us he frequented "very
much out of curiosity, living in it always as

in a foreign country." Here, as elsewhere, Mérimée played the part of the amateur. He liked anecdotes, not great events, in his history; and he was careful to avoid any too serious passions in his search for sensations. There, no doubt, for the sensualist, is happiness, if he can resign himself to it. It is only serious passions which make anybody unhappy; and Mérimée was carefully on the lookout against a possible unhappiness. I can imagine him ending every day with satisfaction, and beginning every fresh day with just enough expectancy to be agreeable, at that period of his life when he was writing the finest of his stories, and dividing the rest of his leisure between the drawing-rooms and the pursuit of uneventful adventures.

Only, though we are *automates autant qu'-esprit,* as Pascal tells us, it is useless to expect that what is automatic in us should remain invariable and unconditioned. If life could be lived on a plan, and for such men on such a plan, if first impulses and profound passions could be kept entirely out of one's own experience, and studied only at a safe distance, then, no doubt, one could go on being happy, in a

not too heroic way. But, with Mérimée as
with all the rest of the world, the scheme
breaks down one day, just when a reasonable
solution to things seems to have been arrived
at. Mérimée had already entered on a peace-
able enough *liaison* when the first letter came
to him from the *Inconnue* to whom he was to
write so many letters, for nine years without
seeing her, and then for thirty years more after
he had met her, the last letter being written
but two hours before his death. These letters,
which we can now read in two volumes, have a
delicately insincere sincerity which makes
every letter a work of art, not because he tried
to make it so, but because he could not help
seeing the form simultaneously with the feeling, and writing genuine love-letters with an
excellence almost as impersonal as that of his
stories. He begins with curiosity, which passes
with singular rapidity into a kind of self-
willed passion; already in the eighth letter,
long before he has seen her, he is speculating
which of the two will know best how to torture
the other: that is, as he views it, love best.
"We shall never love one another really,"
he tells her, as he begins to hope for the con-

trary. Then he discovers, for the first time, and without practical result, "that it is better to have illusions than to have none at all." He confesses himself to her, sometimes reminding her: "You will never know either all the good or all the evil that I have in me. I have spent my life in being praised for qualities which I do not possess, and calumniated for defects which are not mine." And, with a strange, weary humility, which is the other side of his contempt for most things and people, he admits: "To you I am like an old opera, which you are obliged to forget, in order to see it again with any pleasure." He, who has always distrusted first impulses, finds himself telling her (was she really so like him, or was he arguing with himself?): "You always fear first impulses; do not you see that they are the only ones which are worth anything and which always succeed?" Does he realise, unable to change the temperament which he has partly made for himself, that just there has been his own failure?

Perhaps of all love-letters, these of Mérimée show us love triumphing over the most carefully guarded personality. Here the obstacle is not duty, nor circumstance, nor a rival; but (on her side as on his, it would seem) a carefully trained natural coldness, in which action, and even for the most part feeling, are relinquished to the control of second thoughts. A habit of repressive irony goes deep: Mérimée might well have thought himself secure against the outbreak of an unconditional passion. Yet here we find passion betraying itself, often only by bitterness, together with a shy, surprising tenderness, in this curious lovers' itinerary, marked out with all the customary sign-posts, and leading, for all its wilful deviations, along the inevitable road.

It is commonly supposed that the artist, by the habit of his profession, has made for himself a sort of cuirass of phrases against the direct attack of emotion, and so will suffer less than most people if he should fall into love, and things should not go altogether well with him. Rather, he is the more laid open to attack, the more helplessly entangled when once the net has been cast over him. He lives through every passionate trouble, not merely with the daily emotions of the crowd, but with the whole of his imagination. Pain is

multiplied to him by the force of that faculty
by which he conceives delight. What is most
torturing in every not quite fortunate love is
memory, and the artist becomes an artist by
his intensification of memory. Mérimée has
himself defined art as exaggeration *à propos*.
Well, to the artist his own life is an exaggeration not *à propos*, and every hour dramatises
for him its own pain and pleasure, in a tragic
comedy of which he is the author and actor
and spectator. The practice of art is a sharpening of the sensations, and, the knife once
sharpened, does it cut into one's hand less
deeply because one is in the act of using it to
carve wood?

And so we find Mérimée, the most impersonal of artists, and one of those most critical
of the caprices and violences of fate, giving
in to an almost obvious temptation, an anon-
ymous correspondence, a mysterious unknown
woman, and passing from stage to stage of
a finally very genuine love-affair, which kept
him in a fluttering agitation for more than
thirty years. It is curious to note that the
little which we know of this *Inconnue* seems
to mark her out as the realisation of a type

which had always been Mérimée's type of
woman. She has the "wicked eyes" of all
his heroines, from the Mariquita of his first
attempt in literature, who haunts the Inquisitor
with "her great black eyes, like the eyes of a
young cat, soft and wicked at once." He finds
her at the end of his life, in a novel of Tourguenieff, "one of those diabolical creatures whose
coquetry is the more dangerous because it is
capable of passion." Like so many artists,
he has invented his ideal before he meets it,
and must have seemed almost to have fallen
in love with his own creation. It is one of the
privileges of art to create nature, as, according
to a certain mystical doctrine, you can actual-
ise, by sheer fixity of contemplation, your
mental image of a thing into the thing itself.
The *Inconnue* was one of a series, the rest
imaginary; and her power over Mérimée, we
can hardly doubt, came not only from her queer
likeness of temperament to his, but from the
singular, flattering pleasure which it must
have given him to find that he had invented
with so much truth to nature.

2

Mérimée as a writer belongs to the race of
Laclos and of Stendhal, a race essentially
French; and we find him representing, a little
coldly, as it seemed, the claims of mere un-
impassioned intellect, at work on passionate
problems, among those people of the Romantic
period to whom emotion, evident emotion,
was everything. In his subjects he is as
"Romantic" as Victor Hugo or Gautier; he
adds, even, a peculiar flavour of cruelty to
the Romantic ingredients. But he distinguishes sharply, as French writers before him
had so well known how to do, between the
passion one is recounting and the moved or
unmoved way in which one chooses to tell it.
To Mérimée art was a very formal thing,
almost a part of learning; it was a thing to
be done with a clear head, reflectively, with a
calm mastery of even the most vivid material.
While others, at that time, were intoxicating
themselves with strange sensations, hoping
that "nature would take the pen out of their
hands and write," just at the moment when
their own thoughts became least coherent,

Mérimée went quietly to work over something a little abnormal which he had found in nature, with as disinterested, as scholarly, as mentally reserved an interest as if it were one of those Gothic monuments which he inspected to such good purpose, and, as it has seemed to his biographer, with so little sympathy. His own emotion, so far as it is roused, seems to him an extraneous thing, a thing to be concealed, if not a little ashamed of. It is the thing itself he wishes to give you, not his feelings about it; and his theory is that if the thing itself can only be made to stand and speak before the reader, the reader will supply for himself all the feeling that is needed, all the feeling that would be called out in nature by a perfectly clear sight of just such passions in action. It seems to him bad art to paint the picture, and to write a description of the picture as well.

And his method serves him wonderfully up to a certain point, and then leaves him, without his being well aware of it, at the moment even when he has convinced himself that he has realised the utmost of his aim. At a time when he had come to consider

scholarly dexterity as the most important
part of art, Mérimée tells us that *La Vénus
d'Ille* seemed to him the best story he had
ever written. He has often been taken at
his word, but to take him at his word is to
do him an injustice. *La Vénus d'Ille* is a
modern setting of the old story of the Ring
given to Venus, and Mérimée has been
praised for the ingenuity with which he has
obtained an effect of supernatural terror,
while leaving the way open for a material
explanation of the supernatural. What he
has really done is to materialise a myth, by
accepting in it precisely what might be a mere
superstition, the form of the thing, and leaving
out the spiritual meaning of which that form
was no more than a temporary expression.
The ring which the bridegroom sets on the
finger of Venus, and which the statue's finger
closes upon, accepting it, symbolises the pact
between love and sensuality, the lover's abdi-
cation of all but the physical part of love; and
the statue taking its place between husband
and wife on the marriage-night, and crushing
life out of him in an inexorable embrace,
symbolises the merely natural destruction

which that granted prayer brings with it, as a merely human Messalina takes her lover on his own terms, in his abandonment of all to Venus. Mérimée sees a cruel and fantastic superstition, which he is afraid of seeming to take too seriously, which he prefers to leave as a story of ghosts or bogies, a thing at which we are to shiver as at a mere twitch on the nerves, while our mental confidence in the impossibility of what we cannot explain is preserved for us by a hint at a muleteer's vengeance. "Have I frightened you?" says the man of the world, with a reassuring smile. "Think about it no more; I really meant nothing."

And yet, does he after all mean nothing? The devil, the old pagan gods, the spirits of evil incarnated under every form, fascinated him; it gave him a malign pleasure to set them at their evil work among men, while, all the time, he mocks them and the men who believed in them. He is a materialist, and yet he believes in at least a something evil, outside the world, or in the heart of it, which sets humanity at its strange games, relentlessly. Even then he will not surrender his doubts, his ironies, his negations. Is he, perhaps, at times, the athiest who fears that, after all, God may exist, or at least who realises how much he would fear him if he did exist?

Mérimée had always delighted in mystifications; he was always on his guard against being mystified himself, either by nature or by his fellow-creatures. In the early "Romantic" days he had had a genuine passion for various things: "local colour," for instance. But even then he had invented it by a kind of trick, and, later on, he explains what a poor thing "local colour" is, since it can so easily be invented without leaving one's study. He is full of curiosity, and will go far to satisfy it, regretting "the decadence," in our times, "of energetic passions, in favour of tranquillity and perhaps of happiness." These energetic passions he will find, indeed, in our own times, in Corsica, in Spain, in Lithuania, really in the midst of a very genuine and profoundly studied "local colour," and also, under many disguises, in Parisian drawing-rooms. Mérimée prized happiness, material comfort, the satisfaction of one's immediate desires, very highly, and it was his keen sense

of life, of the pleasures of living, that gave
him some of his keenness in the realisation of
violent death, physical pain, whatever disturbs the equilibrium of things with unusual
emphasis. Himself really selfish, he can distinguish the unhappiness of others with a
kind of intuition which is not sympathy, but
which selfish people often have: a dramatic
consciousness of how painful pain must be,
whoever feels it. It is not pity, though it
communicates itself to us, often enough,
as pity. It is the clear-sighted sensitiveness
of a man who watches human things closely,
bringing them home to himself with the
deliberate, essaying art of an actor who has
to represent a particular passion in movement.

And always in Mérimée there is this union
of curiosity with indifference: the curiosity
of the student, the indifference of the man of
the world. Indifference, in him, as in the man
of the world, is partly an attitude, adopted
for its form, and influencing the temperament
just so much as gesture always influences
emotion. The man who forces himself to
appear calm under excitement teaches his
nerves to follow instinctively the way he has

shown them. In time he will not merely seem calm but will be calm, at the moment when he learns that a great disaster has befallen him. But, in Mérimée, was the indifference even as external as it must always be when there is restraint, when, therefore, there is something to restrain? Was there not in him a certain drying up of the sources of emotion, as the man of the world came to accept almost the point of view of society, reading his stories to a little circle of court ladies, when, once in a while, he permitted himself to write a story? And was not this increase of well-bred indifference, now more than ever characteristic, almost the man himself, the chief reason why he abandoned art so early, writing only two or three short stories during the last twenty-five years of his life, and writing these with a labour which by no means conceals itself?

Mérimée had an abstract interest in, almost an enthusiasm for, facts; facts for their meaning, the light they throw on psychology. He declines to consider psychology except through its expression in facts, with an impersonality far more real than that of Flaubert. The document, historical or social, must translate itself into sharp action before he can use it; not that he does not see, and appreciate better than most others, all there is of significance in the document itself; but his theory of art is inexorable. He never allowed himself to write as he pleased, but he wrote always as he considered the artist should write. Thus he made for himself a kind of formula, confining himself, as some thought, within too narrow limits, but, to himself, doing exactly what he set himself to do, with all the satisfaction of one who is convinced of the justice of his aim and confident of his power to attain it.

Look, for instance, at his longest, far from his best work, *La Chronique du Règne de Charles IX*. Like so much of his work, it has something of the air of a *tour de force*, not taken up entirely for its own sake. Mérimée drops into a fashion, half deprecatingly, as if he sees through it, and yet, as with merely mundane elegance, with a resolve to be more scrupulously exact than its devotees. "Belief," says some one in this book, as if speaking for Mérimée, "is a precious gift which has been denied me." Well, he will

do better, without belief, than those who believe. Written under a title which suggests
a work of actual history, it is more than possible
that the first suggestion of this book really
came, as he tells us in the preface, from the
reading of "a large number of memoirs and
pamphlets relating to the end of the sixteenth
century." "I wished to make an epitome of
my reading," he tells us, "and here is the
epitome." The historical problem attracted
him, that never quite explicable Massacre
of St. Bartholomew, in which there was precisely the violence of action and uncertainty
of motive which he liked to set before him at
the beginning of a task in literature. Probable,
clearly defined people, in the dress of the
period, grew up naturally about this central
motive; humour and irony have their part;
there are adventures, told with a sword's
point of sharpness, and in the fewest possible
words; there is one of his cruel and loving
women, in whom every sentiment becomes
action, by some twisted feminine logic of their
own. It is the most artistic, the most clean-
cut, of historical novels; and yet this perfect
neatness of method suggests a certain indif-

ference on the part of the writer, as if he were
more interested in doing the thing well than in
doing it.

And that, in all but the very best of his
stories (even, perhaps, in *Arsène Guillot* only
not in such perfect things as *Carmen*, as
Mateo Falcone), is what Mérimée just lets us
see, underneath an almost faultless skill of
narrative. An incident told by Mérimée at
his best gathers about it something of the
gravity of history, the composed way in which
it is told helping to give it the equivalent of
remoteness, allowing it not merely to be, but,
what is more difficult, to seem classic in its
own time. "Magnificent things, things after
my own heart—that is to say, Greek in their
truth and simplicity," he writes in a letter,
referring to the tales of Poushkin. The phrase
is scarcely too strong to apply to what is best
in his own work. Made out of elemental
passions, hard, cruel, detached as it were from
their own sentiments, the stories that he tells
might in other hands become melodramas:
Carmen, taken thoughtlessly out of his hands,
has supplied the libretto to the most popular of modern light operas. And yet, in his

severe method of telling, mere outlines, it
seems, told with an even stricter watch over
what is significantly left out than over what is
briefly allowed to be said in words, these stories
sum up little separate pieces of the world,
each a little world in itself. And each is a
little world which he has made his own, with a
labor at last its own reward, and taking life
partly because he has put into it more of himself than the mere intention of doing it well.
Mérimée loved Spain, and *Carmen*, which, by
some caprice of popularity, is the symbol of
Spain to people in general, is really, to those
who know Spain well, the most Spanish thing
that has been written since *Gil Blas*. All the
little parade of local colour and philology,
the appendix on the *Calo* of the gipsies, done
to heighten the illusion, has more significance
than people sometimes think. In this story
all the qualities of Mérimée come into agree-
ment; the student of human passions, the
traveller, the observer, the learned man, meet
in harmony; and, in addition, there is the
aficionado, the true *amateur*, in love with Spain
and the Spaniards.

It is significant that at the reception of

Mérimée at the Académie Française in 1845,
M. Étienne thought it already needful to say:
"Do not pause in the midst of your career;
rest is not permitted to your talent." Already
Mérimée was giving way to facts, to facts in
themselves, as they come into history, into
records of scholarship. We find him writing, a
little dryly, on Catiline, on Cæsar, on Don
Pedro the Cruel, learning Russian, and translating from it (yet, while studying the Russians
before all the world, never discovering the
mystical Russian soul), writing learned articles,
writing reports. He looked around on contemporary literature, and found nothing that
he could care for. Stendhal was gone, and
who else was there to admire? Flaubert, it
seemed to him, was "wasting his talent under
the pretence of realism." Victor Hugo was
"a fellow with the most beautiful figures of
speech at his disposal," who did not take the
trouble to think, but intoxicated himself with
his own words. Baudelaire made him furious,
Renan filled him with pitying scorn. In the
midst of his contempt, he may perhaps have
imagined that he was being left behind. For
whatever reason, weakness or strength, he

could not persuade himself that it was worth while to strive for anything any more. He died probably at the moment when he was no longer a fashion, and had not yet become a classic.

1901.

GÉRARD DE NERVAL

1

THIS is the problem of one who lost the whole world and gained his own soul.

"I like to arrange my life as if it were a novel," wrote Gérard de Nerval, and, indeed, it is somewhat difficult to disentangle the precise facts of an existence which was never quite conscious where began and where ended that "overflowing of dreams into real life," of which he speaks. "I do not ask of God," he said, "that he should change anything in events themselves, but that he should change me in regard to things, so that I might have the power to create my own universe about me, to govern my dreams, instead of enduring them." The prayer was not granted, in its entirety; and the tragedy of his life lay in the vain endeavour to hold back the irresistible empire of the unseen, which it was the joy of his life to summon about him. Briefly, we

know that Gérard Labrunie (the name de
Nerval was taken from a little piece of prop-
erty, worth some 1500 francs, which he liked
to imagine had always been in the possession
of his family) was born at Paris, May 22, 1808.
His father was surgeon-major; his mother
died before he was old enough to remember
her, following the *Grande Armée* on the Russian campaign; and Gérard was brought up,
largely under the care of a studious and erratic
uncle, in a little village called Montagny, near
Ermenonville.   He was a precocious schoolboy,
and by the age of eighteen had published six
little collections of verses.   It was during one
of his holidays that he saw, for the first and
last time, the young girl whom he calls Adrienne, and whom, under many names, he loved
to the end of his life.   One evening she had
come from the château to dance with the
young peasant girls on the grass.   She had
danced with Gérard, he had kissed her cheek,
he had crowned her hair with laurels, he had
heard her sing an old song telling of the sorrows
of a princess whom her father had shut in a
tower because she had loved.   To Gérard it
seemed that already he remembered her, and

certainly he was never to forget her. Afterwards, he heard that Adrienne had taken the veil; then, that she was dead. To one who had realised that it is "we, the living, who walk in a world of phantoms," death could not exclude hope; and when, many years later, he fell seriously and fantastically in love with a little actress called Jenny Colon, it was because he seemed to have found, in that blonde and very human person, the re-incarnation of the blonde Adrienne.

Meanwhile Gérard was living in Paris, among his friends the Romantics, writing and living in an equally desultory fashion. *Le bon Gérard* was the best loved, and, in his time, not the least famous, of the company. He led, by choice, now in Paris, now across Europe, the life of a vagabond, and more persistently than others of his friends who were driven to it by need. At that time, when it was the aim of every one to be as eccentric as possible, the eccentricities of Gérard's life and thought seemed, on the whole, less noticeable than those of many really quite normal persons. But with Gérard there was no pose; and when, one day, he was found in the Palais-

Royal, leading a lobster at the end of a blue
ribbon (because, he said, it does not bark, and
knows the secrets of the sea), the visionary had
simply lost control of his visions, and had to be
sent to Dr. Blanche's asylum at Montmartre.
He entered March 21, 1841, and came out,
apparently well again, on the 21st of November.
It would seem that this first access of madness
was, to some extent, the consequence of the
final rupture with Jenny Colon; on June 5,
1842, she died and it was partly in order to put
as many leagues of the earth as possible between him and that memory that Gérard set
out, at the end of 1842, for the East.   It was
also in order to prove to the world, by his consciousness of external things, that he had
recovered his reason.   While he was in Syria,
he once more fell in love with a new incarnation of Adrienne, a young Druse, Saléma, the
daughter of a Sheikh of Lebanon; and it seems
to have been almost by accident that he did
not marry her.   He returned to Paris at the
end of 1843 or the beginning of 1844, and for
the next few years he lived mostly in Paris,
writing charming, graceful, remarkably sane
articles and books and wandering about the

streets, by day and night, in a perpetual dream
from which, now and again, he was somewhat
rudely awakened. When, in the spring of
1853, he went to see Heine, for whom he was
doing an admirable prose translation of his
poems, and told him he had come to return the
money he had received in advance, because
the times were accomplished, and the end of
the world, announced by the Apocalypse, was
at hand, Heine sent for a cab, and Gérard
found himself at Dr. Dubois' asylum, where
he remained two months. It was on coming
out of the asylum that he wrote *Sylvie*, a
delightful idyl, chiefly autobiographical, one
of his three actual achievements. On August
27, 1853, he had to be taken to Dr. Blanche's
asylum at Passy, where he remained till May
27, 1854. Thither, after a month or two spent
in Germany, he returned on August 8, and on
October 19 he came out for the last time, man-
ifestly uncured. He was now engaged on the
narrative o his own madness, and the first
part of *Le Rêve et la Vie* appeared in the *Revue
de Paris* of January 1, 1855. On the 20th he
came into the office of the review, and showed
Gautier and Maxime du Camp an apron-

string which he was carrying in his pocket.
"It is the girdle," he said, "that Madame de
Maintenon wore when she had *Esther* performed at Saint-Cyr." On the 24th he wrote
to a friend: "Come and prove my identity at
the police-station of the Châtelet." The night
before he had been working at his manuscript
in a pot-house of Les Halles, and had been
arrested as a vagabond. He was used to such
little misadventures, but he complained of the
difficulty of writing. "I set off after an idea,"
he said, "and lose myself; I am hours in finding my way back. Do you know I can scarcely
write twenty lines a day, the darkness comes
about me so close!" He took out the apron-
string. "It is the garter of the Queen of
Sheba," he said. The snow was freezing on
the ground, and on the night of the 25th, at
three in the morning, the landlord of a "penny
doss" in the Rue de la Vieille-Lanterne, a
filthy alley lying between the quays and the
Rue de Rivoli, heard some one knocking at
the door, but did not open, on account of the
cold. At dawn, the body of Gérard de Nerval
was found hanging by the apron-string to a
bar of the window.

It is not necessary to exaggerate the importance of the half-dozen volumes which make up the works of Gérard de Nerval. He was not a great writer; he had moments of greatness; and it is the particular quality of these moments which is of interest for us. There is the entertaining, but not more than entertaining, *Voyage en Orient;* there is the estimable translation of *Faust*, and the admirable versions from Heine; there are the volumes of short stories and sketches, of which even *Les Illuminés*, in spite of the promise of its title, is little more than an agreeable compilation. But there remain three compositions: the sonnets, *Le Rêve et la Vie*, and *Sylvie;* of which *Sylvie* is the most objectively achieved, a wandering idyl, full of pastoral delight, and containing some folk-songs of Valois, two of which have been translated by Rossetti; *Le Rêve et la Vie* being the most intensely personal, a narrative of madness, unique as madness itself; and the sonnets, a kind of miracle, which may be held to have created something at least of the method of the later Symbolist. These three compositions, in which alone Gérard is

his finest self, all belong to the periods when
he was, in the eyes of the world, actually
mad. The sonnets belong to two of these
periods, *Le Rêve et la Vie* to the last; *Sylvie*
was written in the short interval between the
two attacks in the early part of 1853. We
have thus the case of a writer, graceful and
elegant when he is sane, but only inspired,
only really wise, passionate, collected, only
really master of himself, when he is insane.
It may be worth looking at a few of the
points which so suggestive a problem presents
to us.

2

Gérard de Nerval lived the transfigured
inner life of the dreamer. "I was very
tired of life!" he says. And like so many
dreamers, who have all the luminous darkness
of the universe in their brains, he found his
most precious and uninterrupted solitude in
the crowded and more sordid streets of great
cities. He who had loved the Queen of
Sheba, and seen the seven Elohims dividing
the world, could find nothing more tolerable

in mortal conditions, when he was truly aware
of them, than the company of the meanest of
mankind, in whom poverty and vice, and the
hard pressure of civilisation, still leave some
of the original vivacity of the human comedy.
The real world seeming to be always so far
from him, and a sort of terror of the gulfs
holding him, in spite of himself, to its flying skirts, he found something at all events
realisable, concrete, in these drinkers of Les
Halles, these vagabonds of the Place du
Carrousel, among whom he so often sought
refuge. It was literally, in part, a refuge.
During the day he could sleep, but night
wakened him, and that restlessness, which
the night draws out in those who are really
under lunar influences, set his feet wandering,
if only in order that his mind might wander
the less. The sun, as he mentions, never
appears in dreams; but, with the approach of
night, is not every one a little readier to believe in the mystery lurking behind the world?

Crains, dans le mur aveugle, un regard qui t'épie!

he writes in one of his great sonnets; and
that fear of the invisible watchfulness of

nature was never absent from him. It is one of the terrors of human existence that we may be led at once to seek and so shun solitude; unable to bear the mortal pressure if its embrace, unable to endure the nostalgia of its absence. "I think man's happiest when he forgets himself," says an Elizabethan dramatist; and, with Gérard, there was Adrienne to forget, and Jenny Colon the actress, and the Queen of Sheba. But to have drunk of the cup of dreams is to have drunk of the cup of eternal memory. The past, and, as it seemed to him, the future were continually with him; only the present fled continually from under his feet. It was only by the effort of this contact with people who lived so sincerely in the day, the minute, that he could find even a temporary foothold. With them, at least, he could hold back all the stars, and the darkness beyond them, and the interminable approach and disappearance of all the ages, if only for the space between tavern and tavern, where he could open his eyes on so frank an abandonment to the common drunkenness of most people in this world, here for once really living the symbolic intoxication of their ignorance.

Like so many dreamers of illimitable dreams, it was the fate of Gérard to incarnate his ideal in the person of an actress. The fatal transfiguration of the footlights, in which reality and the artificial change places with so fantastic a regularity, has drawn many moths into its flame, and will draw more, as long as men persist in demanding illusion of what is real, and reality in what is illusion. The Jenny Colons of the world are very simple, very real, if one will but refrain from assuming them to be a mystery. But it is the penalty of all imaginative lovers to create for themselves the veil which hides from them the features of the beloved. It is their privilage, for it is incomparably more entrancing to fancy oneself in love with Isis than to know that one is in love with Manon Lescaut. The picture of Gérard, after many hesitations, revealing to the astonished Jenny that she is the incarnation of another, the shadow of a dream, that she has been Adrienne and is about to be the Queen of Sheba; her very human little cry of pure incomprehension, *Mais vous ne m'aimez pas!* and her prompt refuge in the arms of the *jeune premier ridé,* if it were not of the acutest pathos, would certainly be of the most quintessential comedy. For Gérard, so sharp an awakening was but like the passage from one state to another, across that little bridge of one step which lies between heaven and hell, to which he was so used in his dreams. It gave permanency to the trivial, crystallising it, in another than Stendhal's sense; and when death came, changing mere human memory into the terms of eternity, the darkness of the spiritual world was lit with a new star, which was henceforth the wandering, desolate guide of so many visions. The tragic figure of Aurélia, which comes and goes through all the labyrinths of dream, is now seen always "as if lit up by a lightning-flash, pale and dying, hurried away by dark horsemen."

The dream or doctrine of the re-incarnation of souls, which has given so much consolation to so many questioners of eternity, was for Gérard (need we doubt?) a dream rather than a doctrine, but one of those dreams which are nearer to a man than his breath. "This vague and hopeless love," he writes in *Sylvie*, "inspired by an actress, which night by night took hold of me at the hour of the performance, leaving me only at the hour of sleep, had its germ in the recollection of Adrienne, flower of the night, unfolding under the pale rays of the moon, rosy and blonde phantom, gliding over the green grass, half bathed in white mist. . . . To love a nun under the form of an actress! . . . and if it were the very same! It is enough to drive one mad!" Yes, *il y a de quoi devenir fou*, as Gérard had found; but there was also, in this intimate sense of the unity, perpetuity, and harmoniously recurring rhythm of nature, not a little of the inner substance of wisdom. It was a dream, perhaps refracted from some broken, illuminating angle by which madness catches unseen light, that revealed to him the meaning of his own superstition, fatality, malady: "During my sleep, I had a marvelous vision. It seemed to me that the goddess appeared before me, saying to me: 'I am the same as Mary, the same as thy mother, the same also whom, under all forms, thou hast always loved. At each of thine ordeals I have dropt yet one more of the masks with which I veil my countenance, and soon thou shalt see me as I am!'" And in perhaps his finest sonnet, the mysterious *Artémis*, we have, under other symbols, and with the deliberate inconsequence of these sonnets, the comfort and despair of the same faith.

La Triezième revient . . . C'est encor la première;
Et c'est toujours la seule,—ou c'est le seul moment:
Car es-tu reine, ô toi! la première ou dernière?
Es-tu roi, toi le seul ou le dernier amant? . . .

Aimez qui vous aima du berceau dans la bière;
Celle que j'aimai seul m'aime encor tendrement;
C'est la mort—ou la morte . . . Ô délice! ô tourment!
La Rose qu'elle tient, c'est la Rose trémière.

Sainte napolitaine aux mains pleines de feux,
Rose au cœur violet, fleur de sainte Gudule;
As-tu trouvé ta croix dans le désert cieux?

Roses blanches, tombez! vous insultez nos dieux:
Tombez, fantômes blancs, de votre ciel qui brûle:
—La Sainte de l'abîme est plus sainte à mes yeux!

Who has not often meditated, above all what artist, on the slightness, after all, of the link which holds our faculties together in that sober health of the brain which we call reason? Are there not moments when that link seems to be worn down to so fine a tenuity that the wing of a passing dream might suffice to snap it? The consciousness seems, as it were, to expand and contract at once, into something too wide for the universe, and too narrow for the thought of self to find room within it. Is it that the sense of identity is about to evaporate, annihilating all, or is it that a more profound identity, the identity of the whole sentient universe, has been at last realised? Leaving the concrete world on these brief voyages, the fear is that we may not have strength to return, or that we may lose the way back. Every artist lives a double life, in which he is for the most part conscious of the illusions of the imagination. He is conscious also of the illusions of the nerves, which he shares with every man of imaginative mind. Nights of insomnia, days of anxious waiting, the sudden shock of an event, and one of these common disturbances may be enough to jangle the tuneless bells of one's nerves. The artist can distinguish these causes of certain of his moods from those other causes which come to him because he is an artist, and are properly concerned with that invention which is his own function. Yet is there not some danger that he may come to confuse one with the other, that he may "lose the thread" which conducts him through the intricacies of the inner world?

The supreme artist, certainly, is the furthest of all men from this danger; for he is the supreme intelligence. Like Dante, he can pass through hell unsinged. With him, imagination is vision; when he looks into the darkness, he sees. The vague dreamer, the insecure artist and the uncertain mystic at once, sees only shadows, not recognising their outlines. He is mastered by the images which have come at his call; he has not the power which chains them for his slaves. "The kingdom of Heaven suffers violence," and the dreamer who has gone tremblingly into the darkness is in peril at the hands of those very real phantoms who are the reflection of his fear.

The madness of Gérard de Nerval, whatever physiological reasons may be rightly given for its outbreak, subsidence, and return,

I take to have been essentially due to the weakness and not the excess of his visionary quality, to the insufficiency of his imaginative energy, and to his lack of spiritual discipline. He was an unsystematic mystic; his "Tower of Babel in two hundred volumes," that medley of books of religion, science, astrology, history, travel, which he thought would have rejoiced the heart of Pico della Mirandola, of Meursius, or of Nicholas of Cusa, was truly, as he says, "enough to drive a wise man mad." "Why not also," he adds, "enough to make a madman wise?" But precisely because it was this *amas bizarre*, this jumble of the perilous secrets in which wisdom is so often folly, and folly so often wisdom. He speaks vaguely of the Cabbala; the Cabbala would have been safety to him, as the Catholic Church would have been, or any other reasoned scheme of things. Wavering among intuitions, ignorances, half-truths, shadows of falsehood, now audacious, now hesitating, he was blown hither and thither by conflicting winds, a prey to the indefinite.

Le Rêve et la Vie, the last fragments of which were found in his pockets after his

suicide, scrawled on scraps of paper, inter-
rupted with Cabbalistic signs and "a demon-
stration of the Immaculate Conception by
geometry," is a narrative of a madman's
visions by the madman himself, yet showing,
as Gautier says, "cold reason seated by the
bedside of hot fever, hallucination analysing
itself by a supreme philosophic effort." What
is curious, yet after all natural, is that part
of the narrative seems to be contemporaneous
with what it describes, and part subsequent
to it; so that it is not as when De Quincey
says to us, such or such was the opium-dream
that I had on such a night; but as if the
opium-dreamer had begun to write down his
dream while he was yet within its coils.
"The descent into hell," he calls it twice;
yet does he not also write: "At times I
imagined that my force and my activity were
doubled; it seemed to me that I knew everything, understood everything; and imagination brought me infinite pleasures. Now that
I have recovered what men call reason, must
I not regret having lost them?" But he had
not lost them; he was still in that state of
double consciousness which he describes in

one of his visions, when, seeing people dressed
in white, "I was astonished," he says, "to
see them all dressed in white; yet it seemed to
me that this was an optical illusion." His
cosmical visions are at times so magnificent
that he seems to be creating myths; and it is
with a worthy ingenuity that he plays the part
he imagines to be assigned to him in his astral
influences.

"First of all I imagined that the persons
collected in the garden (of the madhouse) all
had some influence on the stars, and that the
one who always walked round and round in a
circle regulated the course of the sun. An old
man, who was brought there at certain hours of
the day, and who made knots as he consulted
his watch, seemed to me to be charged with
the notation of the course of the hours. I
attributed to myself an influence over the
course of the moon, and I believed that this
star had been struck by the thunderbolt of the
Most High, which had traced on its face the
imprint of the mask which I had observed.

"I attributed a mystical signification to the
conversations of the warders and of my companions. It seemed to me that they were

the representatives of all the races of the
earth, and that we had undertaken between
us to re-arrange the course of the stars, and
to give a wider development to the system.
An error, in my opinion, had crept into the
general combination of numbers, and thence
came all the ills of humanity. I believed
also that the celestial spirits had taken human
forms, and assisted at this general congress,
seeming though they did to be concerned with
but ordinary occupations. My own part
seemed to me to be the re-establishment of
universal harmony by Cabbalistic art, and I
had to seek a solution by evoking the occult
forces of various religions."

So far we have, no doubt, the confusions of
madness, in which what may indeed be the
symbol is taken for the thing itself. But
now observe what follows:

"I seemed to myself a hero living under the
very eyes of the gods; everything in nature
assumed new aspects, and secret voices came
to me from the plants, the trees, animals, the
meanest insects, to warn and to encourage me.
The words of my companions had mysterious
messages, the sense of which I alone under-

stood; things without form and without life lent themselves to the designs of my mind; out of combinations of stones, the figures of angles, crevices, or openings, the shape of leaves, out of colours, odours, and sounds, I saw unknown harmonies come forth. 'How is it,' I said to myself, 'that I can possibly have lived so long outside Nature, without identifying myself with her! All things live, all things are in motion, all things correspond; the magnetic rays emanating from myself or others traverse without obstacle the infinite chain of created things: a transparent network covers the world, whose loose threads communicate more and more closely with the planets and the stars. Now a captive upon the earth, I hold converse with the starry choir, which is feelingly a part of my joys and sorrows.'"

To have thus realised that central secret of the mystics, from Pythagoras onwards, the secret which the Smaragdine Tablet of Hermes betrays in its "As things are below, so are they above"; which Boehme has classed in his teaching of "signatures," and Swedenborg has systematised in his doctrine of "correspondences"; does it matter very much that he arrived at it by way of the obscure and fatal initiation of madness? Truth, and especially that soul of truth which is poetry, may be reached by many roads; and a road is not necessarily misleading because it is dangerous or forbidden. Here is one who has gazed at light till it has blinded him; and for us all that is important is that he has seen something, not that his eyesight has been too weak to endure the pressure of light overflowing the world from beyond the world.

3

And here we arrive at the fundamental principle which is at once the substance and the æsthetics of the sonnets "composed," as he explains, "in that state of meditation which the Germans would call 'supernatural-istic.'" In one, which I will quote, he is explicit, and seems to state a doctrine.

VERS DORÉS

Homme, libre penseur! te crois-tu seul pensant
Dans ce monde où la vie éclate en toute chose?
Des forces que tu tiens ta liberté dispose,
Mais de tous tes conseils l'univers est absent.

Respecte dans la bête un esprit agissant:
Chaque fleur est une âme à la Nature éclose;
Un mystère d'amour dans le métal repose;
"Tout est sensible!" Et tout sur ton être est puissant.

Crains, dans le mur aveugle, un regard qui t'épie!
A la matière même un verbe est attaché . . .
Ne la fais pas servir à quelque usage impie!

Souvent dans l'être obscur habite un Dieu caché;
Et comme un œil naissant couvert par ses paupières,
Un pur esprit s'accroît sous l'écorce des pierres!

But in the other sonnets, in *Artémis*, which I have quoted, in *El Desdichado*, *Myrtho*, and the rest, he would seem to be deliberately obscure; or at least, his obscurity results, to some extent, from the state of mind which he describes in *Le Rêve et la Vie:* "I then saw, vaguely drifting into form, plastic images of antiquity, which outlined themselves, became definite, and seemed to represent symbols, of which I only seized the idea with difficulty." Nothing could more precisely represent the impression made by these sonnets, in which, for the first time in French, words are used as the ingredients of an evocation, as themselves not merely colour and sound, but symbol. Here are words which create an atmosphere by the actual suggestive quality of their

syllables, as, according to the theory of
Mallarmé, they should do; as, in the recent
attempts of the Symbolists, writer after writer
has endeavoured to lure them into doing.
Persuaded, as Gérard was, of the sensitive
unity of all nature, he was able to trace
resemblances where others saw only diver-
gences; and the setting together of unfamiliar
and apparently alien things, which comes so
strangely upon us in his verse, was perhaps
an actual sight of what it is our misfortune
not to see. His genius, to which madness
had come as the liberating, the precipitating,
spirit, disengaging its finer essence, consisted
in a power of materialising vision, whatever
is most volatile and unseizable in vision
and without losing the sense of mystery, or
that quality which gives its charm to the
intangible. Madness, then, in him, had lit
up, as if by lightning-flashes, the hidden
links of distant and divergent things; perhaps
in somewhat the same manner as that in
which a similarly new, startling, perhaps over-
true sight of things is gained by the artificial
stimulation of haschisch, opium, and those
other drugs by which vision is produced de-

liberately, and the soul, sitting safe within
the perilous circle of its own magic, looks
out on the panorama which either rises out
of the darkness before it, or drifts from itself
into the darkness.   The very imagery of these
sonnets is the imagery which is known to all
dreamers of bought dreams.   *Rose au cœur
violet, fleur de sainte Gudule; le Temple au
péristyle immense; la grotte où nage la syrène:*
the dreamer of· bought dreams has seen
them all.   But no one before Gérard realised that such things as these might be the
basis of almost a new æsthetics.   Did he
himself realise all that he had done, or was
it left for Mallarmé to theorise· upon what
Gérard had but divined?

That he made the discovery, there is no
doubt; and we owe to the fortunate accident
of madness one of the foundations of what
may be called the practical æsthetics of
Symbolism.   Look again at that sonnet *Artémis*, and you will see in it not only the
method of Mallarmé, but much of the most
intimate manner of Verlaine.   The first four
lines, with their fluid rhythm, their repetitions and echoes, their delicate evasions,

might have been written by Verlaine; in the later part the firmness of the rhythms and the jewelled significance of the words are like Mallarmé at his finest, so that in a single sonnet we may fairly claim to see a foreshadowing of the styles of Mallarmé and Verlaine at once. With Verlaine the resemblance goes, perhaps, no further; with Mallarmé it goes to the very roots, the whole man being, certainly, his style.

Gérard de Nerval, then, had divined, before all the world, that poetry should be a miracle; not a hymn to beauty, nor the description of beauty, nor beauty's mirror; but beauty itself, the colour, fragrance, and form of the imagined flower, as it blossoms again out of the page. Vision, the over-powering vision, had come to him beyond, if not against, his will; and he knew that vision is the root out of which the flower must grow. Vision had taught him symbol, and he knew that it is by symbol alone that the flower can take visible form. He knew that the whole mystery of beauty can never be comprehended by the crowd, and that while clearness is a virtue of style, perfect explicitness is not a necessary virtue. So it was with disdain, as well as with confidence, that he allowed these sonnets to be overheard. It was enough for him to say:

J'ai rêvé dans la grotte où nage la syrène;

and to speak, it might be, the siren's language, remembering her. "It will be my last madness," he wrote, "to believe myself a poet: let criticism cure me of it." Criticism, in his own day, even Gautier's criticism, could but be disconcerted by a novelty so unexampled. It is only now that the best critics in France are beginning to realise how great in themselves, and how great in their influence, are these sonnets, which, forgotten by the world for nearly fifty years, have all the while been secretly bringing new æsthetics into French poetry.

THÉOPHILE GAUTIER

1

GAUTIER has spoken for himself in a famous passage of *Mademoiselle de Maupin:* "I am a man of the Homeric age; the world in which I live is not my world, and I understand nothing of the society which surrounds me. For me Christ did not come; I am as much a pagan as Alcibiades or Phidias. I have never plucked on Golgotha the flowers of the Passion, and the deep stream that flows from the side of the Crucified and sets a crimson girdle about the world, has never washed me in its flood; my rebellious body will not acknowledge the supremacy of the soul, and my flesh will not endure to be mortified. I find the earth as beautiful as the sky, and I think that perfection of form is virtue. I have no gift for spirituality; I prefer a statue to a ghost, full noon to twilight. Three things delight me: gold, marble, and purple; brilliance, solidity,

colour. . . . I have looked on love in the light
of antiquity, and as a piece of sculpture more
or less perfect. . . . All my life I have been
concerned with the form of the flagon, never
with the quality of its contents." That is
part of a confession of faith, and it is spoken
with absolute sincerity. Gautier knew himself, and could tell the truth about himself as
simply, as impartially, as if he had been describing a work of art. Or is he not, indeed,
describing a work of art? Was not that very
state of mind, that finished and limited temperament, a thing which he had collaborated
with nature in making, with an effective heightening of what was most natural to him, in the
spirit of art?

Gautier saw the world as mineral, as metal,
as pigment, as rock, tree, water, as architecture, costume, under sunlight, gas, in all the
colours that light can bring out of built or
growing things; he saw it as contour, movement; he saw all that a painter sees, when the
painter sets himself to copy, not to create.
He was the finest copyist who ever used paint
with a pen. Nothing that can be expressed
in technical terms escaped him; there were no

technical terms which he could not reduce to
an orderly beauty. But he absorbed all this
visible world with the hardly discriminating
impartiality of the retina; he had no moods,
was not to be distracted by a sentiment, heard
no voices, saw nothing but darkness, the nega-
tion of day, in night. He was tirelessly attentive, he had no secrets of his own and could keep
none of nature's. He could describe every
ray of the nine thousand precious stones in
the throne of Ivan the Terrible, in the Treasury
of the Kremlin; but he could tell you nothing
of one of Maeterlinck's bees.

The five senses made Gautier for themselves,
that they might become articulate. He speaks
for them all with a dreadful unconcern. All
his words are in love with matter, and they
enjoy their lust and have no recollection. If
the body did not dwindle and expand to some
ignoble physical conclusion; if wrinkles did
not creep yellowing up women's necks, and the
fire in a man's blood did not lose its heat; he
would always be content. Everything that
he cared for in the world was to be had, except,
perhaps, rest from striving after it; only,
everything would one day come to an end,

after a slow spoiling. Decrepit, colourless, uneager things shocked him, and it was with an acute, almost disinterested pity that he watched himself die.

All his life Gautier adored life, and all the processes and forms of life. A pagan, a young Roman, hard and delicate, with something of cruelty in his sympathy with things that could be seen and handled, he would have hated the soul, if he had ever really apprehended it, for its qualifying and disturbing power upon the body. No other modern writer, no writer perhaps, has described nakedness with so abstract a heat of rapture: like d'Albert when he sees Mlle. de Maupin for the first and last time, he is the artist before he is the lover, and he is the lover while he is the artist. It was above all things the human body whose contours and colours he wished to fix for eternity, in the "robust art" of "verse, marble, onyx, enamel." And it was not the body as a frail, perishable thing, and a thing to be pitied, that he wanted to perpetuate; it was the beauty of life itself, imperishable at least in its recurrence.

He loved imperishable things: the body, as generation after generation refashions it, the world, as it is restored and rebuilt, and then gems, and hewn stone, and carved ivory, and woven tapestry. He loved verse for its solid, strictly limited, resistant form, which, while prose melts and drifts about it, remains unalterable, indestructible. Words, he knew, can build as strongly as stones, and not merely rise to music, like the walls of Troy, but be themselves music as well as structure. Yet, as in visible things he cared only for hard outline and rich colour, so in words too he had no love of half-tints, and was content to do without that softening of atmosphere which was to be prized by those who came after him as the thing most worth seeking. Even his verse is without mystery; if he meditates, his meditation has all the fixity of a kind of sharp, precise criticism.

What Gautier saw he saw with unparalleled exactitude; he allows himself no poetic license or room for fine phrases; has his eye always on the object, and really uses the words which best describe it, whatever they may be. So his books of travel are guide-books, in addition to being other things; and not by any means "states of soul" or states of nerves. He is

willing to give you information, and able to
give it to you without deranging his periods.
The little essay on Leonardo is an admirable
piece of artistic divination, and it is also a
clear, simple, sufficient account of the man,
his temperament, and his way of work. The
study of Baudelaire, reprinted in the *édition
définitive* of the "Fleurs du Mal," remains the
one satisfactory summing up, it is not a solution, of the enigma which Baudelaire personi-
fied; and it is almost the most coloured and
perfumed thing in words which he ever wrote.
He wrote equally well about cities, poets,
novelists, painters, or sculptors; he did not
understand one better than the other, or feel
less sympathy for one than for another. He,
the "parfait magicien ès lettres françaises,"
to whom faultless words came in faultlessly
beautiful order, could realise, against Balzac
himself, that Balzac had a style: "he possesses, though he did not think so, a style, and
a very beautiful style, the necessary, inevitable,
mathematical style of his ideas." He appreciated Ingres as justly as he appreciated El
Greco; he went through the Louvre, room
by room, saying the right thing about each

painter in turn. He did not say the final thing; he said nothing which we have to pause and think over before we see the whole of its truth or apprehend the whole of its beauty. Truth, in him, comes to us almost literally through the eyesight, and with the same beautiful clearness as if it were one of those visible things which delighted him most: gold, marble, and purple; brilliance, solidity, colour.

1902.

GUSTAVE FLAUBERT

Salammbô is an attempt, as Flaubert, himself his best critic, has told us, to "perpetuate a mirage by applying to antiquity the methods of the modern novel." By the modern novel he means the novel as he had reconstructed it; he means *Madame Bovary*. That perfect book is perfect because Flaubert had, for once, found exactly the subject suited to his method, had made his method and his subject one. On his scientific side Flaubert is a realist, but there is another, perhaps a more intimately personal side, on which he is lyrical, lyrical in a large, sweeping way. The lyric poet in him made *La Tentation de Saint-Antoine*, the analyst made *L'Education Sentimentale;* but in *Madame Bovary* we find the analyst and the lyric poet in equilibrium. It is the history of a woman, as carefully observed as any story that has ever been written, and observed in surroundings of the most ordinary kind. But Flaubert finds the romantic material which he loved, the materials of beauty, in precisely that temperament which he studies so patiently and so cruelly. Madame Bovary is a little woman, half vulgar and half hysterical, incapable of a fine passion; but her trivial desires, her futile aspirations after second-rate pleasures and second-hand ideals, give to Flaubert all that he wants: the opportunity to create beauty out of reality. What is common in the imagination of Madame Bovary becomes exquisite in Flaubert's rendering of it, and by that counterpoise of a commonness in the subject he is saved from any vague ascents of rhetoric in his rendering of it.

In writing *Salammbô* Flaubert set himself to renew the historical novel, as he had renewed the novel of manners. He would have admitted, doubtless, that perfect success in the historical novel is impossible, by the nature of the case. We are at best only half conscious of the reality of the things about us, only able to translate them approximately into any form of art. How much is left over, in the closest transcription of a

mere line of houses in a street, of a passing
steamer, of one's next-door neighbour, of the
point of view of a foreigner looking along
Piccadilly, of one's own state of mind, moment by moment, as one walks from Oxford
Circus to the Marble Arch? Think, then,
of the attempts to reconstruct no matter what
period of the past, to distinguish the difference in the aspect of a world perhaps bossed
with castles and ridged with ramparts, to
two individualities encased within chain-
armour! Flaubert chose his antiquity wisely:
a period of which we know too little to confuse us, a city of which no stone is left on
another, the minds of Barbarians who have
left us no psychological documents. "Be sure
I have made no fantastic Carthage," he
says proudly, pointing to his documents:
Ammianus Marcellinus, who has furnished
him with "the *exact* form of a door"; the
Bible and Theophrastus, from which he ob-
tains his perfumes and his precious stones;
Gesenius, from whom he gets his Punic
names; the *Mémoires de l'Académie des In-
scriptions.* "As for the temple of Tanit,
I am sure of having reconstructed it as it

was, with the treatise of the Syrian Goddess,
with the medals of the Duc de Luynes, with
what is known of the temple at Jerusalem,
with a passage of St. Jerome, quoted by
Seldon (*De Diis Syriis*), with the plan of the
temple of Gozzo, which is quite Carthaginian,
and best of all, with the ruins of the temple
of Thugga, which I have seen myself, with
my own eyes, and of which no traveller or
antiquarian, so far as I know, has ever
spoken." But that, after all, as he admits
(when, that is, he has proved point by point
his minute accuracy to all that is known
of ancient Carthage, his faithfulness to every
indication which can serve for his guidance,
his patience in grouping rather than his
daring in the invention of action and details),
that is not the question. "I care little enough
for archæology! If the colour is not uniform, if the details are out of keeping, if the
manners do not spring from the religion and the
actions from the passions, if the characters
are not consistent, if the costumes are not
appropriate to the habits and the architecture to the climate, if, in a word, there is not
harmony, I am in error.   If not, no."

And there, precisely, is the definition of
the one merit which can give a historical
novel the right to exist, and at the same
time a definition of the merit which sets
Salammbô above all other historical novels.
Everything in the book is strange, some of it
might easily be bewildering, some revolting;
but all is in harmony. The harmony is like
that of Eastern music, not immediately con-
veying its charm, or even the secret of its
measure, to Western ears; but a monotony
coiling perpetually upon itself, after a severe
law of its own. Or rather, it is like a fresco,
painted gravely in hard, definite colours,
firmly detached from a background of burning sky; a procession of Barbarians, each in
the costume of his country, passes across the
wall; there are battles, in which elephants
fight with men; an army besieges a great
city, or rots to death in a defile between
mountains; the ground is paved with dead
men; crosses, each bearing its living burden,
stand against the sky; a few figures of men
and women appear again and again, expressing by their gestures the soul of the
story.

Flaubert himself has pointed, with his unerring self-criticism, to the main defect of his book: "The pedestal is too large for the statue." There should have been, as he says, a hundred pages more about Salammbô. He declares: "There is not in my book an isolated or gratuitous description; all are useful to my characters, and have an influence, near or remote, on the action." This is true, and yet, all the same, the pedestal is too large for the statue. Salammbô, "always surrounded with grave and exquisite things," has something of the somnambulism which enters into the heroism of Judith; she has a hieratic beauty, and a consciousness as pale and vague as the moon whom she worships. She passes before us, "her body saturated with perfumes," encrusted with jewels like an idol, her head turreted with violet hair, the gold chain tinkling between her ankles; and is hardly more than an attitude, a fixed gesture, like the Eastern women whom one sees passing, with oblique eyes and mouths painted into smiles, their faces curiously traced into a work of art, in the languid movements of a panto-mimic dance. The soul behind those eyes?

the temperament under that at times almost terrifying mask? Salammbô is as inarticulate for us as the serpent, to whose drowsy beauty, capable of such sudden awakenings, hers seems half akin; they move before us in a kind of hieratic pantomime, a coloured, expressive thing, signifying nothing. Mâtho, maddened with love, "in an invincible stupor, like those who have drunk some draught of which they are to die," has the same somnambulistic life; the prey of Venus, he has an almost literal insanity, which, as Flaubert reminds us, is true to the ancient view of that passion. He is the only quite vivid person in the book, and he lives with the intensity of a wild beast, a life "blinded alike" from every inner and outer interruption to one or two fixed ideas. The others have their places in the picture, fall into their attitudes naturally, remain so many coloured outlines for us. The illusion is perfect; these people may not be the real people of history, but at least they have no self-consciousness, no Christian tinge in their minds.

"The metaphors are few, the epithets definite," Flaubert tells us, of his style in this book, where, as he says, he has sacrificed less "to

the amplitude of the phrase and to the period,"
than in *Madame Bovary*. The movement
here is in briefer steps, with a more earnest
gravity, without any of the engaging weakness of adjectives. The style is never archaic,
it is absolutely simple, the precise word being
put always for the precise thing; but it ob-
tains a dignity, a historical remoteness, by the
large seriousness of its manner, the absence of
modern ways of thought, which, in *Madame
Bovary*, bring with them an instinctively
modern cadence.

Salammbô is written with the severity of
history, but Flaubert notes every detail visually, as a painter notes the details of natural
things. A slave is being flogged under a tree:
Flaubert notes the movement of the thong as
it flies, and tells us: "The thongs, as they
whistled through the air, sent the bark of the
plane trees flying." Before the battle of the
Macar, the Barbarians are awaiting the approach of the Carthaginian army. First "the
Barbarians were surprised to see the ground
undulate in the distance." Clouds of dust
rise and whirl over the desert, through which
are seen glimpses of horns, and, as it seems,
wings. Are they bulls or birds, or a mirage of

the desert? The Barbarians watch intently.
"At last they made out several transverse bars,
bristling with uniform points. The bars became denser, larger; dark mounds swayed
from side to side; suddenly square bushes
came into view; they were elephants and
lances. A single shout, 'The Carthaginians!'
arose." Observe how all that is seen, as if the
eyes, unaided by the intelligence, had found out
everything for themselves, taking in one indication after another, instinctively. Flaubert
puts himself in the place of his characters, not
so much to think for them as to see for them.

Compare the style of Flaubert in each of
his books, and you will find that each book
has its own rhythm, perfectly appropriate
to its subject-matter. The style, which has
almost every merit and hardly a fault, becomes
what it is by a process very different from
that of most writers careful of form. Read
Chateaubriand, Gautier, even Baudelaire, and
you will find that the aim of these writers has
been to construct a style which shall be adaptable to every occasion, but without structural
change; the cadence is always the same. The
most exquisite word-painting of Gautier can
be translated rhythm for rhythm into English,

without difficulty; once you have mastered
the tune, you have merely to go on; every
verse will be the same.   But Flaubert is so difficult to translate because he has no fixed
rhythm; his prose keeps step with no regular
march-music.   He invents the rhythm of every
sentence, he changes his cadence with every
mood or for the convenience of every fact.
He has no theory of beauty in form apart
from what it expresses.   For him form is a
living thing, the physical body of thought,
which it clothes and interprets.   "If I call
stones blue, it is because blue is the precise
word, believe me," he replies to Sainte-Beuve's
criticism.   Beauty comes into his words from
the precision with which they express definite
things, definite ideas, definite sensations.   And
in his book, where the material is so hard,
apparently so unmalleable, it is a beauty of
sheer exactitude which fills it from end to end,
a beauty of measure and order, seen equally in
the departure of the doves of Carthage at
the time of their flight into Sicily, and in the
lions feasting on the corpses of the Barbarians,
in the defile between the mountains.

1901.

CHARLES BAUDELAIRE

BAUDELAIRE is little known and much misunderstood in England. Only one English writer has ever done him justice, or said anything adequate about him. As long ago as 1862 Swinburne introduced Baudelaire to English readers: in the columns of the *Spectator*, it is amusing to remember. In 1868 he added a few more words of just and subtle praise in his book on Blake, and in the same year wrote the magnificent elegy on his death, *Ave atque Vale*. There have been occasional outbreaks of irrelevant abuse or contempt, and the name of Baudelaire (generally misspelled) is the journalist's handiest brickbat for hurling at random in the name of respectability. Does all this mean that we are waking up, over here, to the consciousness of one of the great literary forces of the age, a force which has been felt in every other country but ours?

It would be a useful influence for us. Baudelaire desired perfection, and we have never

realised that perfection is a thing to aim at.
He only did what he could do supremely well,
and he was in poverty all his life, not because
he would not work, but because he would work
only at certain things, the things which he
could hope to do to his own satisfaction. Of
the men of letters of our age he was the most
scrupulous. He spent his whole life in writing
one book of verse (out of which all French
poetry has come since his time), one book of
prose in which prose becomes a fine art, some
criticism which is the sanest, subtlest, and
surest which his generation produced, and a
translation which is better than a marvellous
original. What would French poetry be to-
day if Baudelaire had never existed? As
different a thing from what it is as English
poetry would be without Rossetti. Neither
of them is quite among the greatest poets,
but they are more fascinating than the greatest,
they influence more minds. And Baudelaire
was an equally great critic. He discovered
Poe, Wagner, and Manet. Where even Sainte-
Beuve, with his vast materials, his vast general talent for criticism, went wrong in contemporary judgments, Baudelaire was infal-

libly right.   He wrote neither verse nor prose
with ease, but he would not permit himself to
write either without inspiration.   His work
is without abundance, but it is without waste.
It is made out of his whole intellect and all his
nerves.   Every poem is a train of thought and
every essay is the record of sensation.   This
"romantic" had something classic in his moderation, a moderation which becomes at times
as terrifying as Poe's logic.   To "cultivate
one's hysteria" so calmly, and to affront the
reader (*Hypocrite lecteur, mon semblable, mon
frère*) as a judge rather than as a penitent;
to be a casuist in confession; to be so much a
moralist, with so keen a sense of the ecstasy
of evil: that has always bewildered the world,
even in his own country, where the artist is
allowed to live as experimentally as he writes.
Baudelaire lived and died solitary, secret, a
confessor of sins who has never told the whole
truth, *le mauvais moine* of his own sonnet,
an ascetic of passion, a hermit of the brothel.

To understand, not Baudelaire, but what
we can of him, we must read, not only the
four volumes of his collected works, but every
document in Crépet's *Œuvres Posthumes*, and

above all, the letters, and these have only now
been collected into a volume, under the care
of an editor who has done more for Baudelaire
than any one since Crépet. Baudelaire put
into his letters only what he cared to reveal of
himself at a given moment: he has a different
angle to distract the sight of every observer;
and let no one think that he knows Baudelaire
when he has read the letters to Poulet-Malassis,
the friend and publisher, to whom he showed
his business side, or the letters to la Présidente,
the touchstone of his *spleen et idéal*, his chief
experiment in the higher sentiments. Some
of his carefully hidden virtues peep out at
moments, it is true, but nothing that everybody has not long been aware of. We hear
of his ill-luck with money, with proof-sheets,
with his own health. The tragedy of the
life which he chose, as he chose all things
(poetry, Jeanne Duval, the "artificial para-
dises") deliberately, is made a little clearer
to us; we can moralise over it if we like.
But the man remains baffling, and will probably never be discovered.

As it is, much of the value of the book
consists in those glimpses into his mind and

intentions which he allowed people now and then to see. Writing to Sainte-Beuve, to Flaubert, to Soulary, he sometimes lets out, through mere sensitiveness to an intelligence capable of understanding him, some little interesting secret. Thus it is to Sainte-Beuve that he defines and explains the origin and real meaning of the *Petits Poèmes en Prose: Faire cent bagatelles laborieuses qui exigent une bonne humeur constante (bonne humeur nécessaire, même pour traiter des sujets tristes), une excitation bizarre qui a besoin de spectacles, de foules, de musiques, de réverbères même, voilà ce que j'ai voulu faire!* And, writing to some obscure person, he will take the trouble to be even more explicit, as in this symbol of the sonnet: *Avez-vous observé qu'un morceau de ciel aperçu par un soupirail, ou entre deux cheminées, deux rochers, ou par une arcade, donnait une idée plus profonde de l'infini que le grand panorama vu du haut d'une montagne?* It is to another casual person that he speaks out still more intimately (and the occasion of his writing is some thrill of gratitude towards one who had at last done "a little

justice," not to himself, but to Manet): *Eh
bien! on m'accuse, moi, d'imiter Edgar Poe!
Savez-vous pourquoi j'ai si patiemment traduit
Poe? Parce qu'il me resemblait. La première fois que j'ai ouvert un livre de lui, j'ai
vu avec épouvante et ravissement, non seule-
ment des sujets rêvés par moi, mais des phrases,
pensées par moi, et écrites par lui, vingt ans
auparavant.* It is in such glimpses as these
that we see something of Baudelaire in his
letters.

1906.

EDMOND AND JULES DE GONCOURT

My first visit to Edmond de Goncourt was in May, 1892. I remember my immense curiosity about that "House Beautiful," at Auteuil, of which I had heard so much, and my excitement as I rang the bell, and was shown at once into the garden, where Goncourt was just saying good-bye to some friends. He was carelessly dressed, without a collar, and with the usual loosely knotted large white scarf rolled round his neck. He was wearing a straw hat, and it was only afterwards that I could see the fine sweep of the white hair, falling across the forehead. I thought him the most distinguished-looking man of letters I had ever seen; for he had at once the distinction of race, of fine breeding, and of that delicate artistic genius which, with him, was so intimately a part of things beautiful and distinguished. He had the eyes of an old eagle; a general air of dignified collectedness; a rare, and a rarely

charming, smile, which came out, like a ray
of sunshine, in the instinctive pleasure of
having said a witty or graceful thing to
which one's response had been immediate.
When he took me indoors, into that house
which was a museum, I noticed the delicacy
of his hands, and the tenderness with which
he handled his treasures, touching them as
if he loved them, with little, unconscious
murmurs: *Quel goût! quel goût!* These rose-
coloured rooms, with their embroidered ceil-
ings, were filled with cabinets of beautiful
things, Japanese carvings, and prints (the
miraculous "Plongeuses"!), always in perfect
condition (*Je cherche le beau*); albums had
been made for him in Japan, and in these he
inserted prints, mounting others upon silver
and gold paper, which formed a sort of
frame. He showed me his eighteenth-
century designs, among which I remember
his pointing out one (a Chardin, I think) as
the first he had ever bought; he had been
sixteen at the time, and he bought it for
twelve francs.

When we came to the study, the room in
which he worked, he showed me all of his own

first editions, carefully bound, and first editions of Flaubert, Baudelaire, Gautier, with
those, less interesting to me, of the men of
later generations. He spoke of himself and
his brother with a serene pride, which seemed
to me perfectly dignified and appropriate;
and I remember his speaking (with a paren-
thetic disdain of the *brouillard scandinave*,
in which it seemed to him that France was
trying to envelop herself; at the best it
would be but *un mauvais brouillard*) of the
endeavour which he and his brother had
made to represent the only thing worth representing, *le vie vécue, la vraie vérité.* As
in painting, he said, all depends on the way
of seeing, *l'optique:* out of twenty-four men
who will describe what they have all seen,
it is only the twenty-fourth who will find
the right way of expressing it. "There is a
true thing I have said in my journal," he went
on. "The thing is, to find a lorgnette" (and
he put up his hands to his eyes, adjusting them
carefully) "through which to see things. My
brother and I invented a lorgnette, and the
young men have taken it from us."

How true that is, and how significantly it

states just what is most essential in the
work of the Goncourts! It is a new way of
seeing, literally a new way of seeing, which
they have invented; and it is in the invention of this that they have invented that
"new language" of which purists have so
long, so vainly, and so thanklessly complained.
You remember that saying of Masson, the
mask of Gautier, in *Charles Demailly:* "I
am a man for whom the visible world exists."
Well, that is true, also, of the Goncourts;
but in a different way.

"The delicacies of fine literature," that
phrase of Pater always comes into my mind
when I think of the Goncourts; and indeed
Pater seems to me the only English writer
who has ever handled language at all in
their manner or spirit. I frequently heard
Pater refer to certain of their books, to
Madame Gervaisais, to *L'Art du XVIII*
Siècle, to *Chérie;* with a passing objection
to what he called the "immodesty" of this
last book, and a strong emphasis in the
assertion that "that was how it seemed to
him a book should be written." I repeated
this once to Goncourt, trying to give him

some idea of what Pater's work was like;
and he lamented that his ignorance of English prevented him from what he instinctively realised would be so intimate an enjoyment. Pater was of course far more
scrupulous, more limited, in his choice of
epithet, less feverish in his variations of
cadence; and naturally so, for he dealt with
another subject-matter and was careful of
another kind of truth. But with both there
was that passionately intent preoccupation
with "the delicacies of fine literature"; both
achieved a style of the most personal sincerity: *tout grand écrivain de tous les temps*,
said Goncourt, *ne se reconnaît absolument
qu'à cela, c'est qu'il a une langue personnelle,
une langue dont chaque page, chaque ligne, est
signée, pour le lecteur lettré, comme si son nom
était au bas de cette page, de cette ligne:* and
this style, in both, was accused, by the "literary" criticism of its generation, of being
insincere, artificial, and therefore reprehensible.

It is difficult, in speaking of Edmond de
Goncourt, to avoid attributing to him the
whole credit of the work which has so long
borne his name alone. That is an error

which he himself would never have pardoned. *Mon frère et moi* was the phrase constantly on his lips, and in his journal, his prefaces, he has done full justice to the vivid and admirable qualities of that talent which, all the same, would seem to have been the lesser, the more subservient, of the two. Jules, I think, had a more active sense of life, a more generally human curiosity; for the novels of Edmond, written since his brother's death, have, in even that excessively specialised world of their common observation, a yet more specialised choice and direction. But Edmond, there is no doubt, was in the strictest sense the writer; and it is above all for the qualities of its writing that the work of the Goncourts will live. It has been largely concerned with truth—truth to the minute details of human character, sensation, and circumstance, and also of the document, the exact words, of the past; but this devotion to fact, to the curiosities of fact, has been united with an even more persistent devotion to the curiosities of expression. They have invented a new language: that was the old reproach

against them; let it be their distinction.
Like all writers of an elaborate carefulness,
they have been accused of sacrificing both
truth and beauty to deliberate eccentricity.
Deliberate their style certainly was; eccentric it may, perhaps, sometimes have
been; but deliberately eccentric, no. It was
their belief that a writer should have a personal style, a style as peculiar to himself
as his handwriting; and indeed I seem to
see in the handwriting of Edmond de Goncourt just the characteristics of his style.
Every letter is formed carefully, separately,
with a certain elegant stiffness; it is beautiful, formal, too regular in the "continual
slight novelty" of its form to be quite clear
at a glance: very personal, very distinguished
writing.

It may be asserted that the Goncourts are
not merely men of genius, but are perhaps
the typical men of letters of the close of our
century. They have all the curiosities and
the acquirements, the new weaknesses and
the new powers, that belong to our age;
and they sum up in themselves certain theories,
aspirations, ways of looking at things, notions

of literary duty and artistic conscience, which have only lately become at all actual, and some of which owe to them their very origin. To be not merely novelists (inventing a new kind of novel), but historians; not merely historians, but the historians of a particular century, and of what was intimate and what is unknown in it; to be also discriminating, indeed innovating critics of art, but of a certain section of art, the eighteenth century, in France and in Japan; to collect pictures and *bibelots*, beautiful things, always of the French and Japanese eighteenth century: these excursions in so many directions, with their audacities and their careful limitations, their bold novelty and their scrupulous exactitude in detail, are characteristic of what is the finest in the modern conception of culture and the modern ideal in art. Look, for instance, at the Goncourts' view of history. *Quand les civilisations commencent, quand les peuples se forment, l'histoire est drame ou geste. . . . Les siècles qui ont précédé notre siècle ne demandaient à l'historien que le personnage de l'homme, et le portrait de son génie. . . . Le XIXe siècle demande l'homme qui était cet homme*

*d'État, cet homme de guerre, ce poète, ce peintre,
ce grand homme de science ou de métier. L'âme
qui était en cet acteur, le cœur qui a vécu derrière
cet esprit, il les exige et les réclame; et s'il ne
peut recueillir tout cet être moral, toute la vie
intérieure, il commande du moins qu'on lui en
apporte une trace, un jour, un lambeau, une
relique.* From this theory, this conviction,
came that marvellous series of studies in the
eighteenth century in France (*La Femme au
XVIIIe Siècle, Portraits intimes du XVIIIe
Siècle, La du Barry*, and the others), made
entirely out of documents, autograph letters,
scraps of costume, engravings, songs, the unconscious self-revelations of the time, forming,
as they justly say, *l'histoire intime; c'est ce
roman vrai que la postérité appellera peut-
être un jour l'histoire humaine.* To be the
bookworm and the magician; to give the actual
documents, but not to set barren fact by barren
fact; to find a soul and a voice in documents,
to make them more living and more charming
than the charm of life itself: that is what
the Goncourts have done. And it is through
this conception of history that they have
found their way to that new conception of

the novel which has revolutionised the entire art of fiction.

Aujourd'hui, they wrote, in 1864, in the preface to *Germinie Lacerteux, que le Roman s'élargit et grandit, qu'il commence à être la grande forme sérieuse, passionnée, vivante, de l'étude littéraire et de l'enquête sociale, qu'il devient, par l'analyse et par la recherche psychologique, l'Histoire morale contemporaine, aujourd'hui que le Roman s'est imposé les devoirs de la science, il peut en revendiquer les libertés et les franchises. Le public aime les romans faux*, is another brave declaration in the same preface; *ce roman est un roman vrai*. But what, precisely, is it that the Goncourts understood by *un roman vrai?* The old notion of the novel was that it should be an entertaining record of incidents or adventures told for their own sake; a plain, straightforward narrative of facts, the aim being to produce as nearly as possible an effect of continuity, of nothing having been omitted, the statement, so to speak, of a witness on oath; in a word, it is the same as the old notion of history, *drame ou geste*. That is not how the Goncourts apprehend life, or how they conceive it should be

rendered.   As in the study of history they seek
mainly the *inédit*, caring only to record that,
so it is the *inédit* of life that they conceive to
be the main concern, the real "inner history."
And for them the *inédit* of life consists in the
noting of the sensations; it is of the sensations
that they have resolved to be the historians;
not of action, nor of emotion, properly speaking, nor of moral conceptions, but of an inner
life which is all made up of the perceptions of
the senses.   It is scarcely too paradoxical to
say that they are psychologists for whom the
soul does not exist.   One thing, they know,
exists: the sensation flashed through the brain,
the image on the mental retina.   Having
found that, they bodily omit all the rest as of
no importance, trusting to their instinct of
selection, of retaining all that really matters.
It is the painter's method, a selection made
almost visually; the method of the painter
who accumulates detail on detail, in his patient,
many-sided observation of his subject, and
then omits everything which is not an essential
part of the *ensemble* which he sees.   Thus the
new conception of what the real truth of things
consist in has brought with it, inevitably, an

entirely new form, a breaking up of the plain, straightforward narrative into chapters, which are generally quite disconnected, and sometimes of less than a page in length. A very apt image of this new, curious manner of narrative has been found, somewhat maliciously, by M. Lemaître. *Un homme qui marche à l'intérieur d'une maison, si nous regardons du dehors, apparaît successivement à chaque fenêtre, et dans les intervalles nous échappe. Ces fenêtres, ce sont les chapitres de MM. de Goncourt. Encore,* he adds, *y a-t-il plusieurs de ces fenêtres où l'homme que nous attendions ne passe point.* That, certainly, is the danger of the method. No doubt the Goncourts, in their passion for the *inédit,* leave out certain things because they are obvious, even if they are obviously true and obviously important; that is the defect of their quality. To represent life by a series of moments, and to choose these moments for a certain subtlety and rarity in them, is to challenge grave perils. Nor are these the only perils which the Goncourts have constantly before them. There are others, essential to their natures, to their preferences. And, first of all, as we may see on every page

of that miraculous *Journal*, which will remain,
doubtless, the truest, deepest, most poignant
piece of human history that they have ever
written, they are sick men, seeing life through
the medium of diseased nerves. *Notre œuvre
entier*, writes Edmond de Goncourt, *repose
sur la maladie nerveuse; les peintures de la
maladie, nous les avons tirées de nous-mêmes,
et, à force de nous disséquer, nous sommes
arrivés à une sensibilité supra-aiguë que blessaient
les infiniment petits de la vie*. This unhealthy
sensitiveness explains much, the singular merits
as well as certain shortcomings or deviations,
in their work. The Goncourts' vision of
reality might almost be called an exaggerated
sense of the truth of things; such a sense as
diseased nerves inflict upon one, sharpening
the acuteness of every sensation; or somewhat
such a sense as one derives from haschisch,
which simply intensifies, yet in a veiled and
fragrant way, the charm or the disagreeable-
ness of outward things, the notion of time, the
notion of space. What the Goncourts paint
is the subtler poetry of reality, its unusual
aspects, and they evoke it, fleetingly, like
Whistler; they do not render it in hard outline,

like Flaubert, like Manet.   As in the world of
Whistler, so in the world of the Goncourts,
we see cities in which there are always fire-
works at Cremorne, and fair women reflected
beautifully and curiously in mirrors.   It is
a world which is extraordinarily real; but
there is choice, there is curiosity, in the aspect
of reality which it presents.

Compare the descriptions, which form so
large a part of the work of the Goncourts,
with those of Théophile Gautier, who may
reasonably be said to have introduced the
practice of eloquent writing about places, and
also the exact description of them.   Gautier
describes miraculously, but it is, after all, the
ordinary observation carried to perfection, or,
rather, the ordinary pictorial observation.
The Goncourts only tell you the things that
Gautier leaves out; they find new, fantastic
points of view, discover secrets in things, curiosities of beauty, often acute, distressing, in the
aspects of quite ordinary places.   They see
things as an artist, an ultra-subtle artist of the
impressionist kind, might see them; seeing
them indeed always very consciously with a
deliberate attempt upon them, in just that

partial, selecting, creative way in which an artist looks at things for the purpose of painting a picture. In order to arrive at their effects, they shrink from no sacrifice, from no excess; slang, neologism, forced construction, archaism, barbarous epithet, nothing comes amiss to them, so long as it tends to render a sensation. Their unique care is that the phrase should live, should palpitate, should be alert, exactly expressive, super-subtle in expression; and they prefer indeed a certain perversity in their relations with language, which they would have not merely a passionate and sensuous thing, but complex with all the curiosities of a delicately depraved instinct. It is the accusation of the severer sort of French critics that the Goncourts have invented a new language; that the language which they use is no longer the calm and faultless French of the past. It is true; it is their distinction; it is the most wonderful of all their inventions: in order to render new sensations, a new vision of things, they have invented a new language.

1894, 1896.

VILLIERS DE L'ISLE-ADAM

A chacun son infini

1

Count Philippe Auguste Mathias de Villiers de L'Isle-Adam was born at St. Brieuc, in Brittany, November 28, 1838; he died at Paris, under the care of the Frères Saint-Jean-de-Dieu, August 19, 1889. Even before his death, his life had become a legend, and the legend is even now not to be disentangled from the actual occurrences of an existence so heroically visionary. The Don Quixote of idealism, it was not only in philosophical terms that life, to him, was the dream, and the spiritual world the reality; he lived his faith, enduring what others called reality with contempt, whenever, for a moment, he becomes conscious of it. The basis of the character of Villiers was pride, and it was pride which covered

134

more than the universe. And this pride, first
of all, was the pride of race.

Descendant of the original Rodolphe le
Bel, Seigneur de Villiers (1067), through
Jean de Villiers and Maria de l'Isle and
their son Pierre the first Villiers de l'Isle-
Adam, a Villiers de l'Isle-Adam, born in
1384, had been Marshal of France under
Jean-sans-Peur, Duke of Burgundy; he took
Paris during the civil war, and after being
imprisoned in the Bastille, reconquered Pon-
toise from the English, and helped to recon-
quer Paris. Another Villiers de l'Isle-Adam,
born in 1464, Grand Master of the Order of
St. John of Jerusalem, defended Rhodes
against 200,000 Turks for a whole year, in
one of the most famous sieges in history;
it was he who obtained from Charles V.
the concession of the isle of Malta for his
Order, henceforth the Order of the Knights
of Malta.

For Villiers, to whom time, after all, was
but a metaphysical abstraction, the age of
the Crusaders had not passed. From a descendant of the Grand Master of the Knights
of St. John of Jerusalem, the nineteenth

century demanded precisely the virtues which
the sixteenth century had demanded of that
ancestor. And these virtues were all summed
up in one word, which, in its double significance, single to him, covered the whole
attitude of life: the word "nobility." No
word returns oftener to the lips in speaking of what is most characteristic in his
work, and to Villiers moral and spiritual
nobility seemed but the inevitable consequence of that other kind of nobility by
which he seemed to himself still a Knight
of the Order of St. John of Jerusalem. It
was his birthright.

To the aristocratic conception of things,
nobility of soul is indeed a birthright, and
the pride with which this gift of nature is
accepted is a pride of exactly the opposite
kind to that democratic pride to which
nobility of soul is a conquest, valuable in
proportion to its difficulty. This duality,
always essentially aristocratic and democratic,
typically Eastern and Western also, finds its
place in every theory of religion, philosophy,
and the ideal life. The pride of *being*, the
pride of *becoming:* these are the two ulti-

mate contradictions set before every idealist. Villiers' choice, inevitable indeed, was significant. In this measure, it must always be the choice of the artist, to whom, in his contemplation of life, the means is often so much more important than the end. That nobility of soul which comes without effort, which comes only with an unrelaxed diligence over oneself, that I should be I: there can at least be no comparison of its beauty with the stained and dusty onslaught on a never quite conquered fort of the enemy, in a divided self. And, if it be permitted to choose among degrees of sanctity, that, surely, is the highest in which a natural genius for such things accepts its own attainment with the simplicity of a birthright.

And the Catholicism of Villiers was also a part of his inheritance. His ancestors had fought for the Church, and Catholicism was still a pompous flag, under which it was possible to fight on behalf of the spirit, against that materialism which is always, in one way or another, atheist. Thus he dedicates one of his stories to the Pope, chooses ecclesiastical splendours by preference among

the many splendours of the world which go
to make up his stage-pictures, and is learned
in the subtleties of the Fathers. The Church
is his favourite symbol of austere intellectual
beauty; one way, certainly, by which the
temptations of external matter may be van-
quished, and a way, also, by which the desire
of worship may be satisfied.

But there was also, in his attitude towards
the mysteries of the spiritual world, that
"forbidden " curiosity which had troubled
the obedience of the Templars, and which
came to him, too, as a kind of knightly quality. Whether or not he was actually a
Cabbalist, questions of magic began, at an
early age, to preoccupy him, and, from the
first wild experiment of *Isis* to the deliberate
summing up of *Axël*, the "occult" world
finds its way into most of his pages.

Fundamentally, the belief of Villiers is
the belief common to all Eastern mystics.[1]
"Know, once for all, that there is for thee
no other universe than that conception thereof

[1] "I am far from sure," wrote Verlaine, "that the philosophy of Villiers will not one day become the formula of
our century."

which is reflected at the bottom of thy
thoughts." "What is knowledge but a recognition?" Therefore, "forgetting for ever
that which was the illusion of thyself," hasten
to become "an intelligence freed from the
bonds and the desires of the present moment."
"Become the flower of thyself! Thou art
but what thou thinkest: therefore think thyself eternal." "Man, if thou cease to limit
in thyself a thing, that is, to desire it, if, so
doing, thou withdraw thyself from it, it will
follow thee, woman-like, as the water fills
the place that is offered to it in the
hollow of the hand. For thou possessest
the real being of all things, in thy pure
will, and thou art the God that thou art
able to become."

To have accepted the doctrine which thus
finds expression in *Axël*, is to have accepted
this among others of its consequences:
"Science states, but does not explain: she
is the oldest offspring of the chimeras; all
the chimeras, then, on the same terms as
the world (the oldest of them!), are *something more* than nothing!" And in *Elën*
there is a fragment of conversation between

two young students, which has its significance also:

"*Goetze*.   There's my philosopher in full flight
to the regions of the sublime! Happily
we have Science, which is a torch, dear
mystic; we will analyse your sun, if the
planet does not burst into pieces sooner
than it has any right to!
Samuel. Science will not suffice. Sooner or
later you will end by coming to your
knees.
Goetze.   Before what?
Samuel.   Before the darkness!"

Such avowals of ignorance are possible only
from the height of a great intellectual pride.
Villiers' revolt against Science, so far as
Science is materialistic, and his passionate
curiosity in that chimera's flight towards the
invisible, are one and the same impulse of
a mind to which only mind is interesting.
*Toute cette vieille Extériorité, maligne, com-
pliquée, inflexible*, that illusion which Science
accepts for the one reality: it must be the
whole effort of one's consciousness to escape

from its entanglements, to dominate it, or to
ignore it, and one's art must be the building
of an ideal world beyond its access, from
which one may indeed sally out, now and
again, in a desperate enough attack upon
the illusions in the midst of which men live.

And just that, we find, makes up the work
of Villiers, work which divides itself roughly
into two divisions: one, the ideal world, or
the ideal in the world (*Axël*, *Elën*, *Morgane*,
Isis, some of the *contes*, and, intermediary,
La Révolte); the other, satire, the mockery
of reality (*L'Eve Future*, the *Contes Cruels*,
Tribulat Bonhomet). It is part of the originality of Villiers that the two divisions constantly flow into one another; the idealist
being never more the idealist than in his
buffooneries.

2

Axël is the Symbolist drama, in all its
uncompromising conflict with the "modesty"
of Nature and the limitations of the stage.
It is the drama of the soul, and at the same
time it is the most pictorial of dramas; I

should define its manner as a kind of spiritual romanticism. The earlier dramas, *Elën*, *Morgane*, are fixed at somewhat the same point in space; *La Révolte*, which seems to anticipate *The Doll's House*, shows us an artisocratic Ibsen, touching reality with a certain disdain, certainly with far less skill, certainly with far more beauty. But *Axël*, meditated over during a lifetime, shows us Villiers' ideal of his own idealism.

The action takes place, it is true, in this century, but it takes place in corners of the world into which the modern spirit has not yet passed; this *Monastère de Religieuses-trinitaires, le cloître de Sainte Appolodora, situé sur les confins du littoral de l'ancienne Flandre française,* and the *très vieux château fort, le burg des margraves d'Auërsperg, isolé au milieu du Schwartzwald.* The characters, Axël d'Auërsperg, Eve Sara Emmanuèle de Maupers, Maître Janus, the Archidiacre, the Commandeur Kaspar d'Auërsperg, are at once more and less than human beings: they are the types of different ideals, and they are clothed with just enough humanity to give form to what would otherwise remain disembodied spirit. The religious ideal, the occult ideal, the worldly ideal, the passionate ideal, are all presented, one after the other, in these dazzling and profound pages; Axël is the disdainful choice from among them, the disdainful rejection of life itself, of the whole illusion of life, "since infinity alone is not a deception." And Sara? Sara is a superb part of that life which is rejected, which she herself comes, not without reluctance, to reject. In that motionless figure, during the whole of the first act silent but for a single "No," and leaping into a moment's violent action as the act closes, she is the haughtiest woman in literature. But she is a woman, and she desires life, finding it in Axël. Pride, and the woman's devotion to the man, aid her to take the last cold step with Axël, in the transcendental giving up of life at the moment when life becomes ideal.

And the play is written, throughout, with a curious solemnity, a particular kind of eloquence, which makes no attempt to imitate the level of the speech of every day, but which is a sort of ideal language in which beauty is aimed at as exclusively as if it were written in

verse. The modern drama, under the democratic influence of Ibsen, the positive influence
of Dumas *fils*, has limited itself to the expression of temperaments in the one case, of theoretic intelligences in the other, in as nearly
as possible the words which the average man
would use for the statement of his emotions
and ideas. The form, that is, is degraded
below the level of the characters whom it attempts to express; for it is evident that the
average man can articulate only a small enough
part of what he obscurely feels or thinks; and
the theory of Realism is that his emotions and
ideas are to be given only in so far as the words
at his own command can give them. Villiers,
choosing to concern himself only with exceptional characters, and with them only in the
absolute, invents for them a more elaborate
and a more magnificent speech than they
would naturally employ, the speech of their
thoughts, of their dreams.

And it is a world thought or dreamt in
some more fortunate atmosphere than that
in which we live, that Villiers has created for
the final achievement of his abstract ideas.
I do not doubt that he himself always lived

in it, through all the poverty of the precipitous
Rue des Martyrs. But it is in *Axël*, and
in *Axël* only, that he has made us also inhabitants of that world. Even in *Elën* we are
spectators, watching a tragical fairy play (as
if *Fantasio* became suddenly in deadly earnest),
watching some one else's dreams. *Axël* en-
velops us in its own atmosphere; it is as if we
found ourselves on a mountain top on the
other side of the clouds, and without surprise
at finding ourselves there.

The ideal, to Villiers, being the real, spiritual
beauty being the essential beauty, and material beauty its reflection, or its revelation, it is
with a sort of fury that he attacks the materialising forces of the world: science, progress,
the worldly emphasis on "facts," on what is
"positive," "serious," "respectable." Satire,
with him, is the revenge of beauty upon ugliness, the persecution of the ugly; it is not
merely social satire, it is a satire on the material universe by one who believes in a spiritual
universe. Thus it is the only laughter of our
time which is fundamental, as fundamental as
that of Swift or Rabelais. And this lacerating
laughter of the idealist is never surer in its aim

than when it turns the arms of science against itself, as in the vast buffoonery of *L'Eve Future.* A Parisian wit, sharpened to a fineness of irony such as only wit which is also philosophy can attain, brings in another method of attack; humour, which is almost English, another; while again satire becomes tragic, fantastic, macabre. In those enigmatic "tales of the grotesque and arabesque," in which Villiers rivals Poe on his own ground, there is, for the most part, a multiplicity of meaning which is, as it is meant to be, disconcerting. I should not like to say how far Villiers does not, sometimes, believe in his own magic.

It is characteristic of him, at all events, that he employs what we call the supernatural alike in his works of pure idealism and in his works of sheer satire. The moment the world ceased to be the stable object, solidly encrusted with houses in brick and stone, which it is to most of its so temporary inhabitants, Villiers was at home. When he sought the absolute beauty, it was beyond the world that he found it; when he sought horror, it was a breath blowing from an invisible darkness which brought it to his

nerves; when he desired to mock the pre-
tensions of knowledge of or ignorance, it
was always with the unseen that his tragic
buffoonery made familiar.

There is, in everything which Villiers wrote,
a strangeness, certainly both instinctive and
deliberate, which seems to me to be the natural
consequence of that intellectual pride which,
as I have pointed out, was at the basis of his
character. He hated every kind of mediocrity: therefore he chose to analyse exceptional souls, to construct exceptional stories,
to invent splendid names, and to evoke singular landscapes. It was part of his curiosity
in souls to prefer the complex to the simple,
the perverse to the straightforward, the ambiguous to either. His heroes are incar-
nations of spiritual pride, and their tragedies
are the shock of spirit against matter, the
invasion of spirit by matter, the temptation
of spirit by spiritual evil. They seek the
absolute, and find death; they seek wisdom,
find love, and fall into spiritual decay; they
seek reality, and find crime; they seek phantoms, and find themselves. They are on
the borders of a wisdom too great for their

capacity; they are haunted by dark powers, instincts of ambiguous passions; they are too lucid to be quite sane in their extravagances; they have not quite systematically transposed their dreams into action. And his heroines, when they are not, like *L'Eve Future*, the vitalised mechanism of an Edison, have the solemnity of dead people, and a hieratic speech. *Songe, des cœurs condamnés à ce supplice, de ne pas m'aimer!* says Sara, in *Axël. Je ne l'aime pas, ce jeune homme. Qu'ai-je donc fait à Dieu?* says Elën. And their voice is always like the voice of Elën: "I listened attentively to the sound of her voice; it was tactiturn, subdued, like the murmur of the river Lethe, flowing through the region of shadows." They have the immortal weariness of beauty, they are enigmas to themselves, they desire, and know not why they refrain, they do good and evil with the lifting of an eyelid, and are innocent and guilty of all the sins of the earth.

And these strange inhabitants move in as strange a world. They are the princes and châtelaines of ancient castles lost in the depths of the Black Forest; they are

the last descendants of a great race about
to come to an end; students of magic, who
have the sharp and swift swords of the sol-
dier; enigmatic courtesans, at the table of
strange feasts; they find incalculable treasures, *tonnantes et sonnantes cataractes d'or
liquide*, only to disdain them. All the pomp
of the world approaches them, that they may
the better abnegate it, or that it may ruin
them to a deeper degree of their material
hell. And we see them always at the moment
of a crisis, before the two ways of a decision,
hesitating in the entanglements of a great
temptation. And this casuist of souls will
drag forth some horribly stunted or horribly
overgrown soul from under its obscure cov-
ering, setting it to dance naked before our
eyes. He has no mercy on those who have
no mercy on themselves.

In the sense in which that word is ordi-
narily used, Villiers has no pathos. This is
enough to explain why he can never, in the
phrase he would have disliked so greatly,
"touch the popular heart." His mind is too
abstract to contain pity, and it is in his lack
of pity that he seems to put himself outside

humanity. *A chacun son infini*, he has said, and in the avidity of his search for the infinite he has no mercy for the blind weakness which goes stumbling over the earth, without so much as knowing that the sun and stars are overhead. He sees only the gross multitude, the multitude which has the contentment of the slave. He cannot pardon stupidity, for it is incomprehensible to him. He sees, rightly, that stupidity is more criminal than vice; if only because vice is curable, stupidity incurable. But he does not realise, as the great novelists have realised, that stupidity can be pathetic, and that there is not a peasant, nor even a self-satisfied bourgeois, in whom the soul has not its part, in whose existence it is not possible to be interested.

Contempt, noble as it may be, anger, righteous though it may be, cannot be indulged in without a certain lack of sympathy; and lack of sympathy comes from a lack of patient understanding. It is certain that the destiny of the greater part of the human race is either infinitely pathetic or infinitely ridiculous. Under which aspect, then, shall that destiny, and those obscure fractions of human-

ity, be considered? Villiers was too sincere
an idealist, too absolute in his idealism,
to hesitate. "As for living," he cries, in
that splendid phrase of *Axël*, "our servants
will do that for us!" And, in the *Contes
Cruels*, there is this not less characteristic
expression of what was always his mental
attitude: "As at the play, in a central stall,
one sits out, so as not to disturb one's neighbours—out of courtesy, in a word—some play
written in a wearisome style and of which
one does not like the subject, so I lived, out
of politeness": *je vivais par politesse*. In
this haughtiness towards life, in this disdain
of ordinary human motives and ordinary
human beings, there is at once the distinction
and the weakness of Villiers. And he has
himself pointed the moral against himself
in these words of the story which forms the
epilogue to the *Contes Cruels:* "When the
forehead alone contains the existence of a
man, that man is enlightened only from
above his head; then his jealous shadow,
prostrate under him, draws him by the feet,
that it may drag him down into the invisible."

3

All his life Villiers was a poor man; though, all his life, he was awaiting that fortune which he refused to anticipate by any mean employment. During most of his life, he was practically an unknown man. Greatly loved, ardently admired, by that inner circle of the men who have made modern French literature, from Verlaine to Mæterlinck, he was looked upon by most people as an amusing kind of madman, a little dangerous, whose ideas, as they floated freely over the café-table, it was at times highly profitable to steal. For Villiers talked his works before writing them, and sometimes he talked them instead of writing them, in his too royally spendthrift way. To those who knew him he seemed genius itself, and would have seemed so if he had never written a line; for he had the dangerous gift of a personality which seems to have already achieved all that it so energetically contemplates. But personality tells only within hands' reach; and Villiers failed even to startle, failed even to exasperate, the general reader.

That his *Premières Poésies*, published at
the age of nineteen, should have brought him
fame was hardly to be expected, remarkable, especially in its ideas, as that book is.
Nor was it to be expected of the enigmatic
fragment of a romance, *Isis* (1862), antici-
pating, as it does, by so long a period, the
esoteric and spiritualistic romances which were
to have their vogue. But *Elën* (1864) and
Morgane (1865), those two poetic dramas in
prose, so full of distinction, of spiritual rarity;
but two years later, *Claire Lenoir* (afterwards
incorporated in one of his really great books,
Tribulat Bonhomet), with its macabre horror;
but *La Révolte* (1870), for Villiers so "actual,"
and which had its moments of success when
it was revived in 1896 at the Odéon; but *Le
Nouveau Monde* (1880), a drama which, by
some extraordinary caprice, won a prize;
but *Les Contes Cruels* (1880), that collection
of masterpieces, in which the essentially
French *conte* is outdone on its own ground!
It was not till 1886 that Villiers ceased to be
an unknown writer, with the publication of
that phosphorescent buffoonery of science,
that vast parody of humanity, *L'Eve Future*.

Tribulat Bonhomet (which he himself defined
as *bouffonnerie énorme et sombre, couleur du
siècle*) was to come, in its final form, and
the superb poem in prose *Akëdysséril;* and
then, more and more indifferent collections
of stories, in which Villiers, already dying, is
but the shadow of himself: *L'Amour Suprême*
(1886), *Histoires Insolites* (1888), *Nouveaux
Contes Cruels* (1888). He was correcting the
proofs of *Axël* when he died; the volume was
published in 1890, followed by *Propos d'au-
delà*, and a series of articles, *Chez les Passants*.
Once dead, the fame which had avoided him
all his life began to follow him; he had *une
belle presse* at his funeral.

Meanwhile, he had been preparing the spiritual atmosphere of the new generation. Living
among believers in the material world, he
had been declaring, not in vain, his belief in
the world of the spirit; living among Realists
and Parnassians, he had been creating a
new form of art, the art of the Symbolist
drama, and of Symbolism in fiction. He had
been lonely all his life, for he had been living
in his own lifetime, the life of the next generation. There was but one man among his con-

temporaries to whom he could give, and from whom he could receive, perfect sympathy. That man was Wagner. Gradually the younger men came about him; at the end he was not lacking in disciples.

And after all, the last word of Villiers is faith; faith against the evidence of the senses, against the negations of materialistic science, against the monstrous paradox of progress, against his own pessimism in the face of these formidable enemies. He affirms; he " believes in soul, is very sure of God"; requires no witness to the spiritual world of which he is always the inhabitant; and is content to lose his way in the material world, brushing off its mud from time to time with a disdainful gesture, as he goes on his way (to apply a significant word of Pater) "like one on a secret errand."

LÉON CLADEL

I HOPE that the life of Léon Cladel by his
daughter Judith, which Lemerre has brought
out in a pleasant volume, will do something
for the fame of one of the most original writers
of our time. Cladel had the good fortune to
be recognised in his lifetime by those whose
approval mattered most, beginning with Baudelaire, who discovered him before he had
printed his first book, and helped to teach him
the craft of letters. But so exceptional an
artist could never be popular, though he worked
in living stuff and put the whole savour of his
countryside into his tragic and passionate
stories. A peasant, who writes about peasants
and poor people, with a curiosity of style which
not only packs his vocabulary with difficult
words, old or local, and with unheard of
rhythms, chosen to give voice to some never
yet articulated emotion, but which drives
him into oddities of printing, of punctuation,
of the very shape of his accents! A page

of Cladel has a certain visible uncouthness, and at first this seems in keeping with his matter; but the uncouthness, when you look into it, turns out to be itself a refinement, and what has seemed a confused whirl, an improvisation, to be the result really of reiterated labour, whose whole aim has been to bring the spontaneity of the first impulse back into the laboriously finished work.

In this just, sensitive, and admirable book, written by one who has inherited a not less passionate curiosity about life, but with more patience in waiting upon it, watching it, noting its surprises, we have a simple and sufficient commentary upon the books and upon the man. The narrative has warmth and reserve, and is at once tender and clear-sighted. *J'entrevois nettement,* she says with truth, *combien seront précieux pour les futurs historiens de la littérature du xix*$^e_{\downarrow}$ *siècle, les mémoires tracés au contact immédiat de l'artiste, exposés de ses faits et gestes particuliers, de ses origines, de la germination de ses croyances et de son talent; ses critiques à venir y trouveront de solides matériaux, ses admirateurs un aliment à leur piété et les philosophes un des aspects de l'Ame fran-*

çaise. The man is shown to us, *les élans de cette âme toujours grondante et fulgurante comme une forge, et les nuances de ce fiévreux visage d'apôtre, brun, fin et sinueux,* and we see the inevitable growth, out of the hard soil of Quercy and out of the fertilising contact of Paris and Baudelaire, of this whole literature, these books no less astonishing than their titles: *Ompdrailles-le-Tombeau-des-Lutteurs, Celui de la Croix-aux-Bœufs, La Fête Votive de Saint-Bartholomée-Porte-Glaive.* The very titles are an excitement. I can remember how mysterious and alluring they used to seem to me when I first saw them on the cover of what was perhaps his best book, *Les Va-Nu-Pieds.*

It is by one of the stories, and the shortest, in *Les Va-Nu-Pieds,* that I remember Cladel. I read it when I was a boy, and I cannot think of it now without a shiver. It is called *L'Hercule,* and it is about a Sandow of the streets, a professional strong man, who kills himself by an overstrain; it is not a story at all, it is the record of an incident, and there is only the strong man in it and his friend the zany, who makes the jokes while the strong man juggles with bars and cannon-balls. It is all

told in a breath, without a pause, as if someone who had just seen it poured it out in a
flood of hot words. Such vehemence, such
pity, such a sense of the cruelty of the spectacle
of a man driven to death like a beast, for a few
pence and the pleasure of a few children; such
an evocation of the sun and the streets and this
sordid tragic thing happening to the sound of
drum and cymbals; such a vision in sunlight
of a barbarous and ridiculous and horrible
accident, lifted by the telling of it into a new
and unforgettable beauty, I have never felt
or seen in any other story of a like grotesque
tragedy. It realises an ideal, it does for once
what many artists have tried and failed to do;
it wrings the last drop of agony out of that
subject which it is so easy to make pathetic
and effective. Dickens could not have done
it, Bret Harte could not have done it, Kipling
could not do it: Cladel did it only once, with
this perfection.

Something like it he did over and over again,
with unflagging vehemence, with splendid variations, in stories of peasants and wrestlers and
thieves and prostitutes. They are all, as his
daughter says, epic; she calls them Homeric,

but there is none of the Homeric simplicity in this tumult of coloured and clotted speech, in which the language is tortured to make it speak. The comparison with Rabelais is nearer. *La recherche du terme vivant, sa mise en valeur et en saveur, la surabondance des vocables puisés à toutes sources . . . la condensation de l'action autour de ces quelques motifs éternels de l'épopée: combat, ripaille, palabre et luxure*, there, as she sees justly, are links with Rabelais. Goncourt, himself always aiming at an impossible closeness of written to spoken speech, noted with admiration *la vraie photographie de la parole avec ses tours, ses abbréviations ses ellipses, son essoufflement presque*. Speech out of breath, that is what Cladel's is always; his words, never the likely ones, do not so much speak as cry, gesticulate, overtake one another. *L'âme de Léon Cladel*, says his daughter, *était dans un constant et flamboyant automne*. Something of the colour and fever of autumn is in all he wrote. Another writer since Cladel, who has probably never heard of him, has made heroes of peasants and vagabonds. But Maxim Gorki makes heroes of them, consciously, with a mental self-assertion, giving them ideas which he has found in Nietzsche. Cladel put into all his people some of his own passionate way of seeing "scarlet," to use Barbey d'Aurevilly's epithet: *un rural écarlate*. Vehement and voluminous, he overflowed: his whole aim as an artist, as a pupil of Baudelaire, was to concentrate, to hold himself back; and the effort added impetus to the checked overflow. To the realists he seemed merely extravagant; he saw certainly what they could not see; and his romance was always a fruit of the soil. The artist in him, seeming to be in conflict with the peasant, fortified, clarified the peasant, extracted from that hard soil a rare fruit. You see in his face an extraordinary mingling of the peasant, the visionary, and the dandy: the long hair and beard, the sensitive mouth and nose, the fierce brooding eyes, in which wildness and delicacy, strength and a kind of stealthiness, seem to be grafted on an inflexible peasant stock.

1906.

A NOTE ON ZOLA'S METHOD

THE art of Zola is based on certain theories, on a view of humanity which he has adopted as his formula. As a deduction from his formula, he takes many things in human nature for granted, he is content to observe at second-hand; and it is only when he comes to the filling-up of his outlines, the *mise-en-scène*, that his observation becomes personal, minute, and persistent. He has thus succeeded in being at once unreal where reality is most essential, and tediously real where a point-by-point reality is sometimes unimportant. The contradiction is an ingenious one, which it may be interesting to examine in a little detail, and from several points of view.

And, first of all, take *L'Assommoir*, no doubt the most characteristic of Zola's novels, and probably the best; and, leaving out for the present the broader question of his general conception of humanity, let us look at Zola's manner of dealing with his material, noting

162

by the way certain differences between his
manner and that of Goncourt, of Flaubert,
with both of whom he has so often been compared, and with whom he wishes to challenge
comparison.   Contrast *L'Assommoir* with
Germinie Lacerteux, which, it must be remembered, was written thirteen years earlier.
Goncourt, as he incessantly reminds us, was
the first novelist in France to deliberately
study the life of the people, after precise documents; and *Germinie Lacerteux* has this distinction, among others, that it was a new
thing.   And it is done with admirable skill;
as a piece of writing, as a work of art, it is far
superior to Zola.   But, certainly, Zola's work
has a mass and bulk, a *fougue*, a *portée*, which
Goncourt's lacks; and it has a savour of ple-
beian flesh which all the delicate art of Goncourt could not evoke.   Zola sickens you with
it; but there it is.   As in all his books, but
more than in most, there is something greasy,
a smear of eating and drinking; the pages, to
use his own phrase, *grasses des lichades du
lundi*.   In *Germinie Lacerteux* you never forget that Goncourt is an aristocrat; in
L'Assommoir you never forget that Zola

is a bourgeois. Whatever Goncourt touches
becomes, by the mere magic of his touch,
charming, a picture; Zola is totally destitute
of charm. But how, in *L'Assommoir*, he
drives home to you the horrid realities of these
narrow, uncomfortable lives! Zola has made
up his mind that he will say everything, without omitting a single item, whatever he has to
say; thus, in *L'Assommoir*, there is a great
feast which lasts for fifty pages, beginning with
the picking of the goose, the day before, and
going on to the picking of the goose's bones,
by a stray marauding cat, the night after.
And, in a sense, he does say everything; and
there, certainly, is his novelty, his invention.
He observes with immense persistence, but his
observation, after all, is only that of the man
in the street; it is simply carried into detail,
deliberately. And, while Goncourt wanders
away sometimes into arabesques, indulges in
flourishes, so finely artistic is his sense of
words and of the things they represent, so
perfectly can he match a sensation or an impression by its figure in speech, Zola, on the
contrary, never finds just the right word, and
it is his persistent fumbling for it which pro-

duces these miles of description; four pages
describing how two people went upstairs, from
the ground floor to the sixth story, and then
two pages afterwards to describe how they
came downstairs again. Sometimes, by his
prodigious diligence and minuteness, he succeeds in giving you the impression; often,
indeed; but at the cost of what *ennui* to writer
and reader alike! And so much of it all is
purely unnecessary, has no interest in itself
and no connection with the story: the precise
details of Lorilleux's chain-making, bristling
with technical terms: it was *la colonne* that he
made, and only that particular kind of chain;
Goujet's forge, and the machinery in the shed
next door; and just how you cut out zinc with
a large pair of scissors. When Goncourt gives
you a long description of anything, even if you
do not feel that it helps on the story very much,
it is such a beautiful thing in itself, his mere way
of writing it is so enchanting, that you find
yourself wishing it longer, at its longest. But
with Zola, there is no literary interest in the
writing, apart from its clear and coherent
expression of a given thing; and these interminable descriptions have no extraneous, or,

if you will, implicit interest, to save them from
the charge of irrelevancy; they sink by their
own weight.   Just as Zola's vision is the vision
of the average man, so his vocabulary, with
all its technicology, remains mediocre, incapable of expressing subtleties, incapable of a
really artistic effect.   To find out in a slang
dictionary that a filthy idea can be expressed
by an ingeniously filthy phrase in *argot*, and to
use that phrase, is not a great feat, or, on
purely artistic grounds, altogether desirable.
To go to a chainmaker and learn the trade
name of the various kinds of chain which he
manufactures, and of the instruments with
which he manufactures them, is not an elaborate process, or one which can be said to pay
you for the little trouble which it no doubt
takes.   And it is not well to be too certain
after all that Zola is always perfectly accurate
in his use of all this manifold knowledge.   The
slang, for example; he went to books for it, in
books he found it, and no one will ever find
some of it but in books.   However, my
main contention is that Zola's general use of
words is, to be quite frank, somewhat inef-
fectual.   He tries to do what Flaubert did,

without Flaubert's tools, and without the craftsman's hand at the back of the tools. His fingers are too thick; they leave a blurred line. If you want merely weight, a certain kind of force, you get it; but no more.

Where a large part of Zola's merit lies, in his persistent attention to detail, one finds also one of his chief defects. He cannot leave well alone; he cannot omit; he will not take the most obvious fact for granted. *Il marcha le premier, elle le suivit*, well, of course, she followed him, if he walked first: why mention the fact? That beginning of a sentence is absolutely typical; it is impossible for him to refer, for the twentieth time, to some unimportant character, without giving name and profession, not one or the other, but both, invariably both. He tells us particularly that a room is composed of four walls, that a table stands on its four legs. And he does not appear to see the difference between doing that and doing as Flaubert does, namely, selecting precisely the detail out of all others which renders or consorts with the scene in hand, and giving that detail with an ingenious exactness. Here, for instance, in *Madame Bovary*, is a charac-

teristic detail in the manner of Flaubert:
*Huit jours après, comme elle étendait du linge
dans sa cour, elle fut prise d'un crachement
de sang, et le lendemain, tandis que Charles
avait le dos tourné pour fermer le rideau de la
fenêtre, elle dit: "Ah! mon Dieu!" poussa un
soupir et s'évanouit. Elle était morte.* Now
that detail, brought in without the slightest emphasis, of the husband turning his
back at the very instant that his wife dies, is
a detail of immense psychological value; it
indicates to us, at the very opening of the book,
just the character of the man about whom we
are to read so much. Zola would have taken
at least two pages to say that, and, after all,
he would not have said it. He would have told
you the position of the chest of drawers in the
room, what wood the chest of drawers was
made of, and if it had a little varnish knocked
off at the corner of the lower cornice, just
where it would naturally be in the way of
people's feet as they entered the door. He
would have told you how Charles leant against
the other corner of the chest of drawers, and
that the edge of the upper cornice left a slight
dent in his black frock-coat, which remained

visible half an hour afterwards. But that one
little detail, which Flaubert selects from among
a thousand, that, no, he would never have
given us that!

And the language in which all this is written,
apart from the consideration of language as a
medium, is really not literature at all, in any
strict sense. I am not, for the moment, com-
plaining of the colloquialism and the slang.
Zola has told us that he has, in *L'Assommoir*,
used the language of the people in order to
render the people with a closer truth. Whether
he has done that or not is not the question.
The question is, that he does not give one the
sense of reading good literature, whether he
speaks in Delvau's *langue verte*, or according
to the Academy's latest edition of classical
French. His sentences have no rhythm; they
give no pleasure to the ear; they carry no
sensation to the eye. You hear a sentence of
Flaubert, and you see a sentence of Goncourt,
like living things, with forms and voices. But
a page of Zola lies dull and silent before you;
it draws you by no charm, it has no meaning
until you have read the page that goes before
and the page that comes after. It is like

cabinet-makers' work, solid, well fitted together, and essentially made to be used.

Yes, there is no doubt that Zola writes very
badly, worse than any other French writer
of eminence. It is true that Balzac, certainly
one of the greatest, does, in a sense, write
badly; but his way of writing badly is very
different from Zola's, and leaves you with
the sense of quite a different result. Balzac
is too impatient with words; he cannot stay
to get them all into proper order, to pick and
choose among them. Night, the coffee, the
wet towel, and the end of six hours' labour
are often too much for him; and his manner
of writing his novels on the proof-sheets,
altering and expanding as fresh ideas came
to him on each re-reading, was not a way of
doing things which can possibly result in
perfect writing. But Balzac sins from excess, from a feverish haste, the very extravagance of power; and, at all events, he
"sins strongly." Zola sins meanly, he is
penuriously careful, he does the best he possibly
can; and he is not aware that his best does not
answer all requirements. So long as writing
is clear and not ungrammatical, it seems to

him sufficient.   He has not realised that without charm there can be no fine literature, as there can be no perfect flower without fragrance.

And it is here that I would complain, not as a matter of morals, but as a matter of art, of Zola's obsession by what is grossly, uninterestingly filthy.   There is a certain simile in *L'Assommoir*, used in the most innocent connection, in connection with a bonnet, which seems to me the most abjectly dirty phrase which I have ever read.   It is one thing to use dirty words to describe dirty things: that may be necessary, and thus unexceptionable.   It is another thing again, and this, too, may well be defended on artistic grounds, to be ingeniously and wittily indecent.   But I do not think a real man of letters could possibly have used such an expression as the one I am alluding to, or could so meanly succumb to certain kinds of prurience which we find in Zola's work.   Such a scene as the one in which Gervaise comes home with Lantier, and finds her husband lying drunk asleep in his own vomit, might certainly be explained and even excused, though few more disagreeable things were ever written, on the ground of the psychological importance which it undoubtedly has, and the overwhelming way in which it drives home the point which it is the writer's business to make. But the worrying way in which *le derrière* and *le ventre* are constantly kept in view, without the slightest necessity, is quite another thing. I should not like to say how often the phrase "sa nudité de jolie fille" occurs in Zola. Zola's nudities always remind me of those which you can see in the *Foire au pain d'épice* at Vincennes, by paying a penny and looking through a peep-hole. In the laundry scenes, for instance in *L'Assommoir*, he is always reminding you that the laundresses have turned up their sleeves, or undone a button or two of their bodices. His eyes seem eternally fixed on the inch or two of bare flesh that can be seen; and he nudges your elbow at every moment, to make sure that you are looking too. Nothing may be more charming than a frankly sensuous description of things which appeal to the senses; but can one imagine anything less charming, less like art, than this prying eye glued to the peep-hole in the Gingerbread Fair?

Yet, whatever view may be taken of Zola's work in literature, there is no doubt that the life of Zola is a model lesson, and might profitably be told in one of Dr. Smiles's edifying biographies. It may even be brought as a reproach against the writer of these novels, in which there are so many offences against the respectable virtues, that he is too good a bourgeois, too much the incarnation of the respectable virtues, to be a man of genius. If the finest art comes of the intensest living, then Zola has never had even a chance of doing the greatest kind of work. It is his merit and his misfortune to have lived entirely in and for his books, with a heroic devotion to his ideal of literary duty which would merit every praise if we had to consider simply the moral side of the question. So many pages of copy a day, so many hours of study given to mysticism, or Les Halles; Zola has always had his day's work marked out before him, and he has never swerved from it. A recent life of Zola tells us something about his way of getting up a subject. "Immense preparation had been necessary for the *Faute de l'Abbé Mouret*. Mountains of note-books were

heaped up on his table, and for months Zola
was plunged in the study of religious works.
All the mystical part of the book, and notably
the passages having reference to the cultus
of Mary, was taken from the works of the
Spanish Jesuits. The *Imitation of Jesus
Christ* was largely drawn upon, many passages
being copied almost word for word into the
novel—much as in *Clarissa Harlowe*, that
other great realist, Richardson, copied whole
passages from the Psalms. The description
of life in a grand seminary was given him by
a priest who had been dismissed from ecclesiastical service. The little church of Sainte
Marie des Batignolles was regularly visited."

How commendable all that is, but, surely,
how futile! Can one conceive of a more hopeless, a more ridiculous task, than that of
setting to work on a novel of ecclesiastical
life as if one were cramming for an examina-
tion in religious knowledge? Zola apparently
imagines that he can master mysticism in a
fortnight, as he masters the police regulations
of Les Halles. It must be admitted that he
does wonders with his second-hand information, alike in regard to mysticism and Les

Halles. But he succeeds only to a certain point, and that point lies on the nearer side of what is really meant by success. Is not Zola himself, at his moments, aware of this? A letter written in 1881, and printed in Mr. Sherard's life of Zola, from which I have just quoted, seems to me very significant.

"I continue to work in a good state of mental equilibrium. My novel (*Pot-Bouille*) is certainly only a task requiring precision and clearness. No *bravoura*, not the least lyrical treat. It does not give me any warm satisfaction, but it amuses me like a piece of mechanism with a thousand wheels, of which it is my duty to regulate the movements with the most minute care. I ask myself the question: Is it good policy, when one feels that one has passion in one, to check it, or even to bridle it? If one of my books is destined to become immortal, it will, I am sure, be the most passionate one."

Est-elle en marbre ou non, la Vénus de Milo? said the Parnassians, priding themselves on their muse with her *peplum bien sculpté.* Zola will describe to you the exact shape and the exact smell of the rags of his naturalistic muse; but has she, under the tatters, really a human heart? In the whole of Zola's works, amid all his exact and impressive descriptions of misery, all his endless annals of the poor, I know only one episode which brings tears to the eyes, the episode of the child-martyr Lalie in *L'Assommoir*. "A piece of mechanism with a thousand wheels," that is indeed the image of this immense and wonderful study of human life, evolved out of the brain of a solitary student who knows life only by the report of his documents, his friends, and, above all, his formula.

Zola has defined art, very aptly, as nature seen through a temperament. The art of Zola is nature seen through a formula. This professed realist is a man of theories who studies life with a conviction that he will find there such and such things which he has read about in scientific books. He observes, indeed, with astonishing minuteness, but he observes in support of preconceived ideas. And so powerful is his imagination that he has created a whole world which has no existence anywhere but in his own brain, and he has placed there imaginary beings, so much more logical than life, in the midst of surroundings which are themselves so real as to lend almost a semblance of reality to the embodied formulas who inhabit them.

It is the boast of Zola that he has taken up art at the point where Flaubert left it, and that he has developed that art in its logical sequence. But the art of Flaubert, itself a development from Balzac, had carried realism, if not in *Madame Bovary*, at all events in *L'Education Sentimentale*, as far as realism can well go without ceasing to be art. In the grey and somewhat sordid history of Frédéric Moreau there is not a touch of romanticism, not so much as a concession to style, a momentary escape of the imprisoned lyrical tendency. Everything is observed, everything is taken straight from life: realism sincere, direct, implacable, reigns from end to end of the book. But with what consummate art all this mass of observation is disintegrated, arranged, composed! with what infinite delicacy it is manipulated in the service of an unerring sense of construction! And Flaubert has no theory, has no prejudices, has only a certain impatience with human imbecility. Zola, too, gathers his documents, heaps up his mass of observation, and then, in this unhappy "development" of the principles of art which produced *L'Education Sentimentale*, flings everything pell-mell into one overflowing *pot-au-feu*. The probabilities of nature and the delicacies of art are alike drowned beneath a flood of turbid observation, and in the end one does not even feel convinced that Zola really knows his subject. I remember once hearing M. Huysmans, with his look and tone of subtle, ironical malice, describe how Zola, when he was writing *La Terre*, took a drive into the country in a victoria, to see the peasants. The English papers once reported an interview in which the author of *Nana*, indiscreetly questioned as to the amount of personal observation he had put into the book, replied that he had lunched with an actress of the Variétés. The reply was generally taken for a joke, but the lunch was a reality, and it was assuredly a rare experience in the life of solitary diligence to which we owe so many impersonal studies in life. Nor did Zola, as he sat silent by the side of Mlle. X., seem to be making much use of the opportunity. The language of the miners in *Germinal*, how much of local colour is there in that? The interminable additions and divisions, the extracts from a financial gazette, in *L'Argent*, how much of the real temper and idiosyncrasy of the financier do they give us? In his description of places, in his *mise-en-scène*, Zola puts down what he sees with his own eyes, and, though it is often done at utterly disproportionate length, it is at all events done with exactitude. But in the far more important observation of men and women, he is content with second-hand knowledge, the knowledge of a man who sees the world through a formula. Zola sees in humanity *la bête humaine*. He sees the beast in all its transformations, but he sees only the beast. He has never looked at life impartially, he has never seen it as it is. His realism is a distorted idealism, and the man who considers himself the first to paint humanity as it really is will be remembered in the future as the most idealistic writer of his time.

1893.

STÉPHANE MALLARMÉ

1

STÉPHANE MALLARME was one of those who love literature too much to write it except by fragments; in whom the desire of perfection brings its own defeat. With either more or less ambition he would have done more to achieve himself; he was always divided between an absolute aim at the absolute, that is, the unattainable, and a too logical disdain for the compromise by which, after all, literature is literature. Carry the theories of Mallarmé to a practical conclusion, multiply his powers in a direct ratio, and you have Wagner. It is his failure not to be Wagner. And, Wagner having existed, it was for him to be something more, to complete Wagner. Well, not being able to be that, it was a matter of sincere indifference to him whether he left one or two little, limited masterpieces of

formal verse and prose, the more or the less.
It was "the work" that he dreamed of, the
new art, more than a new religion, whose
precise form in the world he was never quite
able to settle.

Un auteur difficile, in the phrase of M.
Catulle Mendès, it has always been to what
he himself calls "a labyrinth illuminated by
flowers" that Mallarmé has felt it due to their
own dignity to invite his readers. To their own
dignity, and also to his. Mallarmé was obscure, not so much because he wrote differently,
as because he thought differently, from other
people. His mind was elliptical, and, relying
with undue confidence on the intelligence of
his readers, he emphasised the effect of what
was unlike other people in his mind by reso-
lutely ignoring even the links of connection
that existed between them. Never having
aimed at popularity, he never needed, as most
writers need, to make the first advances. He
made neither intrusion upon nor concession to
those who, after all, were not obliged to read
him. And when he spoke, he considered it
neither needful nor seemly to listen in order
to hear whether he was heard. To the charge

of obscurity he replied, with sufficient disdain,
that there are many who do not know how to
read—except the newspaper, he adds, in one
of those disconcerting, oddly-printed parentheses, which make his work, to those who
rightly apprehend it, so full of wise limitations,
so safe from hasty or seemingly final conclu-
sions. No one in our time has more significantly vindicated the supreme right of the
artist in the aristocracy of letters; wilfully,
perhaps, not always wisely, but nobly, logically.
Has not every artist shrunk from that making
of himself "a motley to the view," that hand-
ing over of his naked soul to the laughter of
the multitude? But who, in our time, has
wrought so subtle a veil, shining on this side,
where the few are, a thick cloud on the other,
where are the many? The oracles have always
had the wisdom to hide their secrets in the
obscurity of many meanings, or of what has
seemed meaningless; and might it not, after
all, be the finest epitaph for a self-respecting
man of letters to be able to say, even after the
writing of many books: I have kept my
secret, I have not betrayed myself to the
multitude?

But to Mallarmé, certainly, there might be applied the significant warning of Rossetti:

> Yet woe to thee if once thou yield
> Unto the act of doing nought!

After a life of persistent devotion to literature, he has left enough poems to make a single small volume (less, certainly, than a hundred poems in all), a single volume of prose, a few pamphlets, and a prose translation of the poems of Poe. It is because among these there are masterpieces, poems which are among the most beautiful poems written in our time, prose which has all the subtlest qualities of prose, that, quitting the abstract point of view, we are forced to regret the fatal enchantments, fatal for him, of theories which are so greatly needed by others, so valuable for our instruction, if we are only a little careful in putting them into practice.

In estimating the significance of Stéphane Mallarmé, it is necessary to take into account not only his verse and prose, but, almost more than these, the Tuesdays of the Rue de Rome, in which he gave himself freely to more than one generation. No one who has ever climbed those four flights of stairs will

have forgotten the narrow, homely interior,
elegant with a sort of scrupulous Dutch comfort; the heavy, carved furniture, the tall
clock, the portraits, Manet's, Whistler's, on
the walls; the table on which the china bowl,
odorous with tobacco, was pushed from hand
to hand; above all, the rocking-chair, Mallarmé's, from which he would rise quietly,
to stand leaning his elbow on the mantel-
piece, while one hand, the hand which did not
hold the cigarette, would sketch out one of
those familiar gestures: *un peu de prêtre,
un peu de danseuse* (in M. Rodenbach's admirable phrase), *avec lesquels il avait l'air chaque
fois d'entrer dans la conversation, comme on
entre en scène.* One of the best talkers of our
time, he was, unlike most other fine talkers,
harmonious with his own theories in giving no
monologues, in allowing every liberty to his
guests, to the conversation; in his perfect
readiness to follow the slightest indication, to
embroider upon any frame, with any material
presented to him. There would have been
something almost of the challenge of the im-
provisatore in this easily moved alertness of
mental attitude, had it not been for the sin-

gular gentleness with which Mallarmé's intelligence moved, in these considerable feats, with the half-apologetic negligence of the perfect acrobat. He seemed to be no more than brushing the dust off your own ideas, settling, arranging them a little, before he gave them back to you, surprisingly luminous. It was only afterwards that you realised how small had been your own part in the matter, as well as what it meant to have enlightened without dazzling you. But there was always the feeling of comradeship, the comradeship of a master, whom, while you were there at least, you did not question; and that very feeling lifted you, in your own estimation, nearer to art.

Invaluable, it seems to me, those Tuesdays must have been to the young men of two generations who have been making French literature; they were unique, certainly, in the experience of the young Englishman who was always so cordially received there, with so flattering a cordiality. Here was a house in which art, literature, was the very atmosphere, a religious atmosphere; and the master of the house, in his just a little solemn sim-

plicity, a priest. I never heard the price of a
book mentioned, or the number of thousand
francs which a popular author had been paid
for his last volume; here, in this one literary
house, literature was unknown as a trade.
And, above all, the questions that were discussed were never, at least, in Mallarmé's
treatment, in his guidance of them, other than
essential questions, considerations of art in
the abstract, of literature before it coagulates
into a book, of life as its amusing and various
web spins the stuff of art. When, indeed, the
conversation, by some untimely hazard, drifted
too near to one, became for a moment, perhaps
inconveniently, practical, it was Mallarmé's
solicitous politeness to wait, a little constrained,
almost uneasy, rolling his cigarette in silence,
until the disturbing moment had passed.

There were other disturbing moments, sometimes. I remember one night, rather late, the
sudden irruption of M. de Heredia, coming on
after a dinner-party, and seating himself in his
well-filled evening dress, precisely in Mallarmé's favourite chair. He was intensely
amusing, voluble, floridly vehement; Mallarmé, I am sure, was delighted to see him;

but the loud voice was a little trying to his nerves, and then he did not know what to do without his chair. He was like a cat that has been turned out of its favourite corner, as he roamed uneasily about the room, resting an unaccustomed elbow on the sideboard, visibly at a disadvantage.

For the attitude of those young men, some of them no longer exactly young, who frequented the Tuesdays, was certainly the attitude of the disciple. Mallarmé never exacted it, he seemed never to notice it; yet it meant to him, all the same, a good deal; as it meant, and in the best sense, a good deal to them. He loved art with a supreme disinterestedness, and it was for the sake of art that he wished to be really a master. For he knew that he had something to teach, that he had found out some secrets worth knowing, that he had discovered a point of view which he could to some degree perpetuate in those young men who listened to him. And to them this free kind of apprenticeship was, beyond all that it gave in direct counsels, in the pattern of work, a noble influence. Mallarmé's quiet, laborious life was for some of them the only counterpoise

to the Bohemian example of the *d'Harcourt*
or the *Taverne*, where art is loved, but with
something of haste, in a very changing devotion. It was impossible to come away from
Mallarmé's without some tranquillising influence from that quiet place, some impersonal
ambition towards excellence, the resolve, at
least, to write a sonnet, a page of prose, that
should be in its own way as perfect as one
could make it, worthy of Mallarmé.

2

"Poetry," said Mallarmé, "is the language
of a state of crisis"; and all his poems are
the evocation of a passing ecstasy, arrested
in mid-flight. This ecstasy is never the mere
instinctive cry of the heart, the simple human
joy or sorrow, which, like the Parnassians,
but for not quite the same reason, he did not
admit in poetry. It is a mental transposition
of emotion or sensation, veiled with atmosphere, and becoming, as it becomes a poem,
pure beauty. Here, for instance, in a poem,
which I have translated line for line, and almost
word for word, a delicate emotion, a figure

vaguely divined, a landscape magically evoked,
blend in a single effect.

SIGH

My soul, calm sister, towards thy brow, whereon scarce
    grieves
An autumn strewn already with its russet leaves,
And towards the wandering sky of thine angelic eyes,
Mounts, as in melancholy gardens may arise
Some faithful fountain sighing whitely towards the blue!
—Towards the blue pale and pure that sad October knew,
When, in those depths, it mirrored languors infinite,
And agonising leaves upon the waters white,
Windily drifting, traced a furrow cold and dun,
Where, in one long last ray, lingered the yellow sun.

Another poem comes a little closer to
nature, but with what exquisite precautions,
and with what surprising novelty in its un-
hesitating touch on actual things!

SEA-WIND

The flesh is sad, alas! and all the books are read.
Flight, only flight!   I feel that birds are wild to tread
The floor of unknown foam, and to attain the skies!
Nought, neither ancient gardens mirrored in the eyes,
Shall hold this heart that bathes in waters its delight,
O nights! nor yet my waking lamp, whose lonely light
Shadows the vacant paper, whiteness profits best,
Nor the young wife who rocks her baby on her breast.
I will depart.   O steamer, swaying rope and spar,
Lift anchor for exotic lands that lie afar!

A weariness, outworn by cruel hopes, still clings
To the last farewell handkerchief's last beckonings!
And are not these, the masts inviting storms, not these
That an awakening wind bends over wrecking seas,
Lost, not a sail, a sail, a flowering isle, ere long?
But, O my heart, hear thou, hear thou the sailors' song!

These (need I say?) belong to the earlier period, in which Mallarmé had not yet withdrawn his light into the cloud; and to the same period belong the prose-poems, one of which, perhaps the most exquisite, I will translate here.

AUTUMN LAMENT

"Ever since Maria left me, for another star—which? Orion, Altair, or thou, green Venus?—I have always cherished solitude. How many long days I have passed, alone with my cat! By *alone*, I mean without a material being, and my cat is a mystical companion, a spirit. I may say, then, that I have passed long days alone with my cat, and alone, with one of the last writers of the Roman decadence; for since the white creature is no more, strangely and singularly, I have loved all that may be summed up in the word: fall. Thus, in the year, my favourite season is during those last languid summer days which come just before the autumn; and, in the day, the hour when I take my walk is the hour when the sun lingers before fading, with rays of copper-yellow on the grey walls, and of copper-red on the window-panes. And, just so, the literature from which my soul demands delight must be the poetry dying out of the last moments of Rome, provided, nevertheless, that it breathes nothing of the rejuvenating approach of the Barbarians, and does not stammer the infantile Latin of the first Christian prose.

"I read, then, one of those beloved poems (whose streaks of rouge have more charm for me than the fresh cheek of youth), and buried my hand in the fur of the pure animal, when a barrel-organ began to sing, languishingly and melancholy, under my window. It played in the long alley of poplars, whose leaves seem mournful to me even in spring, since Maria passed that way with the tapers, for the last time. Yes, sad people's instrument, truly: the piano glitters, the violin brings one's torn fibres to the

light, but the barrel-organ, in the twilight of
memory, has set me despairingly dreaming.
While it murmured a gaily vulgar air, such
as puts mirth into the heart of the suburbs,
an old-fashioned, an empty air, how came it
that its refrain went to my very soul, and
made me weep like a romantic ballad? I
drank it in, and I did not throw a penny
out of the window, for fear of disturbing my
own impression, and of perceiving that the
instrument was not singing by itself."

Between these characteristic, clear, and
beautiful poems, in verse and in prose, and
the opaque darkness of the later writings,
come one or two poems, perhaps the finest
of all, in which already clearness is "a sec-
ondary grace," but in which a subtle rapture
finds incomparable expression. *L'Après-midi
d'un Faune* and *Hérodiade* have already been
introduced, in different ways, to English
readers: the former by Mr. Gosse, in a
detailed analysis; the latter by a translation into verse. And Debussy, in his new
music, has taken *L'Après-midi d'un Faune*
almost for his new point of departure, interpreting it, at all events, faultlessly. In

these two poems I find Mallarmé at the
moment when his own desire achieves itself;
when he attains Wagner's ideal, that "the
most complete work of the poet should be
that which, in its final achievement, becomes a perfect music": every word is a
jewel, scattering and recapturing sudden fire,
every image is a symbol, and the whole poem
is visible music. After this point began
that fatal "last period" which comes to
most artists who have thought too curiously,
or dreamed too remote dreams, or followed
a too wandering beauty. Mallarmé had long
been too conscious that all publication is
"almost a speculation, on one's modesty, for
one's silence"; that "to unclench the fists,
breaking one's sedentary dream, for a ruffling
face to face with the idea," was after all
unnecessary to his own conception of himself, a mere way of convincing the public
that one exists; and having achieved, as he
thought, "the right to abstain from doing
anything exceptional," he devoted himself,
doubly, to silence. Seldom condescending to
write, he wrote now only for himself, and
in a manner which certainly saved him from

intrusion. Some of Meredith's poems, and
occasional passages of his prose, can alone
give in English some faint idea of the later
prose and verse of Mallarmé. The verse
could not, I think, be translated; of the
prose, in which an extreme lucidity of thought
comes to us but glimmeringly through the
entanglements of a construction, part Latin,
part English, I shall endeavour to translate
some fragments, in speaking of the theoretic writings, contained in the two volumes
of *Vers et Prose* and *Divagations*.

3

It is the distinction of Mallarmé to have
aspired after an impossible liberation of the
soul of literature from what is fretting and
constraining in "the body of that death,"
which is the mere literature of words. Words,
he has realised, are of value only as a notation of the free breath of the spirit; words,
therefore, must be employed with an extreme
care, in their choice and adjustment, in setting them to reflect and chime upon one
another; yet least of all for their own sake,

for what they can never, except by suggestion, express. "Every soul is a melody," he has said, "which needs to be readjusted; and for that are the flute or viol of each." The word, treated indeed with a kind of "adoration," as he says, is so regarded in a magnificent sense, in which it is apprehended as a living thing, itself the vision rather than the reality; at least the philtre of the evocation. The word, chosen as he chooses it, is for him a liberating principle, by which the spirit is extracted from matter; takes form, perhaps assumes immortality. Thus an artificiality, even, in the use of words, that seeming artificiality which comes from using words as if they had never been used before, that chimerical search after the virginity of language, is but the paradoxical outward sign of an extreme discontent with even the best of their service. Writers who use words fluently, seeming to disregard their importance, do so from an unconscious confidence in their expressiveness, which the scrupulous thinker, the precise dreamer, can never place in the most carefully chosen among them. To evoke, by some elaborate, instantaneous magic of language, without the formality of an after all impossible description; to be, rather than to express: that is what Mallarmé has consistently, and from the first, sought in verse and prose. And he has sought this wandering, illusive, beckoning butterfly, the soul of dreams, over more and more entangled ground; and it has led him into the depths of many forests, far from the sunlight. To say that he has found what he sought is impossible; but (is it possible to avoid saying?) how heroic a search, and what marvellous discoveries by the way!

I think I understand, though I cannot claim his own authority for my supposition, the way in which Mallarmé wrote verse, and the reason why it became more and more abstruse, more and more unintelligible. Remember his principle: that to name is to destroy, to suggest is to create. Note, further, that he condemns the inclusion in verse of anything but, "for example, the horror of the forest, or the silent thunder afloat in the leaves; not the intrinsic, dense wood of the trees." He has received, then, a mental sensation: let it be the horror of the forest. This sensation begins to form in his brain, at first probably no more than a rhythm, absolutely without words. Gradually thought begins to concentrate itself (but with an extreme care, lest it should break the tension on which all depends) upon the sensation, already struggling to find its own consciousness. Delicately, stealthily, with infinitely timid precaution, words present themselves, at first in silence. Every word seems like a desecration, seems, the clearer it is, to throw back the original sensation farther and farther into the darkness. But, guided always by the rhythm, which is the executive soul (as, in Aristotle's definition, the soul is the form of the body), words come slowly, one by one, shaping the message. Imagine the poem already written down, at least composed. In its very imperfection, it is clear, it shows the links by which it has been riveted together; the whole process of its construction can be studied. Now most writers would be content; but with Mallarmé the work has only begun. In the final result there must be no sign of the making, there must be only the thing made. He works over it, word by word, changing a word here, for its colour, which is not precisely the colour required, a word there, for the break it makes in the music. A new image occurs to him, rarer, subtler, than the one he has used; the image is transferred. By the time the poem has reached, as it seems to him, a flawless unity, the steps of the progress have been only too effectually effaced; and while the poet, who has seen the thing from the beginning, still sees the relation of point to point, the reader, who comes to it only in its final stage, finds himself in a not unnatural bewilderment. Pursue this manner of writing to its ultimate development; start with an enigma, and then withdraw the key of the enigma; and you arrive, easily, at the frozen impenetrability of those latest sonnets, in which the absence of all punctuation is scarcely a recognisable hindrance.

That, I fancy to myself, was his actual way of writing; here, in what I prefer to give as a corollary, is the theory. "Symbolist, Decadent, or Mystic, the schools thus called by themselves, or thus hastily labelled by our information-press, adopt, for meeting-place,

the point of an Idealism which (similarly as
in fugues, in sonatas) rejects the 'natural'
materials, and, as brutal, a direct thought
ordering them; to retain no more than suggestion. To be instituted, a relation between
images, exact; and that therefrom should
detach itself a third aspect, fusible and clear,
offered to the divination. Abolished, the pre-
tension, æsthetically an error, despite its
dominion over almost all the masterpieces,
to enclose within the subtle paper other than,
for example, the horror of the forest, or the
silent thunder afloat in the leaves; not the
intrinsic, dense wood of the trees. Some few
bursts of personal pride, veridically trumpeted,
awaken the architecture of the palace, alone
habitable; not of stone, on which the pages
would close but ill." For example (it is his
own): "I say: a flower! and out of the oblivion
to which my voice consigns every contour, so
far as anything save the known calyx, music-
ally arises, idea, and exquisite, the one flower
absent from all bouquets." "The pure work,"
then, "implies the elocutionary disappearance
of the poet, who yields place to the words,
immobilised by the shock of their inequality;

they take light from mutual reflection, like an actual trail of fire over precious stones, replacing the old lyric afflatus or the enthusiastic personal direction of the phrase." "The verse which out of many vocables remakes an entire word, new, unknown to the language, and as if magical, attains this isolation of speech." Whence, it being "music which rejoins verse, to form, since Wagner, Poetry," the final conclusion: "That we are now precisely at the moment of seeking, before that breaking up of the large rhythms of literature, and their scattering in articulate, almost instrumental, nervous waves, an art which shall complete the transposition, into the Book, of the symphony or simply recapture our own: for, it is not in elementary sonorities of brass, strings, wood, unquestionably, but in the intellectual word at its utmost, that, fully and evidently, we should find, drawing to itself all the correspondences of the universe, the supreme Music."

Here, literally translated, in exactly the arrangement of the original, are some passages out of the theoretic writings, which I have brought together, to indicate what seem

to me the main lines of Mallarmé's doctrine.
It is the doctrine which, as I have already
said, had been divined by Gérard de Nerval;
but what, in Gérard, was pure vision, becomes in Mallarmé a logical sequence of
meditation. Mallarmé was not a mystic, to
whom anything came unconsciously; he was
a thinker, in whom an extraordinary subtlety
of mind was exercised on always explicit,
though by no means the common, problems.
"A seeker after something in the world, that
is there in no satisfying measure, or not at
all," he pursued his search with unwearying
persistence with a sharp mental division of
dream and idea, certainly very lucid to himself, however he may have failed to render
his expression clear to others. And I, for one,
cannot doubt that he was, for the most part,
entirely right in his statement and analysis of
the new conditions under which we are now
privileged or condemned to write. His obscurity was partly his failure to carry out the
spirit of his own directions; but, apart from
obscurity, which we may all be fortunate
enough to escape, is it possible for a writer,
at the present day, to be quite simple, with the

old, objective simplicity, in either thought or
expression? To be *naïf*, to be archaic, is not
to be either natural or simple; I affirm that
it is not natural to be what is called "natural"
any longer. We have no longer the mental
attitude of those to whom a story was but a
story, and all stories good; we have realised
since it was proved to us by Poe, not merely
that the age of epics is past, but that no long
poem was ever written; the finest long poem
in the world being but a series of short poems
linked together by prose. And, naturally, we
can no longer write what we can no longer
accept. Symbolism, implicit in all literature
from the beginning, as it is implicit in the very
words we use, comes to us now, at last quite
conscious of itself, offering us the only escape
from our many imprisonments. We find a
new, an older, sense in the so worn-out forms
of things; the world, which we can no longer
believe in as the satisfying material object it
was to our grandparents, becomes transfigured
with a new light; words, which long usage
had darkened almost out of recognition, take
fresh lustre. And it is on the lines of that
spiritualising of the word, that perfecting of

form in its capacity for allusion and suggestion, that confidence in the eternal correspondences between the visible and the invisible universe, which Mallarmé taught, and too intermittently practised, that literature must now move, if it is in any sense to move forward.

PAUL VERLAINE

1

"*BIEN affectueusement* . . . yours, P. Verlaine." So, in its gay and friendly mingling of French and English, ended the last letter I had from Verlaine. A few days afterwards came the telegram from Paris telling me of his death, in the Rue Descartes, on that 8th January, 1896.

"Condemned to death," as he was, in Victor Hugo's phrase of men in general, "with a sort of indefinite reprieve," and gravely ill as I had for some time known him to be, it was still with a shock, not only of sorrow, but of surprise, that I heard the news of his death. He had suffered and survived so much, and I found it so hard to associate the idea of death with one who had always been so passionately in love with life, more passionately in love with life than any man I ever knew. Rest was one of the delicate privileges of life which he never loved: he did but endure it with grumbling gaiety when a hospital-bed claimed him. And whenever he spoke to me of the long rest which has now sealed his eyelids, it was with a shuddering revolt from the thought of ever going away into the cold, out of the sunshine which had been so warm to him. With all his pains, misfortunes, and the calamities which followed him step by step all his life, I think few men ever got so much out of their lives, or lived so fully, so intensely, with such a genius for living. That, indeed, is why he was a great poet. Verlaine was a man who gave its full value to every moment, who got out of every moment all that that moment had to give him. It was not always, not often, perhaps, pleasure. But it was energy, the vital force of a nature which was always receiving and giving out, never at rest, never passive, or indifferent, or hesitating. It is impossible for me to convey to those who did not know him any notion of how sincere he was. The word "sincerity" seems hardly to have emphasis enough to say, in regard to this one man, what it says, adequately enough, of others. He sinned, and it was with all his humanity;

he repented, and it was with all his soul.   And
to every occurrence of the day, to every mood
of the mind, to every impulse of the creative
instinct, he brought the same unparalleled
sharpness of sensation.   When, in 1894, he
was my guest in London, I was amazed by the
exactitude of his memory of the mere turnings
of the streets, the shapes and colours of the
buildings, which he had not seen for twenty
years.   He saw, he felt, he remembered, everything, with an unconscious mental selection of
the fine shades, the essential part of things, or
precisely those aspects which most other people
would pass by.

Few poets of our time have been more often
drawn, few have been easier to draw, few have
better repaid drawing, than Paul Verlaine.
A face without a beautiful line, a face all character, full of somnolence and sudden fire, in
which every irregularity was a kind of aid to
the hand, could not but tempt the artist desiring at once to render a significant likeness and
to have his own part in the creation of a picture.   Verlaine, like all men of genius, had
something of the air of the somnambulist:
that profound slumber of the face, as it was in

him, with its startling awakenings. It was a
face devoured by dreams, feverish and som-
nolent; it had earthly passion, intellectual
pride, spiritual humility; the air of one who
remembers, not without an effort, who is listening, half distractedly to something which
other people do not hear; coming back so
suddenly, and from so far, with the relief of
one who steps out of that obscure shadow into
the noisier forgetfulness of life. The eyes,
often half closed, were like the eyes of a cat
between sleeping and waking; eyes in which
contemplation was "itself an act." A remarkable lithograph by Mr. Rothenstein (the face
lit by oblique eyes, the folded hands thrust
into the cheek) gives with singular truth the
sensation of that restless watch on things which
this prisoner of so many chains kept without
slackening. To Verlaine every corner of the
world was alive with tempting and consoling
and terrifying beauty. I have never known
any one to whom the sight of the eyes was so
intense and imaginative a thing. To him,
physical sight and spiritual vision, by some
strange alchemical operation of the brain,
were one. And in the disquietude of his face,

which seemed to take such close heed of things, precisely because it was sufficiently apart from them to be always a spectator, there was a realisable process of vision continually going on, in which all the loose ends of the visible world were being caught up into a new mental fabric.

And along with this fierce subjectivity, into which the egoism of the artist entered so unconsciously, and in which it counted for so much, there was more than the usual amount of childishness, always in some measure present in men of genius. There was a real, almost blithe, childishness in the way in which he would put on his "Satanic" expression, of which it was part of the joke that every one should not be quite in the secret. It was a whim of this kind which made him put at the beginning of *Romances sans Paroles* that very criminal image of a head which had so little resemblance with even the shape, indeed curious enough, of his actual head. "Born under the sign of Saturn," as he no doubt was, with that "old prisoner's head" of which he tells us, it was by his amazing faculty for a simple kind of

happiness that he always impressed me. I
have never seen so cheerful an invalid as he
used to be at that hospital, the Hôpital Saint-
Louis, where at one time I used to go and
see him every week. His whole face seemed
to chuckle as he would tell me, in his emphatic, confiding way, everything that entered
into his head; the droll stories cut short by
a groan, a lamentation, a sudden fury of
reminiscence, at which his face would cloud
or convulse, the wild eyebrows slanting up
and down; and then, suddenly, the good
laugh would be back, clearing the air. No
one was ever so responsive to his own moods
as Verlaine, and with him every mood had
the vehemence of a passion. Is not his
whole art a delicate waiting upon moods,
with that perfect confidence in them as they
are, which it is a large part of ordinary education to discourage in us, and a large part
of experience to repress? But to Verlaine,
happily, experience taught nothing; or
rather, it taught him only to cling the more
closely to those moods in whose succession
lies the more intimate part of our spiritual
life.

It is no doubt well for society that man should learn by experience; for the artist the benefit is doubtful. The artist, it cannot be too clearly understood, has no more part in society than a monk in domestic life: he cannot be judged by its rules, he can be neither praised not blamed for his acceptance or rejection of its conventions. Social rules are made by normal people for normal people, and the man of genius is fundamentally abnormal. It is the poet against society, society against the poet, a direct antagonism; the shock of which, however, it is often possible to avoid by a compromise. So much licence is allowed on the one side, so much liberty foregone on the other. The consequences are not always of the best, art being generally the loser. But there are certain natures to which compromise is impossible; and the nature of Verlaine was one of these natures.

"The soul of an immortal child," says one who has understood him better than others, Charles Morice, "that is the soul of Verlaine, with all the privileges and all the perils of so being; with the sudden

despair so easily distracted, the vivid gaieties
without a cause, the excessive suspicions
and the excessive confidences, the whims so
easily outwearied, the deaf and blind infatua-
tions, with, especially, the unceasing renewal
of impressions in the incorruptible integrity
of personal vision and sensation. Years, influences, teachings, may pass over a temperament such as this, may irritate it, may
fatigue it; transform it, never—never so
much as to alter that particular unity which
consists in a dualism, in the division of forces
between the longing after what is evil and
the adoration of what is good; or rather,
in the antagonism of spirit and flesh. Other
men 'arrange' their lives, take sides, follow
one direction; Verlaine hesitates before a
choice, which seems to him monstrous, for,
with the integral *naïveté* of irrefutable human
truth, he cannot resign himself, however
strong may be the doctrine, however enticing
may be the passion, to the necessity of sacrificing one to the other, and from one to the
other he oscillates without a moment's repose."

It is in such a sense as this that Verlaine

may be said to have learnt nothing from
experience, in the sense that he learnt everything direct from life, and without comparing day with day. That the exquisite
artist of the *Fêtes Galantes* should become
the great poet of *Sagesse*, it was needful that
things should have happened as disastrously
as they did: the marriage with the girl-
wife, that brief idyl, the passion for drink,
those other forbidden passions, vagabondage,
an attempted crime, the eighteen months of
prison, conversion; followed, as it had to be,
by relapse, bodily sickness, poverty, beggary
almost, a lower and lower descent into mean
distresses. It was needful that all this should
happen, in order that the spiritual vision
should eclipse the material vision; but it
was needful that all this should happen in
vain, so far as the conduct of life was concerned. Reflection, in Verlaine, is pure waste;
it is the speech of the soul and the speech of
the eyes, that we must listen to in his verse,
never the speech of the reason. And I call
him fortunate because, going through life with
a great unconsciousness of what most men
spend their lives in considering, he was able

to abandon himself entirely to himself, to his
unimpeded vision, to his unchecked emotion,
to the passionate sincerity which in him was
genius.

2

French poetry, before Verlaine, was an
admirable vehicle for a really fine, a really
poetical, kind of rhetoric. With Victor Hugo,
for the first time since Ronsard (the two or
three masterpieces of Ronsard and his companions) it had learnt to sing; with Baudelaire
it had invented a new vocabulary for the
expression of subtle, often perverse, essentially modern emotion and sensation. But
with Victor Hugo, with Baudelaire, we are
still under the dominion of rhetoric. "Take
eloquence, and wring its neck!" said Verlaine
in his *Art Poétique;* and he showed, by writing it, that French verse could be written
without rhetoric. It was partly from his
study of English models that he learnt the
secret of liberty in verse, but it was much
more a secret found by the way, in the mere
endeavour to be absolutely sincere, to express
exactly what he saw, to give voice to his own

temperament, in which intensity of feeling seemed to find its own expression, as if by accident. *L'art, mes enfants, c'est d'être absolument soi-même,* he tells us in one of his later poems; and, with such a personality as Verlaine's to express, what more has art to do, if it would truly, and in any interesting manner, hold the mirror up to nature?

For, consider the natural qualities which this man had for the task of creating a new poetry. "Sincerity, and the impression of the moment followed to the letter": that is how he defined his theory of style, in an article written about himself.

> Car nous voulons la nuance encor,
> Pas la couleur, rien que la nuance!

as he cries, in his famous *Art Poétique.* Take, then, his susceptibility of the senses, an emotional susceptibility not less delicate; a life sufficiently troubled to draw out every emotion of which he was capable, and, with it, that absorption in the moment, that inability to look before or after; the need to love and the need to confess, each a passion; an art of painting the fine shades of landscape, of evoking atmosphere, which can be compared

With Verlaine the sense of hearing and the
sense of sight are almost interchangeable:
he paints with sound, and his line and atmosphere become music. It was with the most
precise accuracy that Whistler applied the
terms of music to his painting, for painting,
when it aims at being the vision of reality,
pas la couleur, rien que la nuance, passes
almost into the condition of music. Verlaine's
landscape painting is always an evocation, in
which outline is lost in atmosphere.

> C'est des beaux yeux derrière des voiles,
>   C'est le grand jour tremblant de midi,
>   C'est, par un ciel d'automne attiédi,
>   Le bleu fouillis des claires étoiles!

He was a man, certainly, "for whom the
visible world existed," but for whom it existed
always as a vision. He absorbed it through
all his senses, as the true mystic absorbs the
divine beauty. And so he created in verse a
new voice for nature, full of the humble ecstasy
with which he saw, listened, accepted.

> Cette âme qui se lamente
> En cette plaine dormante
>   C'est la nôtre, n'est-ce pas?
> La mienne, dis, et la tienne,
> Dont s'exhale l'humble antienne
>   Par ce tiède soir, tout bas?

And with the same attentive simplicity
with which he found words for the sensations
of hearing and the sensations of sight, he
found words for the sensations of the soul,
for the fine shades of feeling. From the
moment when his inner life may be said to
have begun, he was occupied with the task of
an unceasing confession, in which one seems
to overhear him talking to himself, in that
vague, preoccupied way which he often had.
Here again are words which startle one by
their delicate resemblance to thoughts, by
their winged flight from so far, by their alight-
ing so close. The verse murmurs, with such
an ingenuous confidence, such intimate secrets.
That "setting free" of verse, which is one of
the achievements of Verlaine, was itself mainly
an attempt to be more and more sincere, a
way of turning poetic artifice to new account,
by getting back to nature itself, hidden away
under the eloquent rhetoric of Hugo, Baudelaire, and the Parnassians. In the devotion of rhetoric to either beauty or truth, there
is a certain consciousness of an audience, of
an external judgment: rhetoric would con-
vince, be admired. It is the very essence of

poetry to be unconscious of anything between its own moment of flight and the supreme beauty which it will never attain. Verlaine taught French poetry that wise and subtle unconsciousness. It was in so doing that he "fused his personality," in the words of Verhaeren, "so profoundly with beauty, that he left upon it the imprint of a new and henceforth eternal attitude."

3

J'ai la fureur d'aimer, says Verlaine, in a passage of very personal significance.

> J'ai la fureur d'aimer.   Mon cœur si faible est fou.
> N'importe quand, n'importe quel et n'importe où,
> Qu'un éclair de beauté, de vertu, de vaillance,
> Luise, il s'y précipite, il y vole, il y lance,
> Et, le temps d'une étreinte, il embrasse cent fois
> L'être ou l'objet qu'il a poursuivi de son choix;
> Puis, quand l'illusion a replié son aile,
> Il revient triste et seul bien souvent, mais fidèle,
> Et laissant aux ingrats quelque chose de lui,
> Sang ou chair . . . .
> J'ai la fureur d'aimer.   Qu'y faire?   Ah, laissez faire!

And certainly this admirable, and supremely dangerous, quality was at the root of Verlaine's nature. Instinctive, unreasoning as he was, entirely at the mercy of the emotion or impression which, for the moment, had seized upon him, it was inevitable that he should be completely at the mercy of the most imperious of instincts, of passions, and of intoxications. And he had the simple and ardent nature, in this again consistently childlike, to which love, some kind of affection, given or returned, is not the luxury, the exception, which it is to many natures, but a daily necessity. To such a temperament there may or may not be the one great passion; there will certainly be many passions. And in Verlaine I find that single, childlike necessity of loving and being loved, all through his life and on every page of his works; I find it, unchanged in essence, but constantly changing form, in his chaste and unchaste devotions to women, in his passionate friendships with men, in his supreme mystical adoration of God.

To turn from *La Bonne Chanson*, written for a wedding present to a young wife, to *Chansons pour Elle*, written more than twenty years later, in dubious honour of a middle-aged mistress, is to travel a long road, the hard, long road which Verlaine had travelled during those years. His life was ruinous, a disaster, more sordid perhaps than the life of any other poet; and he could write of it, from a hospital-bed, with this quite sufficient sense of its deprivations. "But all the same, it is hard," he laments, in *Mes Hôpitaux*, "after a life of work, set off, I admit, with accidents in which I have had a large share, catastrophes perhaps vaguely premeditated—it is hard, I say, at forty-seven years of age, in full possession of all the reputation (of the *success*, to use the frightful current phrase) to which my highest ambitions could aspire—hard, hard, hard indeed, worse than hard, to find myself—good God!—to find myself *on the streets*, and to have nowhere to lay my head and support an ageing body save the pillows and the *menus* of a public charity, even now uncertain, and which might at any moment be withdrawn—God forbid!— without, apparently, the fault of any one, oh! not even, and above all, not mine." Yet, after all, these sordid miseries, this poor man's vagabondage, all the misfortunes of one certainly "irreclaimable," on which so much stress has been laid, alike by friends and by foes, are externalities; they are not the man;

the man, the eternal lover, passionate and
humble, remains unchanged, while only his
shadow wanders, from morning to night of the
long day.

The poems to Rimbaud, to Lucien Létinois,
to others, the whole volume of *Dédicaces*,
cover perhaps as wide a range of sentiment
as *La Bonne Chanson* and *Chansons pour Elle*.
The poetry of friendship has never been sung
with such plaintive sincerity, such simple
human feeling, as in some of these poems,
which can only be compared, in modern poetry,
with a poem for which Verlaine had a great
admiration, Tennyson's *In Memoriam*. Only
with Verlaine, the thing itself, the affection or
the regret, is everything; there is no room for
meditation over destiny, or search for a prob-
lematical consolation. Other poems speak a
more difficult language, in which, doubtless,
l'ennui di vivre avec les gens et dans les choses
counts for much, and *la fureur d'aimer* for
more.

In spite of the general impression to the
contrary, an impression which by no means
displeased him himself, I must contend that
the sensuality of Verlaine, brutal as it could

sometimes be, was after all simple rather than complicated, instinctive rather than perverse. In the poetry of Baudelaire, with which the poetry of Verlaine is so often compared, there is a deliberate science of sensual perversity which has something almost monachal in its accentuation of vice with horror, in its passionate devotion to passions. Baudelaire brings every complication of taste, the exasperation of perfumes, the irritant of cruelty, the very odours and colours of corruption, to the creation and adornment of a sort of religion, in which an eternal mass is served before a veiled altar. There is no confession, no absolution, not a prayer is permitted which is not set down in the ritual. With Verlaine, however often love may pass into sensuality, to whatever length sensuality may be hurried, sensuality is never more than the malady of love. It is love desiring the absolute, seeking in vain, seeking always, and, finally, out of the depths, finding God.

Verlaine's conversion took place while he was in prison, during those solitary eighteen months in company with his thoughts, that enforced physical inactivity, which could but concentrate his whole energy on the only kind of sensation then within his capacity, the sensations of the soul and of the conscience. With that promptitude of abandonment which was his genius, he grasped feverishly at the succour of God and the Church, he abased himself before the immaculate purity of the Virgin. He had not, like others who have risen from the same depths to the same height of humiliation, to despoil his nature of its pride, to conquer his intellect, before he could become *l'enfant vêtu de laine et d'innocence*. All that was simple, humble, childlike in him accepted that humiliation with the loving child's joy in penitence; all that was ardent, impulsive, indomitable in him burst at once into a flame of adoration.

He realised the great secret of the Christian mystics: that it is possible to love God with an extravagance of the whole being, to which the love of the creature cannot attain. All love is an attempt to break through the loneliness of individuality, to fuse oneself with something not oneself, to give and to receive, in all the warmth of natural desire, that inmost element which remains, so cold

and so invincible, in the midst of the soul.
It is a desire of the infinite in humanity, and,
as humanity has its limits, it can but return
sadly upon itself when that limit is reached.
Thus human love is not only an ecstasy but
a despair, and the more profound a despair
the more ardently it is returned.

But the love of God, considered only from
its human aspect, contains at least the illusion
of infinity. To love God is to love the absolute, so far as the mind of man can conceive the absolute, and thus, in a sense, to
love God is to possess the absolute, for love
has already possessed that which it appre-
hends. What the earthly lover realises to
himself as the image of his beloved is, after
all, his own vision of love, not her. God must
remain *deus absconditus*, even to love; but the
lover, incapable of possessing infinity, will have
possessed all of infinity of which he is capable.
And his ecstasy will be flawless. The human
mind, meditating on infinity, can but discover
perfection beyond perfection; for it is impossible to conceive of limitation in any
aspect of that which has once been conceived
as infinite. In place of that deception which

comes from the shock of a boundary-line
beyond which humanity cannot conceive of
humanity, there is only a divine rage against
the limits of human perception, which by
their own failure seem at last to limit for us
the infinite itself. For once, love finds itself
bounded only by its own capacity; so far
does the love of God exceed the love of the
creature, and so far would it exceed that love
if God did not exist.

But if He does exist! if, outside humanity,
a conscient, eternal perfection, who has made
the world in his image, loves the humanity
He has made, and demands love in return!
If the spirit of his love is as a breath over
the world, suggesting, strengthening, the love
which it desires, seeking man that man may
seek God, itself the impulse which it humbles
itself to accept at man's hands; if indeed,

Mon Dieu m'a dit: mon fils, il faut m'aimer;

how much more is this love of God, in its
inconceivable acceptance and exchange, the
most divine, the only unending intoxication,
in the world! Well, it is this realised sense
of communion, point by point realised, and

put into words, more simple, more human, more instinctive than any poet since the mediæval mystics has found for the delights of this intercourse, that we find in *Sagesse*, and in the other religious poems of Verlaine.

But, with Verlaine, the love of God is not merely a rapture, it is a thanksgiving for forgiveness. Lying in wait behind all the fair appearances of the world, he remembers the old enemy, the flesh; and the sense of sin (that strange paradox of the reason) is childishly strong in him. He laments his offence, he sees not only the love but the justice of God, and it seems to him, as in a picture, that the little hands of the Virgin are clasped in petition for him. Verlaine's religion is the religion of the Middle Ages. *Je suis catholique,* he said to me, *mais . . . catholique du moyen-âge!* He might have written the ballad which Villon made for his mother, and with the same visual sense of heaven and hell. Like a child, he tells his sins over, promises that he has put them behind him, and finds such *naïve,* human words to express his gratitude. The Virgin

is really, to him, mother and friend; he
delights in the simple, peasant humanity,
still visible in her who is also the Mystical Rose, the Tower of Ivory, the Gate of
Heaven, and who now extends her hands,
in the gesture of pardon, from a throne only
just lower than the throne of God.

4

Experience, I have said, taught Verlaine
nothing; religion had no more stable influence
upon his conduct then experience. In that
apology for himself which he wrote under
the anagram of " Pauvre Lelian," he has
stated the case with his usual sincerity. "I
believe," he says, "and I sin in thought as
in action; I believe, and I repent in thought,
if no more. Or again, I believe, and I am
a good Christian at this moment; I believe,
and I am a bad Christian the instant after.
The remembrance, the hope, the invocation of
a sin delights me, with or without remorse,
sometimes under the very form of sin, and
hedged with all its natural consequences;
more often—so strong, so natural and *animal*,

are flesh and blood—just in the same manner as the remembrances, hopes, invocations of any carnal freethinker. This delight, I, you, some one else, writers, it pleases us to put to paper and publish more or less well expressed: we consign it, in short, into literary form, forgetting all religious ideas, or not letting one of them escape us. Can any one in good faith condemn us as poet? A hundred times no." And, indeed, I would echo, a hundred times no! It is just this apparent complication of what is really a great simplicity which gives its singular value to the poetry of Verlaine, permitting it to sum up in itself the whole paradox of humanity, and especially the weak, passionate, uncertain, troubled century to which we belong, in which so many doubts, negations, and distresses seem, now more than ever, to be struggling towards at least an ideal of spiritual consolation. Verlaine is the poet of these weaknesses and of that ideal.

⌊*See also account given in "Bibliography and Notes," page* 351.⌋

I. JORIS-KARL HUYSMANS

THE novels of Huysmans, however we may regard them as novels, are, at all events, the sincere and complete expression of a very remarkable personality. From *Marthe* to *Là-Bas* every story, every volume, disengages the same atmosphere—the atmosphere of a London November, when mere existence is a sufficient burden, and the little miseries of life loom up through the fog into a vague and formidable grotesqueness. Here, for once, is a pessimist whose philosophy is mere sensation—and sensation, after all, is the one certainty in a world which may be well or ill arranged, for ultimate purposes, but which is certainly, for each of us, what each of us feels it to be. To Huysmans the world appears to be a profoundly uncomfortable, unpleasant, ridiculous place, with a certain solace in various forms of art, and certain possibilities of at least temporary escape. Part of his work presents to us a picture of ordinary life

as he conceives it, in its uniform trivial
wretchedness; in another part he has made
experiment in directions which have seemed
to promise escape, relief; in yet other por-
tions he has allowed himself the delight of
his sole enthusiasm, the enthusiasm of art.
He himself would be the first to acknowledge—indeed, practically, he has acknowledged
that the particular way in which he sees
life is a matter of personal temperament
and constitution, a matter of nerves. The
Goncourts have never tired of insisting on
the fact of their *névrose*, of pointing out its
importance in connection with the form and
structure of their work, their touch on style,
even. To them the *maladie fin de siècle* has
come delicately, as to the chlorotic fine
ladies of the Faubourg Saint-Germain: it
has sharpened their senses to a point of morbid
acuteness, it has given their work a certain
feverish beauty. To Huysmans it has given
the exaggerated horror of whatever is ugly
and unpleasant, with the fatal instinct of
discovering, the fatal necessity of contemplat-
ing, every flaw and every discomfort that a
somewhat imperfect world can offer for in-

spection. It is the transposition of the ideal.
Relative values are lost, for it is the sense of the
disagreeable only that is heightened; and
the world, in this strange disorder of vision,
assumes an aspect which can only be compared with that of a drop of impure water
under the microscope. "Nature seen through
a temperament" is Zola's definition of all
art. Nothing, certainly, could be more exact
and expressive as a definition of the art of
Huysmans.

To realise how faithfully and how completely Huysmans has revealed himself in all
he has written, it is necessary to know the
man. "He gave me the impression of a
cat," some interviewer once wrote of him;
"courteous, perfectly polite, almost amiable,
but all nerves, ready to shoot out his claws
at the least word." And indeed, there is
something of his favourite animal about
him. The face is grey, wearily alert, with
a look of benevolent malice. At first sight
it is commonplace, the features are ordinary,
one seems to have seen it at the Bourse or
the Stock Exchange. But gradually that
strange, unvarying expression, that look of

benevolent malice, grows upon you as the
influence of the man makes itself felt. I
have seen Huysmans in his office—he is an
employé in the Ministry of Foreign Affairs,
and a model employé; I have seen him in a
café, in various houses; but I always see
him in memory as I used to see him at the
house of the bizarre Madame X. He leans
back on the sofa, rolling a cigarette between
his thin, expressive fingers, looking at no
one and at nothing, while Madame X moves
about with solid vivacity in the midst of
her extraordinary menagerie of *bric-à-brac*.
The spoils of all the world are there, in that
incredibly tiny *salon;* they lie underfoot,
they climb up walls, they cling to screens,
brackets, and tables; one of your elbows
menaces a Japanese toy, the other a Dresden
china shepherdess; all the colours of the
rainbow clash in a barbaric discord of notes.
And in a corner of this fantastic room,
Huysmans lies back indifferently on the
sofa, with the air of one perfectly resigned
to the boredom of life. Something is said
by my learned friend who is to write for the
new periodical, or perhaps it is the young

editor of the new periodical who speaks, or
(if that were not impossible) the taciturn
Englishman who accompanies me; and Huysmans, without looking up, and without taking the trouble to speak very distinctly,
picks up the phrase, transforms it, more
likely transpierces it, in a perfectly turned
sentence, a phrase of impromptu elaboration. Perhaps it is only a stupid book that
some one has mentioned, or a stupid woman;
as he speaks, the book looms up before one,
becomes monstrous in its dulness, a masterpiece and miracle of imbecility; the unimportant little woman grows into a slow horror
before your eyes. It is always the unpleasant
aspect of things that he seizes, but the intensity of his revolt from that unpleasantness
brings a touch of the sublime into the very
expression of his disgust. Every sentence is
an epigram, and every epigram slaughters a
reputation or an idea. He speaks with an
accent as of pained surprise, an amused look
of contempt, so profound that it becomes
almost pity, for human imbecility.

Yes, that is the true Huysmans, the Huysmans of *A Rebours*, and it is just such sur-

roundings that seem to bring out his peculiar quality. With this contempt for humanity, this hatred of mediocrity, this passion for a somewhat exotic kind of modernity, an artist who is so exclusively an artist was sure, one day or another, to produce a work which, being produced to please himself, and being entirely typical of himself, would be, in a way, the quintessence of contemporary Decadence. And it is precisely such a book that Huysmans has written, in the extravagant, astonishing *A Rebours*. All his other books are a sort of unconscious preparation for this one book, a sort of inevitable and scarcely necessary sequel to it. They range themselves along the line of a somewhat erratic development, from Baudelaire, through Goncourt, by way of Zola, to the surprising originality of so disconcerting an exception to any and every order of things.

The descendant of a long line of Dutch painters—one of whom, Cornelius Huysmans, has a certain fame among the lesser landscape men of the great period—Joris-Karl Huysmans was born at Paris, February 5, 1848. His first book, *Le Drageoir à Epices,*

published at the age of twenty-six, is a
pasticcio of prose poems, done after Baudelaire, of little sketches, done after Dutch
artists, together with a few studies of
Parisian landscape, done after nature. It
shows us the careful, laboured work of a
really artistic temperament; it betrays here
and there, the spirit of acrimonious observation which is to count for so much with
Huysmans—in the crude malice of *L'Extase*,
for example, in the notation of the "rich-
ness of tone," the "superb colouring," of an
old drunkard. And one sees already something of the novelty and the precision of his
description, the novelty and the unpleasantness of the subjects which he chooses to
describe, in this vividly exact picture of the
carcass of a cow hung up outside a butcher's
shop: "As in a hothouse, a marvellous vegetation flourished in the carcass. Veins shot
out on every side like trails of bind-weed;
dishevelled branch-work extended itself along
the body, an efflorescence of entrails unfurled
their violet-tinted corollas, and big clusters
of fat stood out, a sharp white, against the
red medley of quivering flesh."

In *Marthe: histoire d'une fille*, which followed in 1876, two years later, Huysmans is almost as far from actual achievement as in *Le Drageoir à Epices*, but the book, in its crude attempt to deal realistically, and somewhat after the manner of Goncourt, with the life of a prostitute of the lowest depths, marks a considerable advance upon the somewhat casual experiments of his earlier manner. It is important to remember that *Marthe* preceded *La Fille Elisa* and *Nana*. "I write what I see, what I feel, and what I have experienced," says the brief and defiant preface, "and I write it as well as I can: that is all. This explanation is not an excuse, it is simply the statement of the aim that I pursue in art." Explanation or excuse notwithstanding, the book was forbidden to be sold in France. It is Naturalism in its earliest and most pitiless stage—Naturalism which commits the error of evoking no sort of interest in this unhappy creature who rises a little from her native gutter, only to fall back more woefully into the gutter again. Goncourt's Elisa at least interests us; Zola's Nana at all events appeals to our senses. But Marthe is a mere docu-

ment, like her story. Notes have been taken—
no doubt *sur le vif*—they have been strung together, and here they are with only an interesting brutality, a curious sordidness to note, in
these descriptions that do duty for psychology
and incident alike, in the general flatness of
character, the general dislocation of episode.

Les Sœurs Vatard, published in 1879, and
the short story *Sac au Dos*, which appeared
in 1880 in the famous Zolaist manifesto, *Les
Soirées de Médan*, show the influence of *Les
Rougon-Macquart* rather than of *Germinie
Lacerteux*. For the time the "formula" of
Zola has been accepted: the result is, a remarkable piece of work, but a story without a
story, a frame without a picture. With Zola,
there is at all events a beginning and an end,
a chain of events, a play of character upon
incident. But in *Les Sœurs Vatard* there is
no reason for the narrative ever beginning or
ending; there are miracles of description—the
workroom, the rue de Sèvres, the locomotives,
the *Foire du pain d'épice*—which lead to nothing; there are interiors, there are interviews,
there are the two work-girls, Céline and Dé-
sirée, and their lovers; there is what Zola him-

self described as *tout ce milieu ouvrier, ce coin de misère et d'ignorance, de tranquille ordure et d'air naturellement empesté.* And with it all there is a heavy sense of stagnancy, a dreary lifelessness. All that is good in the book reappears, in vastly better company, in *En Ménage* (1881), a novel which is, perhaps, more in the direct line of heritage from *L'Education Sentimentale*—the starting-point of the Naturalistic novel—than any other novel of the Naturalists.

En Ménage is the story of *"Monsieur Tout-le-monde,* an insignificant personality, one of those poor creatures who have not even the supreme consolation of being able to complain of any injustice in their fate, for an injustice supposes at all events a misunderstood merit, a force." André is the reduction to the bourgeois formula of the invariable hero of Huysmans. He is just enough removed from the commonplace to suffer from it with acuteness. He cannot get on either with or without a woman in his establishment. Betrayed by his wife, he consoles himself with a mistress, and finally goes back to the wife. And the moral of it all is: "Let us be stupidly comfortable, if we can, in any way we can: but it is almost certain that we cannot." In *A Vau-l'Eau*, a less interesting story which followed *En Ménage*, the daily misery of the respectable M. Folantin, the government employé, consists in the impossible search for a decent restaurant, a satisfactory dinner: for M. Folantin, too, there is only the same counsel of a desperate, an inevitable resignation. Never has the intolerable monotony of small inconveniences been so scrupulously, so unsparingly chronicled, as in these two studies in the heroic degree of the commonplace. It happens to André, at a certain epoch in his life, to take back an old servant who had left him many years before. He finds that she has exactly the same defects as before, and "to find them there again," comments the author, "did not displease him. He had been expecting them all the time, he saluted them as old acquaintances, yet with a certain surprise, notwithstanding, to see them neither grown nor diminished. He noted for himself with satisfaction that the stupidity of his servant had remained stationary." On another page, referring to the inventor of cards, Huysmans defines him as one who "did something towards suppressing the free exchange of human imbecility." Having to say in passing that a girl has returned from a ball, "she was at home again," he observes, "after the half-dried sweat of the waltzes." In this invariably sarcastic turn of the phrase, this absoluteness of contempt, this insistence on the disagreeable, we find the note of Huysmans, particularly at this point in his career, when, like Flaubert, he forced himself to contemplate and to analyse the more mediocre manifestations of *la bêtise humaine*.

There is a certain perversity in this furious contemplation of stupidity, this fanatical insistence on the exasperating attraction of the sordid and the disagreeable; and it is by such stages that we come to *A Rebours*. But on the way we have to note a volume of *Croquis Parisiens* (1880), in which the virtuoso who is a part of the artist in Huysmans has executed some of his most astonishing feats; and a volume on *L'Art Moderne* (1883), in which the most modern of artists in literature has applied himself to the criticism—the revelation, rather—of modernity in art. In the latter, Huysmans was the first to declare the supremacy of Degas—"the greatest artist that we

possess to-day in France"—while announcing
with no less fervour the remote, reactionary,
and intricate genius of Gustave Moreau. He
was the first to discover Raffaëlli, "the painter
of poor people and the open sky—a sort of
Parisian Millet," as he called him; the first to
discover Forain, "*le véritable peintre de la
fille*"; the first to discover Odilon Redon, to
do justice to Pissaro and Paul Gauguin. No
literary artist since Baudelaire has made so
valuable a contribution to art criticism, and
the *Curiosités Esthétiques* are, after all, less
exact in their actual study, less revolutionary,
and less really significant in their critical judgments, than *L'Art Moderne*. The *Croquis
Parisiens*, which, in its first edition, was illustrated by etchings of Forain and Raffaëlli, is
simply the attempt to do in words what those
artists have done in aquafortis or in pastel.
There are the same Parisian types—the omni-
bus-conductor, the washerwoman, the man who
sells hot chestnuts—the same impressions of a
sick and sorry landscape, La Bièvre, for preference, in all its desolate and lamentable attraction; there is a marvellously minute series of
studies of that typically Parisian music-hall,

the Folies-Bergère. Huysmans' faculty of description is here seen at its fullest stretch of
agility; precise, suggestive, with all the outline
and colour of actual brush-work, it might even
be compared with the art of Degas, only there
is just that last touch wanting, that breath of
palpitating life, which is what we always get
in Degas, what we never get in Huysmans.

In *L'Art Moderne*, speaking of the water-
colours of Forain, Huysmans attributes to
them "a specious and *cherché* art, demanding,
for its appreciation, a certain initiation, a
certain special sense." To realise the full value,
the real charm, of *A Rebours*, some such initiation might be deemed necessary. In its fantastic unreality, its exquisite artificiality, it is
the natural sequel of *En Ménage* and *A Vau-
l'Eau*, which are so much more acutely sordid
than the most sordid kind of real life; it is the
logical outcome of that hatred and horror of
human mediocrity, of the mediocrity of daily
existence, which we have seen to be the special
form of Huysmans' *névrose*. The motto, taken
from a thirteenth-century mystic, Rusbroeck
the Admirable, is a cry for escape, for the
"something in the world that is there in no

satisfying measure, or not at all": *Il faut que je me réjouisse au-dessus du temps . . . quoique le monde ait horreur de ma joie et que sa grossièreté ne sache pas ce que je veux dire.* And the book is the history of a *Thebaïde raffinée*—a voluntary exile from the world in a new kind of "Palace of Art." Des Esseintes, the vague but typical hero, is one of those half-pathological cases which help us to understand the full meaning of the word *décadence*, which they partly represent. The last descendant of an ancient family, his impoverished blood tainted by all sorts of excesses, Des Esseintes finds himself at thirty *sur le chemin, dégrisé, seul, abominablement lassé.* He has already realised that "the world is divided, in great part, into swaggerers and simpletons." His one desire is to "hide himself away, far from the world, in some retreat, where he might deaden the sound of the loud rumbling of inflexible life, as one covers the street with straw, for sick people." This retreat he discovers, just far enough from Paris to be safe from disturbance, just near enough to be saved from the nostalgia of the unattainable. He succeeds in making his house a paradise of the artificial, choosing

the tones of colour that go best with candle-
light, for it need scarcely be said that Des
Esseintes has effected a simple transposition
of night and day. His disappearance from the
world has been complete; it seems to him that
the "comfortable desert" of his exile need never
cease to be just such a luxurious solitude; it
seems to him that he has attained his desire,
that he has attained to happiness.

Disturbing physical symptoms harass him
from time to time, but they pass. It is an
effect of nerves that now and again he is
haunted by remembrance; the recurrence of
a perfume, the reading of a book, brings
back a period of life when his deliberate perversity was exercised actively in matters of
the senses. There are his fantastic banquets,
his fantastic amours: the *repas de deuil*, Miss
Urania the acrobat, the episode of the ven-
triloquist-woman and the reincarnation of the
Sphinx and the Chimæra of Flaubert, the episode of the boy *chez* Madame Laure. A casual
recollection brings up the schooldays of his
childhood with the Jesuits, and with that the
beliefs of childhood, the fantasies of the Church,
the Catholic abnegation of the *Imitatio* joining

so strangely with the final philosophy of
Schopenhauer. At times his brain is haunted
by social theories—his dull hatred of the
ordinary in life taking form in the region of
ideas. But in the main he feeds himself, with
something of the satisfaction of success, on the
strange food for the sensations with which he
has so laboriously furnished himself. There
are his books, and among these a special library
of the Latin writers of the Decadence. Exas-
perated by Virgil, profoundly contemptuous of
Horace, he tolerates Lucan (which is surprising), adores Petronius (as well he might), and
delights in the neologisms and the exotic novelty of Apuleius. His curiosity extends to the
later Christian poets—from the coloured verse
of Claudian down to the verse which is scarcely
verse of the incoherent ninth century. He is,
of course, an amateur of exquisite printing, of
beautiful bindings, and possesses an incomparable Baudelaire (*édition tirée à un exem-
plaire*), a unique Mallarmé. Catholicism being
the adopted religion of the Decadence—for its
venerable age, valuable in such matters as
the age of an old wine, its vague excitation of
the senses, its mystical picturesqueness—Des

Esseintes has a curious collection of the later
Catholic literature, where Lacordaire and the
Comte de Falloux, Veuillot and Ozanam, find
their place side by side with the half-prophetic,
half-ingenious Hello, the amalgam of a monstrous mysticism and a casuistical sensuality,
Barbey d'Aurevilly.   His collection of "pro-
fane" writers is small, but it is selected for the
qualities of exotic charm that have come to
be his only care in art—for the somewhat diseased, or the somewhat artificial beauty that
alone can strike a responsive thrill from his
exacting nerves.   "Considering within himself,
he realised that a work of art, in order to
attract him, must come to him with that quality of strangeness demanded by Edgar Poe;
but he fared yet further along this route, and
sought for all the Byzantine flora of the brain,
for complicated deliquescences of style; he
required a troubling indecision over which he
could muse, fashioning it after his will to more
of vagueness or of solid form, according to the
state of his mind at the moment.   He delighted in a work of art both for what it was in
itself and for what it could lend him; he would
fain go along with it, thanks to it, as though

sustained by an adjuvant, as though borne in a vehicle, into a sphere where his sublimated sensations would wake in him an unaccustomed stir, the cause of which he would long and vainly seek to determine." So he comes to care supremely for Baudelaire, "who, more than any other, possessed the marvellous power of rendering, with a strange sanity of expression, the most fleeting, the most wavering morbid states of exhausted minds, of desolate souls." In Flaubert he prefers *La Tentation de Saint-Antoine;* in Goncourt, *La Faustin;* in Zola, *La Faute de l'Abbé Mouret*— the exceptional, the most remote and *recherché* outcome of each temperament. And of the three it is the novel of Goncourt that appeals to him with special intimacy—that novel which, more than any other, seems to express, in its exquisitely perverse charm, all that decadent civilisation of which Des Esseintes is the type and symbol. In poetry he has discovered the fine perfume, the evanescent charm, of Paul Verlaine, and near that great poet (forgetting, strangely, Arthur Rimbaud) he places two poets who are curious—the disconcerting, tumultuous Tristan Corbière, and

the painted and bejewelled Théodore Hannon.
With Edgar Poe he has the instinctive sympathy which drew Baudelaire to the enig-
matically perverse Decadent of America; he
delights, sooner than all the world, in the
astonishing, unbalanced, unachieved genius of
Villiers de l'Isle-Adam. Finally, it is in Stéphane Mallarmé that he finds the incarnation
of "the decadence of a literature, irreparably
affected in its organism, weakened in its
ideas by age, exhausted by the excesses of
syntax, sensitive only to the curiosity which
fevers sick people, and yet hastening to say
everything, now at the end, torn by the wish
to atone for all its omissions of enjoyment,
to bequeath its subtlest memories of sorrow
on its death-bed."

But it is not on books alone that Des
Esseintes nurses his sick and craving fancy.
He pushes his delight in the artificial to the
last limits, and diverts himself with a bou-
quet of jewels, a concert of flowers, an orchestra of liqueurs, an orchestra of perfumes.
In flowers he prefers the real flowers that
imitate artificial ones. It is the monstrosities
of nature, the offspring of unnatural adulteries,

that he cherishes in the barbarically coloured
flowers, the plants with barbaric names, the
carnivorous plants of the Antilles—morbid
horrors of vegetation, chosen, not for their
beauty, but for their strangeness. And his
imagination plays harmonies on the sense of
taste, like combinations of music, from the
flute-like sweetness of anisette, the trumpet-
note of kirsch, the eager yet velvety sharpness of curaçao, the clarionet. He combines
scents, weaving them into odorous melodies,
with effects like those of the refrains of certain
poems, employing, for example, the method of
Baudelaire in *L'Irréparable* and *Le Balcon*,
where the last line of the stanza is the echo of
the first, in the languorous progression of the
melody. And above all he has his few, carefully chosen pictures, with their diverse notes
of strange beauty and strange terror—the two
Salomés of Gustave Moreau, the "Religious
Persecutions" of Jan Luyken, the opium-
dreams of Odilon Redon. His favourite artist
is Gustave Moreau, and it is on this superb and
disquieting picture that he cares chiefly to dwell.

A throne, like the high altar of a cathedral, rose beneath innumerable arches springing from columns, thick-

set as Roman pillars, enamelled with vari-coloured bricks,
set with mosaics, incrusted with lapis lazuli and sardonyx,
in a palace like the basilica of an architecture at once
Mussulman and Byzantine. In the centre of the taber-
nacle surmounting the altar, fronted with rows of cir-
cular steps, sat the Tetrarch Herod, the tiara on his head,
his legs pressed together, his hands on his knees. His
face was yellow, parchment-like, annulated with wrinkles,
withered with age; his long beard floated like a white cloud
on the jewelled stars that constellated the robe of netted
gold across his breast. Around this statue, motionless,
frozen in the sacred pose of a Hindu god, perfumes burned,
throwing out clouds of vapour, pierced, as by the phosphorescent eyes of animals, by the fire of precious stones
set in the sides of the throne; then the vapour mounted,
unrolling itself beneath arches where the blue smoke
mingled with the powdered gold of great sunrays, fallen
from the domes.

In the perverse odour of perfumes, in the overheated
atmosphere of this church, Salomé, her left arm extended
in a gesture of command, her bent right arm holding at
the level of the face a great lotus, advances slowly to the
sound of a guitar, thrummed by a woman who crouches
on the floor.

With collected, solemn, almost august countenance,
she begins the lascivious dance that should waken the
sleeping senses of the aged Herod; her breasts undulate,
become rigid at the contact of the whirling necklets;
diamonds sparkle on the dead whiteness of her skin, her
bracelets, girdles, rings, shoot sparks; on her triumphal
robe, sewn with pearls, flowered with silver, sheeted with
gold, the jewelled breastplate, whose every stitch is a
precious stone, bursts into flame, scatters in snakes of

fire, swarms on the ivory-toned, tea-rose flesh, like splendid insects with dazzling wings, marbled with carmine, dotted with morning gold, diapered with steel-blue, streaked with peacock-green.

.   .   .   .

In the work of Gustave Moreau, conceived on no Scriptural data, Des Esseintes saw at last the realisation of the strange, superhuman Salomé that he had dreamed. She was no more the mere dancing-girl who, with the corrupt torsion of her limbs, tears a cry of desire from an old man; who, with her eddying breasts, her palpitating body, her quivering thighs, breaks the energy, melts the will, of a king; she has become the symbolic deity of indestructible Lust, the goddess of immortal Hysteria, the accursed Beauty, chosen among many by the catalepsy that has stiffened her limbs, that has hardened her muscles; the monstrous, indifferent, irresponsible, insensible Beast, poisoning, like Helen of old, all that go near to her, all that look upon her, all that she touches.

It is in such a "Palace of Art" that Des Esseintes would recreate his already over-wrought body and brain, and the monotony of its seclusion is only once broken by a single excursion into the world without. This one episode of action, this one touch of realism in a book given over to the artificial, confined to a record of sensation, is a projected voyage to London, a voyage that never occurs. Des

Esseintes has been reading Dickens, idly, to
quiet his nerves, and the violent colours of
those ultra-British scenes and characters have
imposed themselves upon his imagination.
Days of rain and fog complete the picture of
that *pays de brume et de boue*, and suddenly,
stung by the unwonted desire for change, he
takes the train to Paris, resolved to distract
himself by a visit to London. Arrived in
Paris before his time, he takes a cab to the
office of *Galignani's Messenger*, fancying himself, as the rain-drops rattle on the roof and
the mud splashes against the windows, already
in the midst of the immense city, its smoke
and dirt. He reaches *Galignani's Messenger*,
and there, turning over Baedekers and Mur-
rays, loses himself in dreams of an imagined
London. He buys a Baedeker, and, to pass
the time, enters the "Bodéga" at the corner
of the Rue de Rivoli and the Rue Castiglione.
The wine-cellar is crowded with Englishmen:
he sees, as he drinks his port, and listens to the
unfamiliar accents, all the characters of Dickens
—a whole England of caricature; as he drinks
his Amontillado, the recollection of Poe puts a
new horror into the good-humoured faces

about him. Leaving the "Bodéga," he steps
out again into the rain-swept street, regains
his cab, and drives to the English tavern of
the Rue d'Amsterdam. He has just time for
dinner, and he finds a place beside the *insu-
laires*, with "their porcelain eyes, their crimson
cheeks," and orders a heavy English dinner,
which he washes down with ale and porter,
seasoning his coffee, as he imagines we do in
England, with gin. As time passes, and the
hour of the train draws near, he begins to reflect vaguely on his project; he recalls the disillusion of the visit he had once paid to Holland. Does not a similar disillusion await him
in London? "Why travel, when one can travel
so splendidly in a chair? Was he not at London already, since its odours, its atmosphere,
its inhabitants, its food, its utensils, were all
about him?" The train is due, but he does not
stir. "I have felt and seen," he says to himself, "what I wanted to feel and see. I have
been saturated with English life all this time;
it would be madness to lose, by a clumsy
change of place, these imperishable sensations." So he gathers together his luggage,
and goes home again, resolving never to aban-

don the "docile phantasmagoria of the brain" for the mere realities of the actual world. But his nervous malady, one of whose symptoms had driven him forth and brought him back so spasmodically, is on the increase. He is seized by hallucinations, haunted by sounds: the hysteria of Schumann, the morbid exaltation of Berlioz, communicate themselves to him in the music that besieges his brain. Obliged at last to send for a doctor, we find him, at the end of the book, ordered back to Paris, to the normal life, the normal conditions, with just that chance of escape from death or madness. So suggestively, so instructively, closes the record of a strange, attractive folly—in itself partly a serious ideal (which indeed is Huysmans' own), partly the caricature of that ideal. Des Esseintes, though studied from a real man, who is known to those who know a certain kind of society in Paris, is a type rather than a man: he is the offspring of the Decadent art that he adores, and this book a sort of breviary for its worshippers. It has a place of its own in the literature of the day, for it sums up, not only a talent, but a spiritual epoch.

A Rebours is a book that can only be
written once, and since that date Huysmans
has published a short story, *Un Dilemme*
(1887), which is merely a somewhat lengthy
anecdote; two novels, *En Rade* (1887) and
Là-Bas (1891), both of which are interesting
experiments, but neither of them an entire
success; and a volume of art criticism, *Certains* (1890), notable for a single splendid
essay, that on Félicien Rops, the etcher of
the fantastically erotic. *En Rade* is a sort
of deliberately exaggerated record—vision
rather then record—of the disillusions of a
country sojourn, as they affect the disordered
nerves of a town *névrose*. The narrative
is punctuated by nightmares, marvellously
woven out of nothing, and with no psychological value—the human part of the book
being a sort of picturesque pathology at
best, the representation of a series of states
of nerves, sharpened by the tragic ennui of
the country. There is a cat which becomes
interesting in its agonies; but the long boredom of the man and woman is only too
faithfully shared with the reader. *Là-Bas*
is a more artistic creation, on a more solid

foundation. It is a study of Satanism, a
dexterous interweaving of the history of Gilles
de Retz (the traditional Bluebeard) with the
contemporary manifestations of the Black
Art. "The execration of impotence, the hate
of the mediocre—that is perhaps one of the
most indulgent definitions of Diabolism,"
says Huysmans, somewhere in the book,
and it is on this side that one finds the link
of connection with the others of that series
of pessimist studies in life. *Un naturalisme
spiritualiste*, he defines his own art at this
point in its development; and it is in somewhat the "documentary" manner that he
applies himself to the study of these strange
problems, half of hysteria, half of a real mystical corruption that does actually exist in
our midst. I do not know whether the
monstrous tableau of the Black Mass—so
marvellously, so revoltingly described in the
central episode of the book—is still enacted
in our days, but I do know that all but the
most horrible practices of the sacrilegious
magic of the Middle Ages are yet performed,
from time to time, in a secrecy which is all
but absolute. The character of Madame

Chantelouve is an attempt, probably the first in literature, to diagnose a case of Sadism in a woman. To say that it is successful would be to assume that the thing is possible, which one hesitates to do. The book is even more disquieting, to the normal mind, than *A Rebours*. But it is not, like that, the study of an exception which has become a type. It is the study of an exception which does not profess to be anything but a disease.

Huysmans' place in contemporary literature is not quite easy to estimate. There is a danger of being too much attracted, or too much repelled, by those qualities of deliberate singularity which make his work, sincere expression as it is of his own personality, so artificial and *recherché* in itself. With his pronounced, exceptional characteristics, it would have been impossible for him to write fiction impersonally, or to range himself, for long, in any school, under any master. Interrogated one day as to his opinion of Naturalism, he had but to say in reply: *Au fond, il y a des écrivains qui ont du talent et d'autres qui n'en ont pas, qu'ils soient natu-ralistes, romantiques, décadents, tout ce que*

*vous voudrez, ça m'est égal! il s'agit pour moi
d'avoir du talent, et voilà tout!* But, as we
have seen, he has undergone various influences,
he has had his periods. From the first he
has had a style of singular pungency, novelty,
and colour; and, even in *Le Drageoir à Epices*,
we find such daring combinations as this
(*Camaïeu Rouge*) — *Cette fanfare de rouge
m'étourdissait; cotte gamme d'une intensité
furieuse, d'une violence inouïe, m'aveuglait.*
Working upon the foundation of Flaubert
and of Goncourt, the two great modern
stylists, he has developed an intensely personal style of his own, in which the sense of
rhythm is entirely dominated by the sense
of colour. He manipulates the Franch language with a freedom sometimes barbarous,
"dragging his images by the heels or the
hair" (in the admirable phrase of Léon Bloy)
"up and down the worm-eaten staircase of
terrified syntax," gaining, certainly, the effects
at which he aims. He possesses, in the
highest degree, that *style tacheté et faisandé*
—high-flavoured and spotted with corruption—that he attributes to Goncourt and
Verlaine. And with this audacious and bar-

baric profusion of words—chosen always for
their colour and their vividly expressive
quality—he is able to describe the essentially
modern aspects of things as no one had ever
described them before. No one before him
had ever so realised the perverse charm of
the sordid, the perverse charm of the artificial. Exceptional always, it is for such
qualities as these, rather than for the ordinary qualities of the novelist, that he is
remarkable. His stories are without incident, they are constructed to go on until
they stop, they are almost without characters. His psychology is a matter of the
sensations, and chiefly the visual sensations.
The moral nature is ignored, the emotions
resolve themselves for the most part into a
sordid ennui, rising at times into a rage at
existence. The protagonist of every book
is not so much a character as a bundle of impressions and sensations—the vague outline
of a single consciousness, his own. But it is
that single consciousness—in this morbidly
personal writer—with which we are concerned. For Huysmans' novels, with all
their strangeness, their charm, their repul-

sion, typical too, as they are, of much beside himself, are certainly the expression of a personality as remarkable as that of any contemporary writer.

1892.

II. THE LATER HUYSMANS

In the preface to his first novel, *Marthe: histoire d'une fille*, thirty years ago, Huysmans defined his theory of art in this defiant phrase: "I write what I see, what I feel, and what I have experienced, and I write it as well as I can: that is all." Ten or twelve years ago, he could still say, in answer to an interviewer who asked him his opinion of Naturalism: "At bottom, there are writers who have talent and others who have not; let them be Naturalists, Romantics, Decadents, what you will, it is all the same to me: I only want to know if they have talent." Such theoretical liberality, in a writer of original talent, is a little disconcerting: it means that he is without a theory of his own, that he is not yet conscious of having chosen his own way. And, indeed, it is only with *En Route* that Huysmans can be said to have discovered the direction in which he had really been travelling from the beginning.

In a preface written not long since for
a limited edition of *A Rebours*, Huysmans
confessed that he had never been conscious
of the direction in which he was travelling.
"My life and my literature," he affirmed,
"have undoubtedly a certain amount of pas-
sivity, of the incalculable, of a direction not
mine. I have simply obeyed; I have been
led by what are called 'mysterious ways.'"
He is speaking of the conversion which took
him to La Trappe in 1892, but the words
apply to the whole course of his career as a
man of letters. In *Là-Bas*, which is a sort of
false start, he had, indeed, realised, though
for himself at that time ineffectually, that
"it is essential to preserve the veracity of
the document, the precision of detail, the
fibrous and nervous language of Realism,
but it is equally essential to become the
well-digger of the soul, and not to attempt
to explain what is mysterious by mental
maladies. . . . It is essential, in a word,
to follow the great road so deeply dug out
by Zola, but it is necessary also to trace a
parallel pathway in the air, and to grapple
with the within and the after, to create, in

a word, a spiritual Naturalism." This is
almost a definition of the art of *En Route*,
where this spiritual realism is applied to the
history of a soul, a consciousness; in *La
Cathédrale* the method has still further developed, and Huysmans becomes, in his own
way, a Symbolist.

To the student of psychology few more interesting cases could be presented than the
development of Huysmans. From the first
he has been a man "for whom the visible
world existed," indeed, but as the scene of
a slow martyrdom. The world has always
appeared to him to be a profoundly uncomfortable, unpleasant, and ridiculous place;
and it has been a necessity of his temperament to examine it minutely, with all the
patience of disgust, and a necessity of his
method to record it with an almost ecstatic
hatred. In his first book, *Le Drageoir à
Epices*, published at the age of twenty-six,
we find him seeking his colour by preference in a drunkard's cheek or a carcase outside a butcher's shop. *Marthe*, published at
Brussels in 1876, anticipates *La Fille Elisa*
and *Nana*, but it has a crude brutality of

observation in which there is hardly a touch
of pity. *Les Sœurs Vatard* is a frame without a picture, but in *En Ménage* the dreary
tedium of existence is chronicled in all its
insignificance with a kind of weary and
aching hate. "We, too," is its conclusion,
"by leave of the everlasting stupidity of
things, may, like our fellow-citizens, live
stupid and respected." The fantastic unreality, the exquisite artificiality of *A Rebours*,
the breviary of the decadence, is the first
sign of that possible escape which Huysmans
has always foreseen in the direction of art,
but which he is still unable to make into
more than an artificial paradise, in which
beauty turns to a cruel hallucination and
imprisons the soul still more fatally. The
end is a cry of hopeless hope, in which Huysmans did not understand the meaning till
later: "Lord, have pity of the Christian
who doubts, of the sceptic who would fain
believe, of the convict of life who sets sail
alone by night, under a firmament lighted
only by the consoling watch-lights of the old
hope."

In *Là-Bas* we are in yet another stage of

this strange pilgrim's progress. The disgust
which once manifested itself in the merely
external revolt against the ugliness of streets,
the imbecility of faces, has become more and
more internalised, and the attraction of what
is perverse in the unusual beauty of art has
led, by some obscure route, to the perilous
halfway house of a corrupt mysticism. The
book, with its monstrous pictures of the
Black Mass and of the spiritual abomina-
tions of Satanism, is one step further in the
direction of the supernatural; and this, too,
has its desperate, unlooked-for conclusion:
"Christian glory is a laughing-stock to our
age; it contaminates the supernatural and
casts out the world to come." In *Là-Bas*
we go down into the deepest gulf; *En Route*
sets us one stage along a new way, and at
this turning-point begins the later Huysmans.

The old conception of the novel as an
amusing tale of adventures, though it has
still its apologists in England, has long since
ceased in France to mean anything more
actual than powdered wigs and lace ruffles.
Like children who cry to their elders for "a
story, a story," the English public still wants

its plot, its heroine, its villain. That the
novel should be psychological was a discovery
as early as Benjamin Constant, whose *Adolphe*
anticipates *Le Rouge et le Noir*, that rare,
revealing, yet somewhat arid masterpiece of
Stendahl. But that psychology could be
carried so far into the darkness of the soul,
that the flaming walls of the world themselves faded to a glimmer, was a discovery
which had been made by no novelist before
Huysmans wrote *En Route*. At once the
novel showed itself capable of competing, on
their own ground, with poetry, with the great
"confessions," with philosophy. *En Route*
is perhaps the first novel which does not
set out with the aim of amusing its readers.
It offers you no more entertainment than
Paradise Lost or the *Confessions* of St. Au-
gustine, and it is possible to consider it
on the same level. The novel, which, after
having chronicled the adventures of the Van-
ity Fairs of this world, has set itself with
admirable success to analyse the amorous and
ambitious and money-making intelligence of
the conscious and practical self, sets itself at
last to the final achievement: the revelation

of the sub-conscious self, no longer the intelligence, but the soul. Here, then, purged of the distraction of incident, liberated from the bondage of a too realistic conversation, in which the aim had been to convey the very gesture of breathing life, internalised to a complete liberty, in which, just because it is so absolutely free, art is able to accept, without limiting itself, the expressive medium of a convention, we have in the novel a new form, which may be at once a confession and a decoration, the soul and a pattern.

This story of a conversion is a new thing in modern French; it is a confession, a self-auscultation of the soul; a kind of thinking aloud. It fixes, in precise words, all the uncertainties, the contradictions, the absurd unreasonableness and not less absurd logic, which distract man's brain in the passing over him of sensation and circumstance. And all this thinking is concentrated on one end, is concerned with the working out, in his own singular way, of one man's salvation. There is a certain dry hard casuistry, a subtlety and closeness almost ecclesiastical, in the investigation of an obscure and yet

definite region, whose intellectual passions
are as varied and as tumultuous as those of
the heart. Every step is taken deliberately,
is weighed, approved, condemned, viewed
from this side and from that, and at the same
time one feels behind all this reasoning an
impulsion urging a soul onward against its
will. In this astonishing passage, through
Satanism to faith, in which the cry, "I am
so weary of myself, so sick of my miserable
existence," echoes through page after page,
until despair dies into conviction, the conviction of "the uselessness of concerning oneself about anything but mysticism and the
liturgy, of thinking about anything but about
God," it is impossible not to see the sincerity of an actual, unique experience. The
force of mere curiosity can go far, can penetrate to a certain depth; yet there is a point
at which mere curiosity, even that of genius,
comes to an end; and we are left to the
individual soul's apprehension of what seems
to it the reality of spiritual things. Such
a personal apprehension comes to us out of
this book, and at the same time, just as in
the days when he forced language to express,

in a more coloured and pictorial way than it had ever expressed before, the last escaping details of material things, so, in this analysis of the aberrations and warfares, the confessions and trials of the soul in penitence, Huysmans has found words for even the most subtle and illusive aspects of that inner life which he has come, at the last, to apprehend.

In *La Cathédrale* we are still occupied with this sensitive, lethargic, persevering soul, but with that soul in one of its longest halts by the way, as it undergoes the slow, permeating influence of "*la Cathédrale mystique par excellence*," the cathedral of Chartres. And the greater part of the book is taken up with a study of this cathedral, of that elaborate and profound symbolism by which "the soul of sanctuaries" slowly reveals itself (*quel laconisme hermetique!*) with a sort of parallel interpretation of the symbolism which the Church of the Middle Ages concealed or revealed in colours, precious stones, plants, animals, numbers, odours, and in the Bible itself, in the setting together of the Old and New Testaments.

No doubt, to some extent this book is less

it.   Huysmans began by acquiring so astonishing a mastery of description that he could
describe the inside of a cow hanging in a
butcher's shop as beautifully as if it were
a casket of jewels.   The little work-girls of
his early novels were taken for long walks,
in which they would have seen nothing but
the arm on which they leant and the milliners'
shops which they passed; and what they did
not see was described, marvellously, in twenty
pages.

Huysmans is a brain all eye, a brain which
sees even ideas as if they had a superficies.
His style is always the same, whether he
writes of a butcher's shop or of a stained-
glass window; it is the immediate expression of a way of seeing, so minute and so
intense that it becomes too emphatic for elegance and too coloured for atmosphere or
composition, always ready to sacrifice euphony to either fact or colour.   He cares only
to give you the thing seen, exactly as he sees it,
with all his love or hate, and with all the
exaggeration which that feeling brings into
it.   And he loves beauty as a bulldog loves its
mistress: by growling at all her enemies.   He

honours wisdom by annihilating stupidity. His art of painting in words resembles Monet's art of painting with his brush: there is the same power of rendering a vivid effect, almost deceptively, with a crude and yet sensitive realism. *"C'est pour la gourmandise de l'œil un gala de teintes,"* he says of the provision cellars at Hamburg; and this greed of the eye has eaten up in him almost every other sense. Even of music he writes as a deaf man with an eye for colour might write, to whom a musician had explained certain technical means of expression in music. No one has ever invented such barbarous and exact metaphors for the rendering of visual sensations. Properly, there is no metaphor; the words say exactly what they mean; they become figurative, as we call it, in their insistence on being themselves fact.

Huysmans knows that the motive force of the sentence lies in the verbs, and his verbs are the most singular, precise, and expressive in any language. But in subordinating, as he does, every quality to that of sharp, telling truth, the truth of extremes, his style loses charm; yet it can be dazzling; it has the

solidity of those walls encrusted with gems
which are to be seen in a certain chapel in
Prague; it blazes with colour, and arabesques
into a thousand fantastic patterns.

And now all that laboriously acquired mastery finds at last its use, lending itself to the
new spirit with a wonderful docility. At last
the idea which is beyond reality has been found,
not where Des Esseintes sought it, and a new
meaning comes into what had once been
scarcely more than patient and wrathful observation. The idea is there, visible, in his
cathedral, like the sun which flashes into unity,
into meaning, into intelligible beauty the bewildering lozenges of colour, the inextricable
trails of lead, which go to make up the picture
in one of its painted windows. What, for
instance, could be more precise in its translation of the different aspects under which the
cathedral of Chartres can be seen, merely as
colour, than this one sentence: "Seen as a
whole, under a clear sky, its grey silvers, and,
if the sun shines upon it, turns pale yellow and
then golden; seen close, its skin is like that of
a nibbled biscuit, with its silicious limestone
eaten into holes; sometimes, when the sun is

setting, it turns crimson, and rises up like a
monstrous and delicate shrine, rose and green;
and, at twilight, turns blue, then seems to
evaporate as it fades into violet." Or, again,
in a passage which comes nearer to the conventional idea of eloquence, how absolute an
avoidance of a conventional phrase, a word
used for its merely oratorical value: "High
up, in space, like salamanders, human beings,
with burning faces and flaming robes, lived in a
firmament of fire; but these conflagrations
were circumscribed, limited by an incombus-
tible frame of darker glass, which beat back
the clear young joy of the flames; by that kind
of melancholy, that more serious and more
aged aspect, which is taken by the duller colours. The hue and cry of reds, the limpid
security of whites, the reiterated halleluias
of yellows, the virginal glory of blues, all the
quivering hearth-glow of painted glass, dies
away as it came near this border coloured with
the rust of iron, with the russet of sauce, with
the harsh violet of sandstone, with bottle-
green, with the brown of touchwood, with
sooty black, with ashen grey."

This, in its excess of exactitude (how me-

diæval a quality!) becomes, on one page,
a comparison of the tower without a spire to
an unsharpened pencil which cannot write
the prayers of earth upon the sky. But for
the most part it is a consistent humanising
of too objectively visible things a disengaging
of the sentiment which exists in them, which
is one of the secrets of their appeal to us, but
which for the most part we overlook as we
set ourselves to add up the shapes and colours
which have enchanted us. To Huysmans this
artistic discovery has come, perhaps in the
most effectual way, but certainly in the way
least probable in these days, through faith, a
definite religious faith; so that, beginning
tentatively, he has come, at last, to believe in
the Catholic Church as a monk of the Middle
Ages believed in it. And there is no doubt
that to Huysmans this abandonment to religion
has brought, among other gifts, a certain
human charity in which he was notably lacking,
removing at once one of his artistic limitations.
It has softened his contempt of humanity; it
has broadened his outlook on the world. And
the sense, diffused through the whole of this
book, of the living and beneficent reality of the

Virgin, of her real presence in the cathedral built in her honour and after her own image, brings a strange and touching kind of poetry into these closely and soberly woven pages.

From this time forward, until his death, Huysmans is seen purging himself of his realism, coming closer and closer to that spiritual Naturalism which he had invented, an art made out of an apprehension of the inner meaning of those things which he still saw with the old tenacity of vision. Nothing is changed in him and yet all is changed. The disgust of the world deepens through *L'Oblat*, which is the last stage but one in the pilgrimage which begins with *En Route*. It seeks an escape in poring, with a dreadful diligence, over a saint's recorded miracles, in the life of *Sainte Lydwine de Schiedam*, which is mediæval in its precise acceptance of every horrible detail of the story. *Les Foules de Lourdes* has the same minute attentiveness to horror, but with a new pity in it, and a way of giving thanks to the Virgin, which is in Huysmans yet another escape from his disgust of the world. But it is in the great chapter on Satan as the creator of ugliness that his work seems to end where it had begun, in the service of art, now come from a great way off to join itself with the service of God. And the whole soul of Huysmans characterises itself in the turn of a single phrase there: that "art is the only clean thing on earth, except holiness."

ARTHUR RIMBAUD

THAT story of the Arabian Nights, which is at the same time a true story, the life of Rimbaud, has been told, for the first time, in the extravagant but valuable book of an anarchist of letters, who writes under the name of Paterne Berrichon, and who has since married Rimbaud's sister. *La Vie de Jean-Arthur Rimbaud* is full of curiosity for those who have been mystified by I know not what legends, invented to give wonder to a career, itself more wonderful than any of the inventions. The man who died at Marseilles, at the Hospital of the Conception, on March 10, 1891, at the age of thirty-seven, *négociant*, as the register of his death describes him, was a writer of genius, an innovator in verse and prose, who had written all his poetry by the age of nineteen, and all his prose by a year or two later. He had given up literature to travel hither and thither, first in Europe, then in Africa; he had been an engineer, a leader of

caravans, a merchant of precious merchandise.
And this man, who had never written down a
line after those astonishing early experiments,
was heard, in his last delirium, talking of precisely such visions as those which had haunted
his youth, and using, says his sister, "expres-
sions of a singular and penetrating charm" to
render these sensations of visionary countries.
Here certainly is one of the most curious problems of literature: is it a problem of which we
can discover the secret?

Jean-Nicolas-Arthur Rimbaud was born at
Charleville, in the Ardennes, October 28, 1854.
His father, of whom he saw little, was a captain in the army; his mother, of peasant origin,
was severe, rigid and unsympathetic. At
school he was an unwilling but brilliant scholar,
and by his fifteenth year was well acquainted
with Latin literature and intimately with
French literature. It was in that year that he
began to write poems from the first curiously
original: eleven poems dating from that year
are to be found in his collected works. When
he was sixteen he decided that he had had
enough of school, and enough of home. Only
Paris existed: he must go to Paris. The

first time he went without a ticket; he spent,
indeed, fifteen days in Paris, but he spent them
in Mazas, from which he was released and
restored to his home by his schoolmaster.
The second time, a few days later, he sold his
watch, which paid for his railway ticket.
This time he threw himself on the hospitality
of André Gill, a painter and verse-writer, of
some little notoriety then, whose address he
had happened to come across. The unin-
vited guest was not welcomed, and after some
penniless days in Paris he tramped back to
Charleville. The third time (he had waited
five months, writing poems, and discontented
to be only writing poems) he made his way
to Paris on foot, in a heat of revolutionary
sympathy, to offer himself to the insurgents
of the Commune. Again he had to return
on foot. Finally, having learnt with difficulty that a man is not taken at his own
valuation until he has proved his right to be so
accepted, he sent up the manuscript of his
poems to Verlaine. The manuscript contained *Le Bateau Ivre*, *Les Premières Com-
munions*, *Ma Bohème*, *Roman*, *Les Effarés*, and,
indeed, all but a few of the poems he ever

wrote. Verlaine was overwhelmed with delight, and invited him to Paris. A local admirer lent him the money to get there, and from October, 1871, to July, 1872, he was Verlaine's guest.

The boy of seventeen, already a perfectly original poet, and beginning to be an equally original prose-writer, astonished the whole Parnasse, Banville, Hugo himself. On Verlaine his influence was more profound. The meeting brought about one of those lamentable and admirable disasters which make and unmake careers. Verlaine has told us in his *Confessions* that, "in the beginning, there was no question of any sort of affection or sympathy between two natures so different as that of the poet of the *Assis* and mine, but simply of an extreme admiration and astonishment before this boy of sixteen, who had already written things, as Fénéon has excellently said, 'perhaps outside literature.'" This admiration and astonishment passed gradually into a more personal feeling, and it was under the influence of Rimbaud that the long vagabondage of Verlaine's life began. The two poets wandered together through

Belgium, England, and again Belgium, from July, 1872, to August, 1873, when there occurred that tragic parting at Brussels which left Verlaine a prisoner for eighteen months, and sent Rimbaud back to his family. He had already written all the poetry and prose that he was ever to write, and in 1873 he printed at Brussels *Une Saison en Enfer*. It was the only book he himself ever gave to the press, and no sooner was it printed than he destroyed the whole edition, with the exception of a few copies, of which only Verlaine's copy, I believe, still exists. Soon began new wanderings, with their invariable return to the starting-point of Charleville: a few days in Paris, a year in England, four months in Stuttgart (where he was visited by Verlaine), Italy, France again, Vienna, Java, Holland, Sweden, Egypt, Cyprus, Abyssinia, and then nothing but Africa, until the final return to France. He had been a teacher of French in England, a seller of key-rings in the streets of Paris, had unloaded vessels in the ports, and helped to gather in the harvest in the country; he had been a volunteer in the Dutch army, a military engineer, a trader; and now physical sciences had begun to attract his insatiable curiosity, and dreams of the fabulous East began to resolve themselves into dreams of a romantic commerce with the real East. He became a merchant of coffee, perfumes, ivory, and gold, in the interior of Africa; then an explorer, a predecessor, and in his own regions, of Marchand. After twelve years' wandering and exposure in Africa he was attacked by a malady of the knee, which rapidly became worse. He was transported first to Aden, then to Marseilles, where, in May, 1891, his leg was amputated. Further complications set in. He insisted, first, on being removed to his home, then on being taken back to Marseilles. His sufferings were an intolerable torment, and more cruel to him was the torment of his desire to live. He died inch by inch, fighting every inch; and his sister's quiet narrative of those last months is agonising. He died at Marseilles in November, "prophesying," says his sister, and repeating, "Allah Kerim! Allah Kerim!"

The secret of Rimbaud, I think, and the reason why he was able to do the unique thing in literature which he did, and then

to disappear quietly and become a legend in
the East, is that his mind was not the mind
of the artist but of the man of action.   He
was a dreamer, but all his dreams were discoveries.   To him it was an identical act of
his temperament to write the sonnet of the
Vowels and to trade in ivory and frankincense with the Arabs.   He lived with all his
faculties at every instant of his life, abandoning himself to himself with a confidence
which was at once his strength and (looking
at things less absolutely) his weakness.   To
the student of success, and what is relative
in achievement, he illustrates the danger of
one's over-possession by one's own genius,
just as aptly as the saint in the cloister does,
or the mystic too full of God to speak intel-
ligibly to the world, or the spilt wisdom of
the drunkard.   The artist who is above all
things an artist cultivates a little choice corner
of himself with elaborate care; he brings
miraculous flowers to growth there, but the
rest of the garden is but mown grass or tangled bushes.   That is why many excellent
writers, very many painters, and most musicians are so tedious on any subject but their

own. Is it not tempting, does it not seem a
devotion rather than a superstition, to worship the golden chalice in which the wine has
been made God, as if the chalice were the
reality, and the ¦Real Presence the symbol?
The artist, who is only an artist, circumscribes
his intelligence into almost such a fiction, as
he reverences the work of his own hands. But
there are certain natures (great or small,
Shakespeare or Rimbaud, it makes no difference) to whom the work is nothing; the act
of working, everything. Rimbaud was a small,
narrow, hard, precipitate nature, which had
the will to live, and nothing but the will to live;
and his verses, and his follies, and his wanderings, and his traffickings were but the breathing of different hours in his day.

That is why he is so swift, definite, and
quickly exhausted in vision; why he had his
few things to say, each an action with consequences. He invents new ways of saying
things, not because he is a learned artist, but
because he is burning to say them, and he
has none of the hesitations of knowledge.
He leaps right over or through the conventions that had been standing in everybody's

way; he has no time to go round, and no respect for trespass-boards, and so he becomes the *enfant terrible* of literature, playing pranks (as in that sonnet of the *Vowels*), knocking down barriers for the mere amusement of the thing, getting all the possible advantage of his barbarisms in mind and conduct. And so, in life, he is first of all conspicuous as a disorderly liver, a revolter against morals as against prosody, though we may imagine that, in his heart, morals meant as little to him, one way or the other, as prosody. Later on, his revolt seems to be against civilisation itself, as he disappears into the deserts of Africa. And it is, if you like, a revolt against civilisation, but the revolt is instinctive, a need of the organism; it is not doctrinal, cynical, a conviction, a sentiment.

Always, as he says *révant univers fantastiques*, he is conscious of the danger as well as the ecstasy of that divine imitation; for he says: "My life will always be too vast to be given up wholly to force and beauty." *J'attends Dieu avec gourmandise*, he cries, in a fine rapture; and then, sadly enough: "I have created all the feasts, all the triumphs, all the dramas of the world. I have set myself to invent new flowers, a new flesh, a new language. I have fancied that I have attained supernatural power. Well, I have now only to put my imagination and my memories in the grave. What a fine artist's and story-teller's fame thrown away!" See how completely he is conscious, and how completely he is at the mercy, of that hallucinatory rage of vision, vision to him being always force, power, creation, which, on some of his pages, seems to become sheer madness, and on others a kind of wild but absolute insight. He will be silent, he tells us, as to all that he contains within his mind, "greedy as the sea," for otherwise poets and visionaries would envy him his fantastic wealth. And, in that *Nuit d'Enfer*, which does not bear that title in vain, he exalts himself as a kind of saviour; he is in the circle of pride in Dante's hell, and he has lost all sense of limit, really believes himself to be "no one and some one." Then, in the *Alchimie du Verbe*, he becomes the analyst of his own hallucinations. "I believe in all the enchantments," he tells us; "I invented the colour of the vowels; A, black; E, white; I, red; O, blue;

U, green.   I regulated the form and the movement of every consonant, and, with instinctive
rhythms, I flattered myself that I had invented a poetic language accessible, one day or
another, to every shade of meaning.   I reserved to myself the right of translation [1]

[1] Here is the famous sonnet, which must be taken, as it
was meant, without undue seriousness, and yet as something
more than a mere joke.

VOYELLES

A noir, E blanc, I rouge, U vert, O bleu, voyelles,
  Je dirai quelque jour vos naissances latentes.
  A, noir corset velu des mouches éclatantes
Qui bombillent autour des puanteurs cruelles,

Golfe d'ombre; E, candeur des vapeurs et des tentes,
  Lance des glaciers fiers, rois blancs, frissons d'ombelles;
  I, pourpres, sang craché, rire des lèvres belles
Dans la colère ou les ivresses pénitentes;

U, cycles, vibrements divins des mers virides,
Paix des pâtis semés d'animaux, paix des rides
Que l'alchemie imprime aux grands fronts studieux;

O, suprême clairon plein de strideurs étranges,
Silences traversés des mondes et des Anges;
—O l'Oméga, rayon violet de Ses Yeux!

Coincidence or origin, it has lately been pointed out that
Rimbaud may formerly have seen an old A B C book in which
the vowels are coloured for the most part as his are (A, black;
E, white; I, red; O, blue; U, green).   In the little illus-
trative pictures around them some are oddly in keeping
with the image of Rimbaud.

. . . I accustomed myself to simple hallucination: I saw, quite frankly, a mosque in place
of a factory, a school of drums kept by the
angels, post-chaises on the roads of heaven,
a drawing-room at the bottom of a lake;
monsters, mysteries; the title of a vaudeville
raised up horrors before me. Then I explained my magical sophisms by the hallucination of words! I ended by finding something
sacred in the disorder of my mind." Then
he makes the great discovery. Action, one
sees, this fraudulent and insistent will to live,
has been at the root of all these mental and
verbal orgies, in which he has been wasting
the very substance of his thought. Well,
"action," he discovers, "is not life, but a
way of spoiling something." Even this is a
form of enervation, and must be rejected from
the absolute. *Mon devoir m'est remis. Il ne
faut plus songer à cela. Je suis réellement
d'outre-tombe, et pas de commissions.*

It is for the absolute that he seeks, always;
the absolute which the great artist, with his
careful wisdom, has renounced seeking. And
he is content with nothing less; hence his own
contempt for what he has done, after all,

so easily; for what has come to him, perhaps
through his impatience, but imperfectly.   He
is a dreamer in whom dream is swift, hard in
outline, coming suddenly and going suddenly,
a real thing, but seen only in passing.   Visions
rush past him, he cannot arrest them; they
rush forth from him, he cannot restrain their
haste to be gone, as he creates them in the
mere indiscriminate idleness of energy.   And
so this seeker after the absolute leaves but
a broken medley of fragments, into each of
which he has put a little of his personality,
which he is forever dramatising, by multi-
plying one facet, so to speak, after another.
Very genuinely, he is now a beaten and wandering ship, flying in a sort of intoxication
before the wind, over undiscovered seas; now
a starving child outside a baker's window, in
the very ecstasy of hunger; now *la victime et la
petite épouse* of the first communion; now:

> Je ne parlerai pas, je ne penserai rien;
> Mais l'amour infini me montera dans l'âme,
> Et j'irai loin, bien loin, comme un bohémien,
> Par la Nature, heureux comme avec une femme!

He catches at verse, at prose, invents a
sort of *vers libre* before any one else, not

quite knowing what to do with it, invents
a quite new way of writing prose, which
Laforgue will turn to account later on; and
having suggested, with some impatience, half
the things that his own and the next generation are to busy themselves with developing,
he gives up writing, as an inadequate form,
to which he is also inadequate.

What, then, is the actual value of Rimbaud's work, in verse and prose, apart from
its relative values of so many kinds? I
think, considerable; though it will probably
come to rest on two or three pieces of verse,
and a still vaguer accomplishment in prose.
He brought into French verse something of
that "gipsy way of going with nature, as
with a woman"; a very young, very crude,
very defiant and sometimes very masterly
sense of just these real things which are too
close to us to be seen by most people with
any clearness. He could render physical sensation, of the subtlest kind, without making
any compromise with language, forcing language to speak straight, taming it as one would
tame a dangerous animal. And he kneaded
prose as he kneaded verse, making it a dis-

articulated, abstract, mathematically lyrical
thing. In verse, he pointed the way to certain new splendours, as to certain new *naï-
vetés*; there is the *Bateau Ivre*, without which
we might never have had Verlaine's *Crimen
Amoris*. And, intertangled with what is ingenuous, and with what is splendid, there is a
certain irony, which comes into that youth-
ful work as if youth were already reminiscent
of itself, so conscious is it that youth is youth,
and that youth is passing.

In all these ways, Rimbaud had his influence upon Verlaine, and his influence upon
Verlaine was above all the influence of the
man of action upon the man of sensation;
the influence of what is simple, narrow,
emphatic, upon what is subtle, complex,
growing. Verlaine's rich, sensitive nature was
just then trying to realise itself. Just because
it had such delicate possibilities, because
there were so many directions in which it
could grow, it was not at first quite sure of
its way. Rimbaud came into the life and
art of Verlaine, troubling both, with that
trouble which reveals a man to himself.
Having helped to make Verlaine a great

poet, he could go. Note that he himself could never have developed: writing had been one of his discoveries; he could but make other discoveries, personal ones. Even in literature he had his future; but his future was Verlaine.

JULES LAFORGUE

Jules Laforgue was born at Montevideo,
of Breton parents, August 20, 1860. He died
in Paris in 1887, two days before his twenty-
seventh birthday. From 1880 to 1886 he
had been reader to the Empress Augusta at
Berlin. He married only a few months before his death. *D'allures?* says M. Gustave
Kahn, *fort correctes, de hauts gibus, des cra-
vates sobres, des vestons anglais, des pardessus
clergymans, et de par les nécessités, un para-
pluie immuablement placé sous le bras.* His
portraits show us a clean-shaved, reticent
face, betraying little. With such a personality anecdotes have but small chance of
appropriating those details by which ex-
pansive natures express themselves to the
world. We know nothing about Laforgue
which his work is not better able to tell us,
even now that we have all his notes, un-
finished fragments, and the letters of an
almost virginal *naïveté* which he wrote to

the woman whom he was going to marry.
His entire work, apart from these additions,
is contained in two small volumes, one of
prose, the *Moralités Légendaires*, the other
of verse, *Les Complaintes*, *L'Imitation de
Notre-Dame la Lune*, and a few other pieces,
all published during the last three years of
his life.

The prose and verse of Laforgue, scrupulously correct, but with a new manner of
correctness, owe more than any one has realised to the half-unconscious prose and verse
of Rimbaud. Verse and prose are alike a
kind of travesty, making subtle use of colloquialism, slang, neologism, technical terms,
for their allusive, their factitious, their reflected meanings, with which one can play,
very seriously. The verse is alert, troubled,
swaying, deliberately uncertain, hating rhetoric so piously that it prefers, and finds its
piquancy in, the ridiculously obvious. It is
really *vers libre*, but at the same time correct
verse, before *vers libre* had been invented.
And it carries, as far as that theory has
ever been carried, the theory which demands
an instantaneous notation (Whistler, let us

say) of the figure or landscape which one
has been accustomed to define with such
rigorous exactitude.   Verse, always elegant, is
broken up into a kind of mockery of prose.

> Encore un de mes pierrots mort;
>   Mort d'un chronique orphelinisme;
>   C'était un cœur plein de dandysme
> Lunaire, en un drôle de corps;

he will say to us, with a familiarity of manner, as of one talking languidly, in a low
voice, the lips always teased into a slightly
bitter smile; and he will pass suddenly into
the ironical lilt of

> Hotel garni
> De l'infini,
>
> Sphinx et Joconde
> Des défunts mondes;

and from that into this solemn and smiling end of one of his last poems, his own
epitaph, if you will:

> Il prit froid l'autre automne,
> S'étant attardi vers les peines des cors,
> Sur la fin d'un beau jour.
> Oh! ce fut pour vos cors, et ce fut pour l'automne.
> Qu'il nous montra qu' "on meurt d'amour!"
> On ne le verra plus aux fêtes nationales,
> S'enfermer dans l'Histoire et tirer les verrous,
> Il vint trop tard, il est reparti sans scandale;
> O vous qui m'écoutez, rentrez chacun chez vous.

The old cadences, the old eloquence, the
ingenuous seriousness of poetry, are all banished, on a theory as self-denying as that
which permitted Degas to dispense with
recognisable beauty in his figures. Here, if
ever, is modern verse, verse which dispenses
with so many of the privileges of poetry, for
an ideal quite of its own. It is, after all,
a very self-conscious ideal, becoming artificial through its extreme naturalness; for
in poetry it is not "natural" to say things
quite so much in the manner of the moment,
with however ironical an intention.

The prose of the *Moralités Légendaires* is
perhaps even more of a discovery. Finding
its origin, as I have pointed out, in the ex-
perimental prose of Rimbaud, it carries that
manner to a singular perfection. Disartic-
ulated, abstract, mathematically lyrical, it
gives expression, in its icy ecstasy, to a
very subtle criticism of the universe, with
a surprising irony of cosmical vision. We
learn from books of mediæval magic that
the embraces of the devil are of a coldness
so intense that it may be called, by an allow-
able figure of speech, fiery. Everything may

be as strongly its opposite as itself, and that is why this balanced, chill, colloquial style of Laforgue has, in the paradox of its intensity, the essential heat of the most obviously emotional prose. The prose is more patient than the verse, with its more compassionate laughter at universal experience. It can laugh as seriously, as profoundly, as in that graveyard monologue of Hamlet, Laforgue's Hamlet, who, Maeterlinck ventures to say, "is at moments more Hamlet than the Hamlet of Shakespeare." Let me translate a few sentences from it.

"Perhaps I have still twenty or thirty years to live, and I shall pass that way like the others. Like the others? O Totality, the misery of being there no longer! Ah! I would like to set out to-morrow, and search all through the world for the most adamantine processes of embalming. They, too, were, the little people of History, learning to read, trimming their nails, lighting the dirty lamp every evening, in love, gluttonous, vain, fond of compliments, handshakes, and kisses, living on bell-tower gossip, saying, 'What sort of weather shall we have to-morrow? Winter

has really come. . . . We have had no plums
this year.' Ah! everything is good, if it would
not come to an end. And thou, Silence,
pardon the Earth; the little madcap hardly
knows what she is doing; on the day of the
great summing-up of consciousness before the
Ideal, she will be labelled with a pitiful *idem*
in the column of the miniature evolutions
of the Unique Evolution, in the column
of negligeable quantities. . . . To die! Evidently, one dies without knowing it, as,
every night, one enters upon sleep. One
has no consciousness of the passing of the
last lucid thought into sleep, into swooning,
into death. Evidently. But to be no more,
to be here no more, to be ours no more!
Not even to be able, any more, to press
against one's human heart, some idle after-
noon, the ancient sadness contained in one
little chord on the piano!"

In these always "lunar" parodies, *Salomé,
Lohengrin, Fils de Parsifal, Persée et An-
dromède,* each a kind of metaphysical myth,
he realises that *la créature va hardiment à
être cérébrale, anti-naturelle,* and he has invented these fantastic puppets with an al-

most Japanese art of spiritual dislocation.
They are, in part, a way of taking one's
revenge upon science, by an ironical borrow-
ing of its very terms, which dance in his
prose and verse, derisively, at the end of a
string.

In his acceptance of the fragility of things
as actually a principle of art, Laforgue is a
sort of transformed Watteau, showing his
disdain for the world which fascinates him,
in quite a different way. He has constructed
his own world, lunar and actual, speaking
slang and astronomy, with a constant disengaging of the visionary aspect, under which
frivolity becomes an escape from the arro-
gance of a still more temporary mode of
being, the world as it appears to the sober
majority. He is terribly conscious of daily
life, cannot omit, mentally, a single hour of
the day; and his flight to the moon is in sheer
desperation. He sees what he calls *l'Incon-
scient* in every gesture, but he cannot see it
without these gestures. And he sees, not only
as an imposition, but as a conquest, the possibilities for art which come from the sickly
modern being, with his clothes, his nerves:

the mere fact that he flowers from the soil of
his epoch.

It is an art of the nerves, this art of Laforgue, and it is what all art would tend
towards if we followed our nerves on all
their journeys. There is in it all the restlessness of modern life, the haste to escape
from whatever weighs too heavily on the
liberty of the moment, that capricious liberty
which demands only room enough to hurry
itself weary. It is distressingly conscious of
the unhappiness of mortality, but it plays,
somewhat uneasily, at a disdainful indifference. And it is out of these elements of
caprice, fear, contempt, linked together by
an embracing laughter, that it makes its
existence.

Il n'y a pas de type, il y a la vie, Laforgue
replies to those who come to him with classical ideals. *Votre idéal est bien vite magni-
fiquement submergé,* in life itself, which should
form its own art, an art deliberately ephem-
eral, with the attaching pathos of passing
things. There is a great pity at the root
of this art of Laforgue: self-pity, which
extends, with the artistic sympathy, through

mere clearness of vision, across the world.
His laughter, which Maeterlinck has defined
so admirably as "the laughter of the soul,"
is the laughter of Pierrot, more than half a
sob, and shaken out of him with a deplorable
gesture of the thin arms, thrown wide. He is
a metaphysical Pierrot, *Pierrot lunaire*, and
it is of abstract notions, the whole science of
the unconscious, that he makes his showman's
patter. As it is part of his manner not to
distinguish between irony and pity, or even
belief, we need not attempt to do so. Heine
should teach us to understand at least so
much of a poet who could not otherwise
resemble him less. In Laforgue, sentiment
is squeezed out of the world before one begins
to play at ball with it.

And so, of the two, he is the more hopeless. He has invented a new manner of
being René or Werther: an inflexible politeness towards man, woman, and destiny. He
composes love-poems hat in hand, and smiles
with an exasperating tolerance before all
the transformations of the eternal feminine.
He is very conscious of death, but his *blague*
of death is, above all things, gentlemanly.

He will not permit himself, at any moment, the luxury of dropping the mask: not at any moment.

Read this *Autre Complainte de Lord Pierrot*, with the singular pity of its cruelty, before such an imagined dropping of the mask:

> Celle qui doit me mettre au courant de la Femme!
>   Nous lui dirons d'abord, de mon air le moins froid:
> "La somme des angles d'un triangle, chère âme,
>   Est égale à deux droits."
>
> Et si ce cri lui part: "Dieu de Dieu que je t'aime!"
>   —"Dieu reconnaîtra les siens."   Ou piquée au vif:
> —"Mes claviers ont du cœur, tu sera mon seul thème."
>   Moi· "Tout est relatif."
>
> De tous ses yeux, alors! se sentant trop banale:
>   "Ah! tu ne m'aime pas; tant d'autres sont jaloux!"
> Et moi, d'un œil qui vers l'Inconscient s'emballe:
>   "Merci, pas mal; et vous?
>
> "Jouons au plus fidèle!"—A quoi bon, ô Nature!
>   "Autant à qui perd gagne."   Alors, autre couplet.
> —"Ah! tu te lasseras le premier, j'en suis sûre."
>   —"Après vous, s'il vous plaît."
>
> Enfins, si, par un soir, elle meurt dans mes livres,
>   Douce; feignant de n'en pas croire encor mes yeux,
> J'aurai un: "Ah çà, mais, nous avions De Quoi vivre!
>   C'était donc sérieux?"

And yet one realises, if one but reads him attentively enough, how much suffering and despair, and resignation to what is, after all, the inevitable, are hidden away under this disguise, and also why this disguise is possible. Laforgue died at twenty-seven: he had been a dying man all his life, and his work has the fatal evasiveness of those who shrink from remembering the one thing which they are unable to forget. Coming as he does after Rimbaud, turning the divination of the other into theories, into achieved results, he is the eternally grown up, mature to the point of self-negation, as the other is the eternal *enfant terrible*. He thinks intensely about life, seeing what is automatic, pathetically ludicrous in it, almost as one might who has no part in the comedy. He has the double advantage, for his art, of being condemned to death, and of being, in the admirable phrase of Villiers, "one of those who come into the world with a ray of moonlight in their brains."

MAETERLINCK AS A MYSTIC

THE secret of things which is just beyond
the most subtle words, the secret of the expressive silences, has always been clearer to
Maeterlinck than to most people; and, in
his plays, he has elaborated an art of sensitive, tactiturn, and at the same time highly
ornamental simplicity, which has come nearer
than any other art to being the voice of
silence. To Maeterlinck the theatre has been,
for the most part, no more than one of the
disguises by which he can express himself,
and with his book of meditations on the
inner life, *Le Trésor des Humbles*, he may
seem to have dropped his disguise.

All art hates the vague; not the mysterious, but the vague; two opposites very
commonly confused, as the secret with the
obscure, the infinite with the indefinite. And
the artist who is also a mystic hates the
vague with a more profound hatred than
any other artist. Thus Maeterlinck, endea-

307

vouring to clothe mystical conceptions in
concrete form, has invented a drama so
precise, so curt, so arbitrary in its limits,
that it can safely be confided to the masks
and feigned voices of marionettes. His
theatre of artificial beings, who are at once
more ghostly and more mechanical than the
living actors whom we are accustomed to see,
in so curious a parody of life, moving with
a certain freedom of action across the stage,
may be taken as itself a symbol of the aspect
under which what we fantastically term "real
life" presents itself to the mystic. Are we
not all puppets, in a theatre of marionettes,
in which the parts we play, the dresses we
wear, the very emotion whose dominance
gives its express form to our faces, have all
been chosen for us; in which I, it may be,
with curled hair and a Spanish cloak, play
the romantic lover, sorely against my will,
while you, a "fair penitent" for no repented
sin, pass quietly under a nun's habit? And
as our parts have been chosen for us, our
motions controlled from behind the curtain,
so the words we seem to speak are but spoken
through us, and we do but utter fragments

of some elaborate invention, planned for larger
ends than our personal display or convenience,
but to which, all the same, we are in a humble
degree necessary. This symbolical theatre,
its very existence being a symbol, has per-
plexed many minds, to some of whom it has
seemed puerile, a child's mystification of small
words and repetitions, a thing of attitudes
and omissions; while others, yet more un-
wisely, have compared it with the violent,
rhetorical, most human drama of the Eliza-
bethans, with Shakespeare himself, to whom
all the world was a stage, and the stage all
this world, certainly. A sentence, already
famous, of the *Trésor des Humbles*, will tell
you what it signifies to Maeterlinck himself.

"I have come to believe," he writes, in
Le Tragique Quotidien, "that an old man
seated in his armchair, waiting quietly under
the lamplight, listening without knowing it
to all the eternal laws which reign about his
house, interpreting without understanding it
all that there is in the silence of doors and
windows, and in the little voice of light, enduring the presence of his soul and of his
destiny, bowing his head a little, without

suspecting that all the powers of the earth
intervene and stand on guard in the room like
attentive servants, not knowing that the sun
itself suspends above the abyss the little table
on which he rests his elbow, and that there is
not a star in the sky nor a force in the soul
which is indifferent to the motion of a falling eyelid or a rising thought—I have come
to believe that this motionless old man
lived really a more profound, human, and
universal life than the lover who strangles
his mistress, the captain who gains a victory,
or the husband who 'avenges his honour.'"

That, it seems to me, says all there is
to be said of the intention of this drama
which Maeterlinck has evoked; and, of its
style, this other sentence, which I take from
the same essay: "It is only the words that
at first sight seem useless which really count
in a work."

This drama, then, is a drama founded on
philosophical ideas, apprehended emotionally;
on the sense of the mystery of the universe,
of the weakness of humanity, that sense which
Pascal expressed when he said: *Ce qui m'étonne
le plus est de voir que tout le monde n'est pas*

étonné de sa faiblesse; with an acute feeling
of the pathetic ignorance in which the souls
nearest to one another look out upon their
neighbours. It is a drama in which the interest is concentrated on vague people, who are
little parts of the universal consciousness,
their strange names being but the pseudonyms
of obscure passions, intimate emotions. They
have the fascination which we find in the eyes
of certain pictures, so much more real and
disquieting, so much more permanent with
us, than living people. And they have the
touching simplicity of children; they are
always children in their ignorance of themselves, of one another, and of fate. And,
because they are so disembodied of the
more trivial accidents of life, they give themselves without limitation to whatever passionate instinct possesses them. I do not
know a more passionate love-scene than
that scene in the wood beside the fountain,
where Pelléas and Mélisande confess the
strange burden which has come upon them.
When the soul gives itself absolutely to love.
all the barriers of the world are burnt away,
and all its wisdom and subtlety are as in-

cense poured on a flame. Morality, too,
is burnt away, no longer exists, any more
than it does for children or for God.

Maeterlinck has realised, better than any
one else, the significance, in life and art, of
mystery. He has realised how unsearchable
is the darkness out of which we have but
just stepped, and the darkness into which
we are about to pass. And he has realised
how the thought and sense of that twofold
darkness invade the little space of light in
which, for a moment, we move; the depth to
which they shadow our steps, even in that
moment's partial escape. But in some of his
plays he would seem to have apprehended
this mystery as a thing merely or mainly terrifying; the actual physical darkness sur-
rounding blind men, the actual physical approach of death as the intruder; he has shown
us people huddled at a window, out of which
they are almost afraid to look, or beating at a
door, the opening of which they dread. Fear
shivers through these plays, creeping across
our nerves like a damp mist coiling up out of a
valley. And there is beauty, certainly, in
this "vague spiritual fear"; but a less obvious

kind of beauty than that which gives its profound pathos to *Aglavaine et Sélysette*, the one
play written since the writing of the essays.
Here is mystery, which is also pure beauty, in
these delicate approaches of intellectual pathos,
in which suffering and death and error become
transformed into something almost happy, so
full is it of strange light.

And the aim of Maeterlinck, in his plays,
is not only to render the soul and the soul's
atmosphere, but to reveal this strangeness,
pity, and beauty through beautiful pictures.
No dramatist has ever been so careful that
his scenes should be in themselves beautiful,
or has made the actual space of forest, tower,
or seashore so emotionally significant.   He has
realised, after Wagner, that the art of the stage
is the art of pictorial beauty, of the correspondence in rhythm between the speakers,
their words, and their surroundings.   He has
seen how, in this way, and in this way alone,
the emotion, which it is but a part of the
poetic drama to express, can be at once inten-
sified and purified.

It is only after hinting at many of the
things which he had to say in these plays,

which have, after all, been a kind of subter-
fuge, that Maeterlinck has cared, or been able,
to speak with the direct utterance of the
essays. And what may seem curious is that
this prose of the essays, which is the prose of
a doctrine, is incomparably more beautiful
than the prose of the plays, which was the
prose of an art. Holding on this point a
different opinion from one who was, in many
senses, his master, Villiers de l'Isle-Adam, he
did not admit that beauty of words, or even
any expressed beauty of thoughts, had its
place in spoken dialogue, even though it was
not two living actors speaking to one another
on the stage, but a soul speaking to a soul,
and imagined speaking through the mouths of
marionettes. But that beauty of phrase which
makes the profound and sometimes obscure
pages of *Axël* shine as with the crossing fire
of jewels, rejoices us, though with a softer, a
more equable, radiance, in the pages of these
essays, in which every sentence has the in-
dwelling beauty of an intellectual emotion,
preserved at the same height of tranquil
ecstasy from first page to last. There is a
sort of religious calm in these deliberate sen-

tences, into which the writer has known how
to introduce that divine monotony which is
one of the accomplishments of great style.
Never has simplicity been more ornate or a
fine beauty more visible through its self-
concealment.

But, after all, the claim upon us of this
book is not the claim of a work of art, but
of a doctrine, and more than that, of a system. Belonging, as he does, to the eternal
hierarchy, the unbroken succession, of the
mystics, Maeterlinck has apprehended what
is essential in the mystical doctrine with a
more profound comprehension, and thus more
systematically, than any mystic of recent
times. He has many points of resemblance
with Emerson, on whom he has written an
essay which is properly an exposition of his
own personal ideas; but Emerson, who pro-
claimed the supreme guidance of the inner
light, the supreme necessity of trusting instinct, of honouring emotion, did but proclaim
all this, not without a certain anti-mystical
vagueness: Maeterlinck has systematised it.
A more profound mystic than Emerson, he
has greater command of that which comes to

him unawares, is less at the mercy of visiting angels.

Also, it may be said that he surrenders himself to them more absolutely, with less reserve and discretion; and, as he has infinite leisure, his contemplation being subject to no limits of time, he is ready to follow them on unknown rounds, to any distance, in any direction, ready also to rest in any wayside inn, without fearing that he will have lost the road on the morrow.

This old gospel, of which Maeterlinck is the new voice, has been quietly waiting until certain bankruptcies, the bankruptcy of Science, of the Positive Philosophies, should allow it full credit. Considering the length even of time, it has not had an unreasonable space of waiting; and remember that it takes time but little into account. We have seen many little gospels demanding of every emotion, of every instinct, "its certificate at the hand of some respectable authority." Without confidence in themselves or in things, and led by Science, which is as if one were led by one's note-book, they demand a reasonable explanation of every mystery. Not finding that explanation, they reject the mystery; which is as if the fly on the wheel rejected the wheel because it was hidden from his eyes by the dust of its own raising.

The mystic is at once the proudest and the humblest of men. He is as a child who resigns himself to the guidance of an unseen hand, the hand of one walking by his side; he resigns himself with the child's humility. And he has the pride of the humble, a pride manifesting itself in the calm rejection of every accepted map of the roads, of every offer of assistance, of every painted signpost pointing out the smoothest ways on which to travel. He demands no authority for the unseen hand whose fingers he feels upon his wrist. He conceives of life, not, indeed, so much as a road on which one walks, very much at one's own discretion, but as a blown and wandering ship, surrounded by a sea from which there is no glimpse of land; and he conceives that to the currents of that sea he may safely trust himself. Let his hand, indeed, be on the rudder, there will be no miracle worked for him; it is enough miracle that the sea should be there, and the ship, and he himself. He will never know why

his hand should turn the rudder this way
rather than that.

Jacob Boehme has said, very subtly, "that
man does not perceive the truth but God
perceives the truth in man"; that is, that
whatever we perceive or do is not perceived
or done consciously by us, but unconsciously
through us. Our business, then, is to tend
that "inner light" by which most mystics
have symbolised that which at once guides us
in time and attaches us to eternity. This
inner light is no miraculous descent of the
Holy Spirit, but the perfectly natural, though
it may finally be overcoming, ascent of the
spirit within us. The spirit, in all men, being
but a ray of the universal light, it can, by
careful tending, by the removal of all obstruc-
tion, the cleansing of the vessel, the trimming
of the wick, as it were, be increased, made to
burn with a steadier, a brighter flame. In
the last rapture it may become dazzling, may
blind the watcher with excess of light, shutting
him in within the circle of transfiguration,
whose extreme radiance will leave all the
rest of the world henceforth one darkness.

All mystics being concerned with what is

divine in life, with the laws which apply
equally to time and eternity, it may happen
to one to concern himself chiefly with time
seen under the aspect of eternity, to another
to concern himself rather with eternity seen
under the aspect of time.   Thus many mystics
have occupied themselves, very profitably,
with showing how natural, how explicable on
their own terms, are the mysteries of life; the
whole aim of Maeterlinck is to show how
mysterious all life is, "what an astonishing
thing it is, merely to live." What he had
pointed out to us, with certain solemn gestures, in his plays, he sets himself now to
affirm, slowly, fully, with that "confidence
in mystery" of which he speaks. Because
"there is not an hour without its familiar
miracles and its ineffable suggestions," he
sets himself to show us these miracles and
these meanings where others have not always
sought or found them, in women, in children,
in the theatre.   He seems to touch, at one
moment or another, whether he is discussing
La Beauté Intérieure or *Le Tragique Quotidien*,
on all of these hours, and there is no hour so
dark that his touch does not illuminate it.

And it is characteristic of him, of his "confidence in mystery," that he speaks always
without raising his voice, without surprise or
triumph, or the air of having said anything
more than the simplest observation. He
speaks, not as if he knew more than others, or
had sought out more elaborate secrets, but as
if he had listened more attentively.

Loving most those writers "whose works
are nearest to silence," he begins his book,
significantly, with an essay on Silence, an
essay which, like all these essays, has the
reserve, the expressive reticence, of those
"active silences" of which he succeeds in
revealing a few of the secrets.

"Souls," he tells us, "are weighed in silence,
as gold and silver are weighed in pure water,
and the words which we pronounce have no
meaning except through the silence in which
they are bathed. We seek to know that we
may learn not to know"; knowledge, that
which can be known by the pure reason, meta-
physics, "indispensable" on this side of the
"frontiers," being after all precisely what is
least essential to us, since least essentially
ourselves. "We possess a self more profound

and more boundless than the self of the passions or of pure reason. . . . There comes a moment when the phenomena of our customary consciousness, what we may call the consciousness of the passions or of our normal relationships, no longer mean anything to us, no longer touch our real life. I admit that this consciousness is often interesting in its way, and that it is often necessary to know it thoroughly. But it is a surface plant, and its roots fear the great central fire of our being. I may commit a crime without the least breath stirring the tiniest flame of this fire; and, on the other hand, the crossing of a single glance, a thought which never comes into being, a minute which passes without the utterance of a word, may rouse it into terrible agitations in the depths of its retreat, and cause it to overflow upon my life. Our soul does not judge as we judge; it is a capricious and hidden thing. It can be reached by a breath and unconscious of a tempest. Let us find out what reaches it; everything is there, for it is there that we ourselves are."

And it is towards this point that all the words of this book tend. Maeterlinck, unlike

most men ("What is man but a God who is
afraid?"), is not "miserly of immortal things."
He utters the most divine secrets without
fear, betraying certain hiding-places of the
soul in those most nearly inaccessible retreats
which lie nearest to us. All that he says we
know already; we may deny it, but we know
it. It is what we are not often at leisure
enough with ourselves, sincere enough with
ourselves, to realise; what we often dare not
realise; but, when he says it, we know that
it is true, and our knowledge of it is his
warrant for saying it. He is what he is
precisely because he tells us nothing which
we do not already know, or it may be, what
we have known and forgotten.

The mystic, let it be remembered, has
nothing in common with the moralist. He
speaks only to those who are already prepared
to listen to him, and he is indifferent to the
"practical" effect which these or others may
draw from his words. A young and profound
mystic of our day has figured the influence of
wise words upon the foolish and headstrong
as "torches thrown into a burning city."
The mystic knows well that it is not always

the soul of the drunkard or the blasphemer
which is farthest from the eternal beauty.   He
is concerned only with that soul of the soul,
that life of life, with which the day's doings
have so little to do; itself a mystery, and at
home only among those supreme mysteries
which surround it like an atmosphere.   It is
not always that he cares that his message, or
his vision, may be as clear to others as it is to
himself.   But, because he is an artist, and
not only a philosopher, Maeterlinck has taken
especial pains that not a word of his may go
astray, and there is not a word of this book
which needs to be read twice, in order that it
may be understood, by the least trained of
attentive readers.   It is, indeed, as he calls
it, "The Treasure of the Lowly."

CONCLUSION

OUR only chance, in this world, of a complete happiness, lies in the measure of our success in shutting the eyes of the mind, and deadening its sense of hearing, and dulling the keenness of its apprehension of the unknown. Knowing so much less than nothing, for we are entrapped in smiling and many-coloured appearances, our life may seem to be but a little space of leisure, in which it will be the necessary business of each of us to speculate on what is so rapidly becoming the past and so rapidly becoming the future, that scarcely existing present which is after all our only possession. Yet, as the present passes from us, hardly to be enjoyed except as memory or as hope, and only with an at best partial recognition of the uncertainty or inutility of both, it is with a kind of terror that we wake up, every now and then, to the whole knowledge of our ignorance, and to some perception of where it is leading us. To live

324

through a single day with that overpowering consciousness of our real position, which, in the moments in which alone it mercifully comes, is like blinding light or the thrust of a flaming sword, would drive any man out of his senses. It is our hesitations, the excuses of our hearts, the compromises of our intelligence, which save us. We can forget so much, we can bear suspense with so fortunate an evasion of its real issues; we are so admirably finite.

And so there is a great, silent conspiracy between us to forget death; all our lives are spent in busily forgetting death. That is why we are active about so many things which we know to be unimportant; why we are so afraid of solitude, and so thankful for the company of our fellow-creatures. Allowing ourselves, for the most part, to be but vaguely conscious of that great suspense in which we live, we find our escape from its sterile, annihilating reality in many dreams, in religion, passion, art; each a forgetfulness, each a symbol of creation; religion being the creation of a new heaven, passion the creation of a new earth, and art, in its mingling of

heaven and earth, the creation of heaven out
of earth. Each is a kind of sublime sel-
fishness, the saint, the lover, and the artist
having each an incommunicable ecstasy which
he esteems as his ultimate attainment, however, in his lower moments, he may serve
God in action, or do the will of his mistress,
or minister to men by showing them a little
beauty.   But it is, before all things, an escape·
and the prophets who have redeemed the
world, and the artists who have made the
world beautiful, and the lovers who have
quickened the pulses of the world, have really,
whether they knew it or not, been fleeing
from the certainty of one thought: that we
have, all of us, only our one day; and from
the dread of that other thought: that the day,
however used, must after all be wasted.

The fear of death is not cowardice; it is,
rather, an intellectual dissatisfaction with an
enigma which has been presented to us, and
which can be solved only when its solution
is of no further use. All we have to ask
of death is the meaning of life, and we are
waiting all through life to ask that question.
That life should be happy or unhappy, as

those words are used, means so very little; and the heightening or lessening of the general felicity of the world means so little to any individual. There is something almost vulgar in happiness which does not become joy, and joy is an ecstasy which can rarely be maintained in the soul for more than the moment during which we recognize that it is not sorrow. Only very young people want to be happy. What we all want is to be quite sure that there is something which makes it worth while to go on living, in what seems to us our best way, at our finest intensity; something beyond the mere fact that we are satisfying a sort of inner logic (which may be quite faulty) and that we get our best makeshift for happiness on that so hazardous assumption.

Well, the doctrine of Mysticism, with which all this symbolical literature has so much to do, of which it is all so much the expression, presents us, not with a guide for conduct, not with a plan for our happiness, not with an explanation of any mystery, but with a theory of life which makes us familiar with mystery, and which seems to harmonise those instincts which make for religion, passion, and art, freeing us at once of a great bondage. The final uncertainty remains, but we seem to knock less helplessly at closed doors, coming so much closer to the once terrifying eternity of things about us, as we come to look upon these things as shadows, through which we have our shadowy passage. "For in the particular acts of human life," Plotinus tells us, "it is not the interior soul and the true man, but the exterior shadow of the man alone, which laments and weeps, performing his part on the earth as in a more ample and extended scene, in which many shadows of souls and phantom scenes appear." And as we realise the identity of a poem, a prayer, or a kiss, in that spiritual universe which we are weaving for ourselves, each out of a thread of the great fabric; as we realise the infinite insignificance of action, its immense distance from the current of life; as we realise the delight of feeling ourselves carried onward by forces which it is our wisdom to obey; it is at least with a certain relief that we turn to an ancient doctrine, so much the more likely to be true because it has so much the air of a dream. On this theory alone does all life become worth living, all art worth making, all worship worth offering. And because it might slay as well as save, because the freedom of its sweet captivity might so easily become deadly to the fool, because that is the hardest path to walk in where you are told only, walk well; it is perhaps the only counsel of perfection which can ever really mean much to the artist.

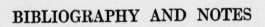

BIBLIOGRAPHY AND NOTES

BIBLIOGRAPHY AND NOTES

THE essays contained in this book are not intended to give information. They are concerned with ideas rather than with facts; each is a study of a problem, only in part a literary one, in which I have endeavoured to consider writers as personalities under the action of spiritual forces, or as themselves so many forces. But it has seemed to me that readers have a right to demand information in regard to writers who are so often likely to be unfamiliar to them. I have, therefore, given a bibliography of the works of each writer with whom I have dealt, and I have added a number of notes, giving various particulars which I think are likely to be useful in fixing more definitely the personal characteristics of these writers.

HONORÉ DE BALZAC

(1799–1850)

La Comédie Humaine

Scènes de la Vie Privée

Préface. La Maison du Chat-qui-pelote, 1829; *Le Bal de Sceaux,* 1829; *Mémoires de deux jeunes Mariées,* 1841; *La Bourse,* 1832; *Modeste Mignon,* 1844; *Un Début dans la vie,* 1842; *Albert Savarus,* 1842; *La Vendetta,* 1830; *La Paix du ménage,* 1829; *Madame Firmiani,* 1832; *Étude de femme,* 1830; *La Fausse maîtresse,* 1842; *Une Fille d'Ève,* 1838; *Le Message,* 1832; *La Grenadière,* 1832; *La Femme abandonnée,* 1832; *Honorine,* 1843; *Béatrix,* 1838; *Gobseck,* 1830; *La Femme de trente ans,* 1834; *La Père Goriot,* 1834; *Le Colonel Chabert,* 1832; *La Messe de l'Athée,* 1836; *L'Interdiction,* 1836; *Le Contrat de mariage,* 1835; *Autre étude de femme,* 1839; *La Grande Bretéche,* 1832.

Scènes de la vie de Province

Ursule Mirouët, 1841; *Eugénie Grandet,* 1833; *Le Lys dans la vallée,* 1835; *Pierrette,* 1839; *Le Curé de Tours,* 1832; *La Ménage d'un garçon,* 1842; *L'illustre Gaudissart,* 1833; *La Muse du département,* 1843; *Le Vieille fille,* 1836; *Le Cabinet des Antiques,* 1837; *Les Illusions Perdues,* 1836.

Scènes de la Vie Parisienne

Ferragus, 1833; *La Duchesse de Langeais*, 1834; *La Fille aux yeux d'or*, 1834; *La Grandeur et la Décadence de César Birotteau*, 1837; *La Maison Nucingen*, 1837; *Splendeurs et misères des courtisanes*, 1838; *Les Secrets de la Princesse de Cadignan*, 1839; *Facino Cane*, 1836; *Sarrasine*, 1830; *Pierre Grassou*, 1839; *La Cousine Bette*, 1846; *Le Cousin Pons*, 1847; *Un Prince de la Bohême*, 1839; *Gaudissart II*, 1844; *Les Employés*, 1836; *Les Comédiens sans le savoir*, 1845; *Les Petits Bourgeois*, 1845;

Scènes de la Vie Militarie

Les Chouans, 1827; *Une Passion dans le désert*, 1830.

Scènes de la Vie Politique

Un Épisode sous la Terreur, 1831; *Une Ténébreuse Affaire*, 1841; *Z. Marcas*, 1840; *L'Envers de l'Histoire contemporaine*, 1847; *Le Député d'Arcis*.

Scènes de la Vie de Campagne

Le Médecin de campagne, 1832; *Le Curé de village*, 1837; *Lès Paysans*, 1845.

Études Philosophiques

La Peau de Chagrin, 1830; *Jésus-Christ en Flandres*, 1831; *Melmoth réconcilié*, 1835; *Le Chef-d'œuvre inconnu*, 1832; *Gambara*, 1837; *Massimilla Doni*, 1839; *La Recherche de l'Absolu*, 1834; *L'Enfant Maudit*, 1831; *Les Maranas*, 1832; *Adieu*, 1830; *Le Réquisitionnaire*, 1831;

El Verdugo, 1829; *Un Drame au bord de la mer*, 1834; *L'Auberge rouge*, 1831; *L'Élixir de longue vie*, 1830; *Maître Cornélius*, 1831; *Cathérine de Médicis*, 1836; *Les Proscrits*, 1831; *Louis Lambert*, 1832; *Séraphita*, 1833.

Études Analytiques

La Physiologie du mariage, 1829; *Petites misères de la vie conjugale.*

Théâtre

Vautrin, Drame 5 Actes, 1840; *Les Ressources de Quinola*, Comédie 5 Actes, 1842; *Paméla Giraud*, Drame 5 Actes, 1843; *La Marâtre*, Drame 5 Actes, 1848; *La Faiseur* (*Mercadet*), Comédie 5 Actes, 1851; *Les Contes Drolatiques*, 1832, 1833, 1839.

PROSPER MÉRIMÉE

(1803–1870)

La Guzla, 1827; *La Jacquerie*, 1828; *Le Chronique du Temps de Charles IX*, 1829; *La Vase Etrusque*, 1829; *Vénus d'Ille*, 1837; *Colomba*, 1846; *Carmen*, 1845; *Lokis*, 1869; *Mateo Falcone*, 1876; *Melanges Historiques et Littéraires*, 1855; *Les Cosaques d'Autre-fois*, 1865; *Étude sur les Arts au Moyen-Age*, 1875; *Les Faux Démétrius*, 1853; *Étude sur l'Histoire Romaine*, 1844; *Histoire de Dom Pedro*, 1848; *Lettres à une Inconnue*, 1874.

GÉRARD DE NERVAL

(1808–1855)

Napoléon et la France Guerrière, élégies nationales,
1826; *La mort de Talma,* 1826; *L'Académie, ou les Mem-*
bres Introuvables, comédie satirique en vers, 1826; *Napoléon*
et Talma, élégies nationales nouvelles, 1826; *M. Dentscurt,*
ou le Cuisinier Grand Homme, 1826; *Elégies Nationales et*
Satires Politiques, 1827; *Faust, tragédie de Goethe,* 1828
(suivi du second *Faust,* 1840); *Couronne Poétique de*
Béranger, 1828; *Le Peuple, ode,* 1830; *Poésies Allemandes,*
Morçeaux cho sis et traduits, 1830; *Choix de Poésies de*
Ronsard et de Regnier, 1830; *Nos Adieux à la Chambre*
de Députés de l'an 1830, 1831; *Lénore, traduite de Burger,*
1835; *Piquilo, opéra comique* (with Dumas), 1837; *L'Al-*
chimiste, drame en vers (with Dumas), 1839; *Léo Burck-*
hardt, drame en prose (with Dumas), 1839; *Scènes de la*
Vie Orientale, 2 vols., 1848–1850; *Les Monténegrins, opéra*
comique (with Alboize), 1849; *Le Chariot d'Enfant, drame*
en vers (with Méry), 1850; *Les Nuits du Ramazan,* 1850;
Voyage en Orient, 1851; *L'Imagier de Harlem, légende*
en prose et en vers (with Méry and Bernard Lopez),
1852; *Contes et Facéties,* 1852; *Lorely, souvenirs d'Alle-*
magne, 1852; *Les Illuminés,* 1852; *Petits Châteaux de*
Bohême, 1853; *Les Filles du Feu,* 1854; *Misanthropie et*
Repentir, drame de Kotzebue, 1855; *La Bohême galante,*
1855; *Le Rêve et la Vie; Aurélia,* 1855; *Le Marquis de*

Fayolle (with E. Gorges), 1856; *Œuvres Complètes*, 6 vols.
(1, *Les Deux Faust de Goethe;* 2, 3, *Voyage en Orient;* 4,
Les Illuminés, Les Faux Saulniers; 5, *Le Rêve et la Vie, Les
Filles du Feu, La Bohême galante;* 6, *Poésies Complètes*),
1867.

The sonnets, written at different periods and published
for the first time in the collection of 1854, "Les Filles du
Feu," which also contains "Sylvie," were reprinted in the
volume of *Poésies Complètes*, where they are imbedded in
the midst of deplorable juvenilia. All, or almost all, of the
verse worth preserving was collected, in 1897, by that
delicate amateur of the curiosities of beauty, M. Remy
de Gourmont, in a tiny volume called *Les Chimères*,
which contains the six sonnets of "Les Chimères," the
sonnet called "Vers Dorés," the five sonnets of "Le Christ
aux Oliviers," and, in facsimile of the autograph, the
lyric called "Les Cydalises." The true facts of the life
of Gérard have been told for the first time, from original
documents, by Mme. Arvède Barine, in two excellent
articles in the *Revue des Deux Mondes*, October 15 and
November 1, 1897, since reprinted in *Les Nevrosés*, 1898.

THÉOPHILE GAUTIER

(1811–1872)

Les Poésies, 1830; *Albertus, où l'êmet le Péché*, 1833; *Les Jeunes-France*, 1833; *Mademoiselle de Maupin*, 1835; *Fortunio*, 1838.

La Comédie de la Mort, 1838; *Tras les Montes*, 1839; *Une Larme du Diable*, 1839; *Gisèle, ballet*, 1841; *Une Voyage en Espagne*, 1843; *Le Peri, ballet*, 1843; *Les Grotesques*, 1844.

Une Nuit de Cléopâtre, 1845; *Premières Poèsies*, 1845; *Zigzags*, 1845; *Le Tricorne Enchanté*, 1845; *La Turquie*, 1846.

La Juive de Constantine, drama, 1846; *Jean et Jeannette*, 1846; *Le Roi Candaule*, 1847.

Les Roués innocents, 1847; *Histoire des Peintres*, 1847; *Regardez, mais n'y touche pas*, 1847; *Les Fêtes de Madrid*, 1847; *Partie carrée*, 1851; *Italia*, 1852; *Les Émaux et Camées*, 1852; *L'Art Moderne*, 1859; *Les Beaux Arts en Europe*, 1852; *Caprices et Zigzags*, 1852; *Aria Marcella*, 1852; *Les Beaux-arts en Europe*, 1855; *Constantinople*, 1854; *Théâtre de poche*, 1855; *Le Roman de la Momie*, 1856; *Jettatura*, 1857; *Avatar*, 1857; *Sakountala, Ballet*, 1858; *Honoré de Balzac*, 1859; *Les Vosges*, 1860; *Trésors d'Art de la Russie*, 1860–1863; *Histoire de l'art théâtrale en France depuis vingt-cinq ans*, 1860; *Le Capitaine Fracasse*, 1863; *Les Dieux et les Demi-Dieux de la peintre*, 1863;

Poésies nouvelles, 1863; *Loin de Paris*, 1864; *La Belle Jenny*, 1864; *Voyage en Russie*, 1865; *Spirite*, 1866; *Le Palais pompeien de l'Avenue Montaigne*, 1866; *Rapport sur le progrès des Lettres*, 1868; *Ménagere intime*, 1869; *La Nature chez Elle*, 1870; *Tableaux de Siege*, 1871; *Théâtre*, 1872; *Portraits Contemporaines*, 1874; *Histoire du Romantisme*, 1874; *Portraits et Souvenirs littéraires*, 1875; *Poésies complètes*, 1876: 2 vols.; *L'Orient*, 1877; *Fusins et eaux-Fortes*, 1880; *Tableaux à la Plume*, 1880; *Mademoiselle Daphné*, 1881; *Guide de l'Amateur au Musés du Louvre.* 1882; *Souvenirs de Théâtre d'Art et de critique*, 1883.

GUSTAVE FLAUBERT

(1821–1880)

Madame Bovary, 1857; *Salammbô*, 1863; *La Tentation de Saint Antoine*, 1874; *L'Education Sentimentale*, 1870; *Trois Contes*, 1877; *Bouvard et Péchuché*, 1881; *Le Candidat*, 1874; *Sur les Champs et par les Grèves*, 1886; *Lettres à George Sand*, 1884; *Correspondances*, 1887–1893.

CHARLES BAUDELAIRE

(1821–1867)

Salon de 1845, 1845; *Salon de 1846*, 1846; *Histoires Extraordinaires, traduit de Poe*, 1856; *Nouvelle Histoires Extraordinaires*, 1857; *Les Fleurs du Mal*, 1857; *Aventures d'Arthur Gordon Pym (Poe)*, 1858; *Théophile Gautier*, 1859; *Les Paradis Artificiels: Opium et Haschisch*, 1860; *Richard Wagner et Tannhäuser à Paris*, 1861; *Euréka: Poe*, 1864; *Histoires Grotesques: Poe*, 1865; *Les Épaves de Charles Baudelaire*, 1866.

EDMOND AND JULES DE GONCOURT

(1822–1896; 1830–1870)

En 18, 1851; *Salon de 1852*, 1852; *La Lorette*, 1853; *Mystères des Théâtres*, 1853; *La revolution dans les Mœurs*, 1854; *Histoire de la Société Française pendent la Revolution*, 1854; *Histoire de la Société Française pendent la Directoire*, 1855; *Le Peinture à l'Exposition de Paris de 1855*, 1855; *Une Voiture des Masques*, 1856; *Les Actrices*, 1856; *Sophie Arnauld*, 1857; *Portraits intimes du XVIII Siècle*, 1857–1858; *Histoire de Marie Antoinette*, 1858; *L'Art du XVIII Siècle*, 1859–1875; *Les Hommes de Lettres*, 1860; *Les Maîtresses de Louis VI*, 1860; *Sœur Philomène*, 1861; *Les Femmes au XVIII Siècle*, 1864; *Renée Mauperin*, 1864; *Germinie Lacerteux*, 1864; *Idées et Sensations*, 1860; *Manette Salomon*, 1867; *Madame Gervaisais*, 1869; *Gavarni*, 1873; *La Patrie en Danger*, 1879; *L'Amour au XVIII Siècle*, 1873; *La du Barry*, 1875; *Madame de Pompadour*, 1878; *La Duchesse de la Châteauroux*, 1879; *Pages retrouvées*, 1886; *Journal des Goncourts*, 1887–1896, 9 Vols.; *Préfaces et manifestes littéraires*, 1888; *L'Italie d'hier*, 1894; *Edmond de Goncourt: Catalogue raisonée de l'œuvre peinte, dessiné et grave d'Antoine Watteau*, 1873; *Catalogue de l'œuvre de P. Proudhun*, 1876; *La Fille Élisa*, 1879; *Les Frères Zamganno*, 1879; *La Maison d'un Artiste*, 1881; *La Faustin*, 1882; *La Saint-Hubert*, 1882; *Chérie*, 1884; *Germinie Lacerteux, pièce*, 1888; *Mademoiselle Clairon*, 1890; *Outamoro, le peintre des maisons vertes*, 1891; *La Gumiard*, 1893; *À bas le progrès*, 1893; *Hokouseï*, 1896.

VILLIERS DE L'ISLE-ADAM

(1838–1889)

Premières Poésies, 1859; *Isis*, 1862; *Elën*, 1864; *Morgane*, 1865; *Claire Lenoir* (in the *Revue des Lettres et des Arts*), 1867; *L'Evasion*, 1870; *La Révolte*, 1870; *Azraël*, 1878; *Le Nouveau Monde*, 1880; *Contes Cruels*, 1880; *L'Eve Future*, 1886; *Akëdysséril*, 1886; *L'Amour Suprême*, 1886; *Tribulat Bonhomet*, 1887; *Histoires Insolites*, 1888; *Nouveaux Contes Cruels*, 1889; *Axël*, 1890; *Chez les Passants*, 1890; *Propos d'Au-delà*, 1893; *Histoires Souveraines*, 1899 (a selection).

Among works announced, but never published, it may be interesting to mention: *Seid, William de Strally, Faust, Poésies Nouvelles* (*Intermèdes; Gog; Ave, Mater Victa; Poésies diverses*), *La Tentation sur la Montagne, Le Vieux de la Montagne, L'Adoration des Mages, Méditations Littéraires, Mélanges, Théâtre* (2 vols.), *Documents sur les Règnes de Charles VI. et de Charles VII., L'Illusionisme, De la Connaissance de l'Utile, L'Exégèse Divine.*

A sympathetic, but slightly vague, Life of Villiers was written by his cousin, Vicomte Robert du Pontavice de Heussey: *Villiers de l'Isle-Adam*, 1893; it was translated into English by Lady Mary Lloyd, 1894. See Verlaine's *Poétes Maudits*, 1884, and his biography of Villiers in *Les Hommes d'Aujourd'hui*, the series of penny biographies, with caricature portraits, published by Vanier; also Mallarmé's *Villiers de l'Isle-Adam,* the reprint of a lecture given at Brussels a few months after Villiers' death. *La Révolte* was translated by Mrs. Theresa Barclay in the *Fortnightly Review,* December, 1897, and acted in London by the New Stage Club in 1906. I have translated a little poem, *Aveu,* from the interlude of verse in the *Contes Cruels* called *Chant d'Amour,* in *Days and Nights,* 1889. An article of mine, the first, I believe, to be written on Villiers in English, appeared in the *Woman's World* in 1889; another in the *Illustrated London News* in 1891.

LÉON CLADEL

(1835–1892)

Les Martyrs Ridicules. *Préface par Charles Baudelaire,*
1862; *Pierre Patient,* 1862; *L'Amour Romantique,* 1882;
Le Deuxième Mystère de l'Incarnation, 1883; *Le Bous-*
cassié, 1889; *La Fête-Votive de Saint Bartholomée Porte-*
Glaive, 1872; *Les Vas- nu-Pieds,* 1874; *Celui de la Croix*
—aux Bœufs, 1878; *Bonshommes,* 1879; *Ompdrailles*
Le Tombeau des Lutteurs, 1879; *N'a q'un Oeil,* 1885;
Tity Foyssac IV, 1886; *Petits Chiens de Léon Cladel,*
1879; *Par Devant Notaire,* 1880; *Crête-Rouge,* 1880;
Six Morceaux de la Littérature, 1880; *Kerkades Garde-*
Barrière, 1884; *Urbains et Ruraux,* 1884; *Léon Cladel et*
ses Kyrielle des Chiens, 1885; *Héros et Pantins,* 1885;
Quelques Sires, 1885; *Mi-Diable,* 1886; *Gueux de Marque,*
1887; *Effigies d'Inconnus,* 1888; *Raca,* 1888; *Seize*
Morceaux de Littérature, 1889; *L'ancien,* 1889; *Juive-*
Errante, 1897.

ÉMILE ZOLA

(1840–1902)

Les Rougon-Maequart, 1871–1893; *La Fortune des Rougons*, 1871; *La Curée*, 1872; *Le Ventre de Paris*, 1873; *La Conquête de Pluisans*, 1874; *La Faute de l'abbe Mouret*, 1875; *Son Excellence Eugène Rougon*, 1876; *L'Assommoir*, 1876; *Une Page d'Amour*, 1878; *Nana*, 1880; *Pot.-Bouille*, 1882; *Au Bonheur des Dames*, 1883; *La Joie de Vivre*, 1884; *Madeleine Ferat*, 1885; *La Confession de Claude*, 1886; *Contes à Ninon*, 1891; *Nouveaux Contes à Ninon*, 1874; *Le Capitaine Burle*, 1883; *La joie de vivre*, 1884; *Les Mystères de Marseilles*, 1885; *Mes Haines*, 1866; *Le Roman Expérimental*, 1881; *Nos Auteurs dramatiques*, 1881; *Documents littéraires*, 1881; *Une Compagne*, 1882. *Théâtre: Thérèse Raquin, Les Héritiers Rabourdin, La Bouton de Rose*, 1890; *L'Argent*, 1891; *L'Attaque du Moulin*, 1890; *La Bête Humaine*, 1890; *La Débâcle*, 1892; *Le Doctor Pascal*, 1893; *Germinie*, 1885; *Mon Salon*, 1886; *Le naturalisme au Théâtre*, 1889; *L'Œuvre*, 1886; *Le Rêve*, 1892; *Paris*, 1898; *Rome*, 1896; *Lourdes*, 1894; *Fécondité*, 1899; *Travail*, 1901; *Verité*, 1903.

STÉPHANE MALLARMÉ

(1842–1898)

Le Corbeau (traduit de Poe), 1875; *La Dernière Mode,* 1875; *L'Après-Midi d'un Faune,* 1876; *Le Vathek de Beckford,* 1876; *Petite Philologie à l'Usage des Classes et du Monde: Les Mots Anglais,* 1877; *Poésies Complètes* (photogravées sur le manuscrit), 1887; *Les Poèms de Poe,* 1888; *Le Ten o'Clock de M. Whistler,* 1888; *Pages,* 1891; *Les Miens: Villiers de l'Isle-Adam,* 1892; *Vers et Prose,* 1892; *La Musique et les Lettres* (Oxford, Cambridge), 1894; *Divagations,* 1897; *Poésies,* 1899.

See, on this difficult subject, Edmund Gosse, *Questions at Issue,* 1893, in which will be found the first study of Mallarmé that appeared in English; and Vittorio Pica, *Letteratura d'Eccezione,* 1899, which contains a carefully-documented study of more than a hundred pages. There is a translation of the poem called " Fleurs " in Mr. John Gray's *Silverpoints,* 1893, and translations of " Hérodiade " and three shorter poems will be found in the first volume of my collected poems. Several of the poems in prose have been translated into English; my translation of the " Plainte d'Automne," contained in this volume, was made in momentary forgetfulness that the same poem in prose had already been translated by Mr. George Moore in *Confessions of a Young Man.* Mr. Moore also translated " Le Phénomène Futur " in the *Savoy,* July, 1896.

PAUL VERLAINE

(1844–1896)

Poèmes Saturniens, 1866; *Fêtes Galantes*, 1869; *La Bonne Chanson*, 1870; *Romances sans Paroles*, 1874; *Sagesse*, 1881; *Les Poètes Maudits*, 1884; *Jadis et Naguère*, 1884; *Les Mémoires d'un Veuf*, 1886; *Louise Leclercq* (suivi de *Le Poteau, Pierre Duchatelet, Madame Aubin*), 1887; *Amour*, 1888; *Parallèlement*, 1889; *Dédicaces*, 1890; *Bonheur*, 1891; *Mes Hôpitaux*, 1891; *Chansons pour Elle*, 1891; *Liturgies Intimes*, 1892; *Mes Prisons*, 1893; *Odes en son Honneur*, 1893; *Elégies*, 1893; *Quinze Jours en Hollande*, 1894; *Dans les Limbes*, 1894; *Epigrammes*, 1894; *Confessions*, 1895; *Chair*, 1896; *Invectives*, 1896; *Voyage en France d'un Français* (posthumous), 1907.

The complete works of Verlaine are now published in six volumes at the Librairie Léon Vanier (now Messein); the text is very incorrectly printed, and it is still necessary to refer to the earlier editions in separate volumes. A *Choix de Poésies*, 1891, with a preface by François Coppée, and a reproduction of Carrière's admirable portrait, is published in one volume by Charpentier; the series of *Hommes d'Aujourd'hui* contains twenty-seven biographical notices by Verlaine; and a considerable number of poems and prose articles exists, scattered in various magazines, some of them English, such as the *Senate;* in some cases the articles themselves are translated into English, such as "My Visit to London," in the *Savoy* for April, 1896, and " Notes on England: Myself as a French Master," and " Shakespeare and Racine," in the *Fortnightly Review* for July, 1894, and September, 1894. The first English translation in verse from Verlaine is Arthur O'Shaughnessy's rendering of " Clair de Lune " in *Fêtes Galantes,* under the title " Pastel," in *Songs of a Worker,* 1881. A volume of translations in verse, *Poems of Verlaine,* by Gertrude Hall, was published in America in 1895. In Mr. John Gray's *Silverpoints,* 1893, there are translations of " Parsifal," " A Crucifix," " Le Chevalier Malheur," " Spleen," " Clair de Lune," " Mon Dieu m'a dit," and " Green."

As I have mentioned, there have been many portraits of Verlaine. The three portraits drawn on lithographic paper by Mr. Rothenstein, and published in 1898, are but the latest, if also among the best, of a long series, of which Mr. Rothenstein himself has done two or three others, one of which was reproduced in the *Pall Mall Gazette* in 1894, when Verlaine was in London. M. F. A. Cazals, a young artist who was one of Verlaine's most intimate friends, has done I should not like to say how many portraits, some of which he has gathered together in a little book, *Paul Verlaine: ses Portraits,* 1898. There are portraits in nine of Verlaine's own books, several of them by M. Cazals (roughly jotted, expressive notes of moments), one by M. Anquetin (a strong piece of thinking flesh and blood), and in the *Choix de Poésies* there is a reproduction of the cloudy, inspired poet of M. Eugène Carrière's painting. Another portrait, which I have not seen, but which Verlaine himself calls, in the *Dédicaces, un portrait enfin reposé,* was done by

M. Aman-Jean. M. Niederhausern has done a bust in bronze, Mr. Rothenstein a portrait medallion. A new edition of the *Confessions*, 1899, contains a number of sketches; *Verlaine Dessinateur*, 1896, many more; and there are yet others in the extremely objectionable book of M. Charles Donos, *Verlaine Intime*, 1898. The *Hommes d'Aujourd'hui* contains a caricature-portrait, many other portraits have appeared in French and English and German and Italian magazines, and there is yet another portrait in the admirable little book of Charles Morice, *Paul Verlaine*, 1888, which contains by far the best study that has ever been made of Verlaine as a poet. I believe Mr. George Moore's article, " A Great Poet," reprinted in *Impressions and Opinions*, 1891, was the first that was written on Verlaine in England; my own article in the *National Review* in 1892 was, I believe, the first detailed study of the whole of his work up to that date. At last, in the *Vie de Paul Verlaine*, of Edmund Lepelletier, there has come the authentic record.

An honest and instructed life of Verlaine has long been wanted, if only as an antidote to the defamatory production called *Verlaine Intime*, made up out of materials collected by the publisher Léon Vanier in his own defense, in order that a hard taskmaster might be presented to the world in the colours of a benefactor. A " legend " which may well have seemed plausible to those who knew Verlaine only at the end of his life, has obtained currency; and a comparison of Verlaine with Villon, not only as a poet (which is to his honour), but also as a man, has been made, and believed. Lepelletier's book is an exact chronicle of a friendship which lasted, without a break, for thirty-six years—that is, from the time when Verlaine was sixteen to the time of his death;

and a more sane, loyal and impartial chronicle of any man's life we have never read. It is written with full knowledge of every part of the career which it traces; and it is written by a man who puts down whatever he knows exactly as he believes it to have been. His conclusion is that "on peut fouiller sa vie au microscope: on y reconnaîtra des fautes, des folies, des faiblesses, bien des souffrances aussi, avec de la fatalitéau fond, pas de honte véritable, pas une vile et indigne action. Les vrais amis du poète peuvent donc revendiquer pour lui l'épithete d'honnête homme, sans doute très vulgaire, mais qui, aux yeux de certains, a encore du prix."

In 1886 Verlaine dedicated *Les Mémoires d'un Veuf* to Lepelletier, affirming the resolve, on his part, to "garder intacte la vielle amitié si forte et si belle." The compact has been kept nobly by the survivor.

It may, indeed, be questioned whether Lepelletier does not insist a little too much on the bourgeois element which he finds in Verlaine. When a man has suffered under unjust accusations, it is natural for his friends to defend him under whatever aspect seems to them most generally convincing. So it is interesting to know that for seven years Verlaine was in a municipal office, the Bureau des Budgets et Comptes, and that later, in 1882, he made an application, which was refused, for leave to return to his former post. Lepelletier reproaches the authorities for an action which he takes to have precipitated Verlaine into the final misery of his vagabondage. He would have lived quietly, he says, and written in security. Both assumptions may be doubted. What was bourgeois, and contented with quiet, was a small part of the nature of one who was too strong as well as too weak to remain within limits. The terrible force of

Verlaine's weakness would always, in the process of making him a poet, have carried him far from that "tranquilité d'une sinécure bureaucratique" which Lepelletier strangely regrets for him. It is hardly permitted, in looking back over a disastrous life which has expressed itself in notable poetry, to regret that the end should have been attained, by no matter what means.

On moral questions Lepelletier speaks with the authority of an intimate friendship, and from a point of view which seems wholly without prejudice. He defends Verlaine with evident conviction against the most serious charges brought against him, and he shows at least, on documentary evidence, that nothing of the darker part of his "legend" was ever proved against him in any of his arrests and imprisonments. Drink, and mad rages let loose by drink, account, ignobly enough, for all of them. In the famous quarrel with Rimbaud, which brought him into prison for eighteen months, the accusation reads:

"Pour avoir, à Bruxelles, le 10 juillet, 1873, volontairement portés des coups et fait des blessures ayant entraîné une incapacité de travail personnel à Arthur Rimbaud."

The whole account of this episode is given by M. Lepelletier in great detail, and from this we learn that it was by the merest change of mind on the part of Rimbaud, or by sudden treachery, that the matter came into the courts at all. Lepelletier supplies an unfavourable account of Rimbaud, whom he looks upon as the evil counsellor of Verlaine—probably with justice. There is little doubt that Rimbaud, apart from his genuine touch of precocious power, which had its influence on the genius of Verlaine, was a "mauvais sujet" of a selfish and mischievous kind. He was destructive and

pitiless; and having done his worst, he went off carelessly into Africa.

It will surprise some readers to learn that Verlaine
took his degree of "bachelier-ès-lettres," and that on
leaving the Lycée Bonaparte he received a certificate
placing him "au nombre des sujets distingués que compte
l'établissement." He was well grounded in Latin, and
fairly well in English, and at several intervals in his
life attempted to master Spanish, with the vague desire
of translating Calderon. At an early period he read
French literature, classical and modern, with avidity;
translations of English, German and Eastern classics;
books of criticism and philosophy.

"Il admirait beaucoup Joseph de Maîstre. *Le Rouge
et le Noir* de Stendhal avait producé sur lui une forte
impression. Il avait deniché, on ne sait où, une Vie
de sainte Thérèse, qu'il lisait avec ravissement."

He was absorbed in Baudelaire, Gautier, Leconte
de Lisle, Banville; he read Pétrus Borel and Aloysius
Bertrand. The only poem that remains of this early
period is the "Nocturne Parisien" of the *Poèmes Saturniens*, which dates from about his twentieth year. Jules
de Goncourt defined it as "un beau poème sinistre mêlant
comme une Morgue à Notre-Dame." Baudelaire, as
Sainte-Beuve, in a charming letter of real appreciation,
pointed out, is here the evident "point de départ, pour
aller au delà."

The chapter in which Lepelletier tells the story of the
origin of the most famous literary movement since that
of 1830, the "Parnasse," is one of the most entertaining
in the book, and gives, in its narrative of the receptions
"chez Nina" (a *salon* which Lepelletier describes as
the ancestor of the "Chat Noir"), a vivid picture of

the days when Villiers de l'Isle-Adam and François
Coppée were beginners together. Nina de Villars was
one of the oddest people of her time: she made a kind of
private Bohemia for poets, musicians, all kinds of artists
and eccentric people, herself the most eccentric of them
all. It was at her house that the members of the " Parnasse " gathered, while they selected as their more formal
meeting-place the *salon* of Madame Ricard. It is not
generally known that Verlaine's *Poèmes Saturniens* was
the third volume to be issued by the house of Lemerre,
afterwards to become a famous " publisher of poets,"
and it was in this volume that the new laws of the Parnasse were first formulated—that impassivity, that
" marble egoism," which Verlaine was so soon to reject
for a more living impulse, but which neither Leconte de
Lisle nor Héredia was ever to abandon. When one
thinks of the later Verlaine, it is curious to turn to that
first formula:

Est-elle en marvre où non, le Vénus de Milo?

Verlaine's verse suddenly becomes human with *La
Bonne Chanson*, though the humanity in it is not yet
salted as with fire. It is the record of the event which,
as Lepelletier says, dominated his whole life; the marriage
with Mathilde Maute, the young girl with whom he
had fallen in love at first sight, and whose desertion of
him, however explicable, he never forgot nor forgave.
Nothing could be more just or delicate than Lepelletier's
treatment of the whole situation and there is no doubt
that he is right in saying that the young wife " eût une
grande responsabilité dans les désordres de l'éxistence
désorbitée du poète." Verlaine, as he says, " était bon,
aimant, et c'était comme un souffrant qu'il fallait le

traiter." "Vous n'avez rien compris à ma simplicité," he wrote long afterwards, addressing the woman of whom Lepelletier says, " Il l'aima toujours, il n'aima qu'elle."

With his marriage Verlaine's disasters begin. Rimbaud enters his life and turns the current of it; the vagabondage begins, in France and England, and the letters written from London are among the most vivid documents in the book: thumbnail sketches full of keen observation. Then comes his imprisonment and conversion to Catholicism. Here Lepelletier, while he gives us an infinity of details which he alone could give, adopts an attitude which we cannot think to be justified, and which, as a matter of fact, Verlaine protested against during his lifetime. "Cette conversion fut-elle profonde et véridique?" he asks; and he answers, "Je ne le crois pas." That his conversion had much influence on Verlaine's conduct cannot be contended, but conduct and belief are two different things. Sincerity of the moment was his fundamental characteristic, but the moments made and remade his moods in their passing. The religion of *Sagesse* is not the less genuine because that grave and sacred book was followed by the revolt of *Parallèment*. Verlaine tried to explain—in the poems themselves, in prefaces, and in conversation with friends— how natural it was to sin and to repent, and to use the same childlike words in the immediate rendering of sin and of repentance. This *naïveté*, which made any regular existence an impossibility, was a part of him which gave a quality to his work unlike that of any other poet of our time. At the end of his life hardly anything but the *maïveté* was left, and the poems became mere outcries and gestures. Lepelletier is justly indignant at the action of Vanier in publishing after Verlaine's death the collection called *Invectives*, made up of scraps and impromptus which the poet certainly never intended to publish. Here we see part of the weakness of a great man, who becomes petty when he puts off his true character and tries to be angry. " J'ai la fureur d'aimer," he says somewhere, and there is no essential part of his work which is not the expression of some form of love, grotesque or heroic, human or divine.

Of all this later, more and more miserable part of the life of Verlaine, Lepelletier has less to tell us. It has been sufficiently commented on, not always by friendly or understanding witnesses. What we get in this book, for the first time, is a view of the life as a whole, with all that is beautiful, tragic, and desperate in it. It is not an apology: it is a statement. It not only does honor to a great and unhappy man of genius: it does him justice.

JORIS-KARL HUYSMANS

(1848–1907)

Le Drageoir à Épices, 1874; *Marthe: Histoire d'une Fille*, 1876; *Les Sœurs Vatard*, 1879; *Croquis Parisiens*, 1880; *En Ménage*, 1881; *A Vau-l'Eau*, 1882; *L'Art Moderne*, 1883; *A Rebours*, 1884; *Un Dilemme*, 1887; *En Rade*, 1887; *Certains*, 1889; *La Bièvre*, 1890; *Là-Bas*, 1891; *En Route*, 1895; *La Cathédrale*, 1898; *La Bièvre et Saint-Séverin*, 1898; *Pages Catholiques*, 1900; *Sainte Lydwine de Schiedam*, 1901; *De Tout*, 1902; *L'Oblat*, 1903; *Trois Primitifs*, 1905; *Les Foules de Lourdes*, 1906; See also the short story, *Sac au Dos*, in the *Soirées de Medan*, 1880, and the pantomime, *Pierrot Sceptique*, 1881, in collaboration with Léon Hennique. *En Route* was translated into English by Mr. Kegan Paul, in 1896; and *La Cathédrale* by Miss Clara Bell, in 1898.

MAURICE MAETERLINCK

(1862)

Serres Chaudes, 1889; *La Princesse Maleine*, 1890; *Les Aveugles (L'Intruse, Les Aveugles)*, 1890; *L'Ornement des Noces Spirituelles, de Ruysbroeck l'Admirable*, 1891; *Les Sept Princesses*, 1891; *Pelléas et Mélisande*, 1892; *Alladine et Palomides, Intérieur, La Mort de Tintagiles*, 1894; *Annabella, de John Ford*, 1895; *Les Disciples à Saïs et les Fragments de Novalis*, 1895; *Le Trésor des Humbles*, 1896; *Douze Chansons*, 1896; *Aglavaine et Sélysette*, 1896; *La Sagesse et la Destinée*, 1898; *Théâtre*, 1901 (3 vols.); *La Vie des Abeilles*, 1901; *Monna Vanna*, 1902; *Le Temple Enseveli*, 1902; *Joyzelle*, 1903; *Le Double Jardin*, 1904; *L'Intelligence des Fleurs*, 1907.

M. Maeterlinck has had the good or bad fortune to be more promptly, and more violently, praised at the beginning of his career than at all events any other writer of whom I have spoken in this volume. His fame in France was made by a flaming article of M. Octave Mirbeau in the *Figaro* of August 24, 1890. M. Mirbeau greeted him as the " Belgian Shakepeare," and expressed his opinion of *La Princesse Maleine* by saying " M. Maeterlinck has given us the greatest work of genius that has been produced in our time, and the most extraordinary and the most naïve too, comparable (dare I say?) superior in beauty to what is most beautiful in Shakespeare . . .

more tragic than *Macbeth*, more extraordinary in thought
than *Hamlet*." Mr. William Archer introduced M.
Maeterlinck to England in an article called " A Pessimist
Playwright " in the *Fortnightly Review*, September, 1891.
Less enthusiastic than M. Mirbeau, he defined the author
of *La Princesse Maleine* as " a Webster who had read
Alfred de Musset." A freely adapted version of *L'Intruse*
was given by Mr. Tree at the Haymarket Theatre, January 27, 1892, and since that time many of M. Maeterlinck's plays have been acted, without cuts, or with but
few cuts, at various London theatres. Several of his
books have also been translated into English: *The Princesse Maleine* (by Gerard Harry) and *The Intruder* (by
William Wilson), 1892; *Pelleas and Melisande* and *The
Sightless* (by Laurence Alma-Tadema), 1892; *Ruysbroeck
and the Mystics* (by J. T. Stoddart), 1894; *The Treasure of
the Humble* (by A. Sutro), 1897; *Aglavaine and Selysette*
(by A. Sutro), 1897; *Wisdom and Destiny* (by A. Sutro),
1898; *Alladine and Palomides* (by A. Sutro), *Interior* (by
William Archer), and *The Death of Tintagiles* (by A. Sutro),
1899.

I have spoken, in this volume, chiefly of Maeterlinck's
essays, and but little of his plays, and I have said all that
I had to say without special reference to the second volume of essays, *La Sagesse et la Destinée*. Like *Le Trésor
des Humbles*, that book is a message, a doctrine, even more
than it is a piece of literature. It is a treatise on wisdom
and happiness, on the search for happiness because it is
wisdom, not for wisdom because it is happiness. It is a
book of patient and resigned philosophy, a very Flemish
philosophy, more resigned than even *Le Trésor des Humbles*. In a sense it seems to aim less high. An ecstatic
mysticism has given way to a kind of prudence. Is this

coming nearer to the earth really an intellectual ascent
or descent? At least it is a divergence, and it probably
indicates a divergence in art as well as in meditation.
Yet, while it is quite possible to at least indicate Maeterlinck's position as a philosopher, it seems to me prema-
ture to attempt to define his position as a dramatist.
Interesting as his dramatic work has always been, there
is, in the later dramas, so singular an advance in all the
qualities that go to make great art, that I find it impossible
at this stage of his development, to treat his dramatic
work as in any sense the final expression of a personality.
What the next stage of his development may be it is
impossible to say. He will not write more beautiful
dramas than he has written in *Aglavaine et Sélysette* and
in *Péleas et Mélisande*. But he may, and he probably
will, write something which will move the general world
more profoundly, touching it more closely, in the manner
of the great writers, in whom beauty has not been more
beautiful than in writers less great, but has come to men
with a more splendid energy.

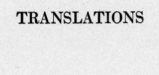

TRANSLATIONS

I. HÉRODIADE

HERODIADE.

To mine own self I am a wilderness.
You know it, amethyst gardens numberless
Enfolded in the flaming, subtle deep,
Strange gold, that through the red earth's
     heavy sleep
Has cherished ancient brightness like a dream,
Stones whence mine eyes, pure jewels, have
     their gleam
Of icy and melodious radiance, you,
Metals, which into my young tresses drew
A fatal splendour and their manifold grace!
Thou, woman, born into these evil days
Disastrous to the cavern sibylline,
Who speakest, prophesying not of one divine,
But of a mortal, if from that close sheath,
My robes, rustle the wild enchanted breath
In the white quiver of my nakedness,
In the warm air of summer, O prophetess,

369

(And woman's body obeys that ancient claim)
Behold me in my shivering starry shame,
I die!
The horror of my virginity
Delights me, and I would envelop me
In the terror of my tresses, that, by night,
Inviolate reptile, I might feel the white
And glimmering radiance of thy frozen fire,
Thou that art chaste and diest of desire,
White night of ice and of the cruel snow!
Eternal sister, my lone sister, lo
My dreams uplifted before thee! now, apart,
So rare a crystal is my dreaming heart,
I live in a monotonous land alone,
And all about me lives but in mine own
Image, the idolatrous mirror of my pride,
Mirroring this Hérodiade diamond-eyed.
I am indeed alone, O charm and curse!

NURSE.
O lady, would you die then?

HERODIADE.
No, poor nurse;
Be calm, and leave me; prithee, pardon me,
But, ere thou go, close to the casement; see

How the seraphical blue in the dim glass smiles,
But I abhor the blue of the sky!
Yet miles
On miles of rocking waves! Know'st not a
    land
Where, in the pestilent sky, men see the hand
Of Venus, and her shadow in dark leaves?
Thither I go.
Light thou the wax that grieves
In the swift flame, and sheds an alien tear
Over the vain gold; wilt not say in mere
Childishness?

NURSE.
Now?

HERODIADE.
Farewell.   You lie, O flower
Of these chill lips!
I wait the unknown hour,
Or, deaf to your crying and that hour supreme,
Utter the lamentation of the dream
Of childhood seeing fall apart in sighs
The icy chaplet of its reveries.

II. SIGH

My soul, calm sister, towards thy brow,
    whereon scarce grieves
An autumn strewn already with its russet
    leaves,
And towards the wandering sky of thine angelic
    eyes,
Mounts, as in melancholy gardens may arise
Some faithful fountain sighing whitely towards
    the blue!
Towards the blue pale and pure that sad
    October knew,
When, in those depths, it mirrored languors
    infinite,
And agonising leaves upon the waters white,
Windily drifting, traced a furrow cold and dun,
Where, in one long last ray, lingered the yellow
    sun.

III. SEA-WIND

The flesh is sad, alas! and all the books are
    read.
Flight, only flight! I feel that birds are wild
    to tread
The floor of unknown foam, and to attain the
    skies!
Nought, neither ancient gardens mirrored
    in the eyes,
Shall hold this heart that bathes in waters its
    delight,
O nights! nor yet my waking lamp, whose
    lonely light
Shadows the vacant paper, whiteness profits
    best,
Nor the young wife who rocks her baby on her
    breast.
I will depart! O steamer, swaying rope and
    spar,
Lift anchor for exotic lands that lie afar!
A weariness, outworn by cruel hopes, still
    clings
To the last farewell handkerchief's last beckon-
    ings!

And are not these, the masts inviting storms,
    not these
That an awakening wind bends over wrecking
    seas,
Lost, not a sail, a sail, a flowering isle, ere long?
But, O my heart, hear thou, hear thou the
    sailors' song!

IV. ANGUISH

To-night I do not come to conquer thee,
O Beast that dost the sins of the whole world
        bear,
Nor with my kisses' weary misery
Wake a sad tempest in thy wanton hair;
It is that heavy and that dreamless sleep
I ask of the close curtains of thy bed,
Which, after all thy treacheries, folds thee
        deep,
Who knowest oblivion better than the dead.
For Vice, that gnaws with keener tooth than
        Time,
Brands me as thee, of barren conquest proud;
But while thou guardest in thy breast of stone
A heart that fears no fang of any crime,
I wander palely, haunted by my shroud,
Fearing to die if I but sleep alone.

From Paul Verlaine: Fêtes Galantes

I.   CLAIR DE LUNE

Your soul is a sealed garden, and there go
With masque and bergamasque fair companies
Playing on lutes and dancing and as though
Sad under their fantastic fripperies.

Though they in minor keys go carolling
Of love the conqueror and of life the boon
They seem to doubt the happiness they sing
And the song melts into the light of the moon,

The sad light of the moon, so lovely fair
That all the birds dream in the leafy shade
And the slim fountains sob into the air
Among the marble statues in the glade.

II. PANTOMIME

Pierrot, no sentimental swain,
Washes a paté down again
With furtive flagons, white and red.

Cassandre, with demure content,
Greets with a tear of sentiment
His nephew disinherited.

That blackguard of a Harlequin
Pirouettes, and plots to win
His Columbine that flits and flies.

Columbine dreams, and starts to find
A sad heart sighing in the wind,
And in her heart a voice that sighs.

III. SUR L'HERBE

The Abbé wanders.—Marquis, now
Set straight your periwig, and speak!
—This Cyprus wine is heavenly, how
Much less, Camargo, than your cheek!

—My goddess . . . —Do, mi, sol, la, si.
—Abbé, such treason who'll forgive you?
—May I die, ladies, if there be
A star in heaven I will not give you!

—I'd be my lady's lapdog; then . . .
—Shepherdess, kiss your shepherd soon,
Shepherd, come kiss . . . —Well, gentlemen?
—Do, mi, so.   —Hey, good-night, good moon!

IV. L'ALLÉE

As in the age of shepherd king and queen,
Painted and frail amid her nodding bows,
Under the sombre branches and between
The green and mossy garden-ways she goes,
With little mincing airs one keeps to pet
A darling and provoking perroquet.
Her long-trained robe is blue, the fan she holds
With fluent fingers girt with heavy rings,
So vaguely hints of vague erotic things
That her eye smiles, musing among its folds.
—Blonde too, a tiny nose, a rosy mouth,
Artful as that sly patch that makes more sly,
In her divine unconscious pride of youth,
The slightly simpering sparkle of the eye.

V. A LA PROMENADE

The sky so pale, and the trees, such frail things,
Seem as if smiling on our bright array
That flits so light and gay upon the way
With indolent airs and fluttering as of wings.

The fountain wrinkles under a faint wind,
And all the sifted sunlight falling through
The lime-trees of the shadowy avenue
Comes to us blue and shadowy-pale and
    thinned.

Faultlessly fickle, and yet fond enough,
With fonds hearts not too tender to be free,
We wander whispering deliciously,
And every lover leads a lady-love,

Whose imperceptible and roguish hand
Darts now and then a dainty tap, the lip
Revenges on an extreme finger-tip,
The tip of the left little finger, and,

The deed being so excessive and uncouth,
A duly freezing look deals punishment,
That in the instant of the act is blent
With a shy pity pouting in the mouth.

VI. DANS LA GROTTE

Stay, let me die, since I am true,
For my distress will not delay,
And the Hyrcanian tigress ravening for prey
Is as a little lamb to you.

Yes, here within, cruel Clymène,
This steel which in how many wars
How many a Cyrus slew, or Scipio, now pre-
    pares
To end my life and end my pain.

But nay, what need of steel have I
To haste my passage to the shades?
Did not Love pierce my heart, beyond all
    mortal aids,
With the first arrow of your eye?

VII. LES INGENUS

High heels and long skirts intercepting them,
So that, according to the wind or way,
An ankle peeped and vanished as in play;
And well we loved the malice of the game.

Sometimes an insect with its jealous sting
Some fair one's whiter neck disquieted,
From which the gleams of sudden whiteness
    shed
Met in our eyes a frolic welcoming.

The stealthy autumn evening faded out,
And the fair creatures dreaming by our side
Words of such subtle savour to us sighed
That since that time our souls tremble and
    doubt.

VIII. CORTÈGE

A silver-vested monkey trips
And pirouettes before the face
Of one who twists a kerchief's lace
Between her well-gloved finger-tips.

A little negro, a red elf,
Carries her dropping train, and holds
At arm's length all the heavy folds,
Watching each fold displace itself.

The monkey never lets his eyes
Wander from the fair woman's breast,
White wonder that to be possessed
Would call a god out of the skies.

Sometimes the little negro seems
To lift his sumptuous burden up
Higher than need be, in the hope
Of seeing what all night he dreams.

She goes by corridor and stair,
Still to the insolent appeals
Of her familiar animals
Indifferent or unaware.

IX.   LES COQUILLAGES

Each shell incrusted in the grot
Where we two loved each other well
An aspect of its own has got.

The purple of a purple shell
Is our souls' colour when they make
Our burning heart's blood visible.

This pallid shell affects to take
Thy languors, when thy love-tired eyes
Rebuke me for my mockery's sake.

This counterfeits the harmonies
Of thy pink ear, and this might be
Thy plump short nape with rosy dyes.

But one, among these, troubled me.

X. EN PATINANT

We were the victims, you and I,
Madame, of mutual self deceits;
And that which set our brains awry
May well have been the summer heats.

And the spring too, if I recall,
Contributed to spoil our play,
And yet its share, I think, was small
In leading you and me astray.

For air in springtime is so fresh
That rose-buds Love has surely meant
To match the roses of the flesh
Have odours almost innocent;

And even the lilies that outpour
Their biting odours where the sun
Is new in heaven, do but the more
Enliven and enlighten one,

So stealthily the zephyr blows
A mocking breath that renders back
The heart's rest and the soul's repose
And the flower's aphrodisiac,

And the five senses, peeping out,
Take up their station at the feast,
But, being by themselves, without
Troubling the reason in the least.

That was the time of azure skies,
(Madame, do you remember it?)
And sonnets to my lady's eyes,
And cautious kisses not too sweet.

Free from all passion's idle pother,
Full of mere kindliness, how long,
How well we liked not loved each other,
Without one rapture or one wrong!

Ah, happy hours!   But summer came:
Farewell, fresh breezes of the spring!
A wind of pleasure like a flame
Leapt on our senses wondering.

Strange flowers, fair crimson-hearted flowers
Poured their ripe odours over us,
And evil voices of the hours
Whispered above us in the boughs.

We yielded to it all, ah me!
What vertigo of fools held fast
Our senses in its ecstasy
Until the heat of summer passed?

There were vain tears and vainer laughter,
And hands indefinitely pressed,
Moist sadnesses, and swoonings after,
And what vague void within the breast?

But autumn came to our relief,
Its light grown cold, its gusts grown rough,
Came to remind us, sharp and brief,
That we had wantoned long enough,

And led us quickly to recover
The elegance demanded of
Every quite irreproachable lover
And every seemly lady-love.

Now it is winter, and, alas,
Our backers tremble for their stake;
Already other sledges pass
And leave us toiling in their wake.

Put both your hands into your muff,
Sit back, now, steady! off we go.
Fanchon will tell us soon enough
Whatever news there is to know.

XI. FANTOCHES

Scaramouche waves a threatening hand
To Pulcinella, and they stand,
Two shadows, black against the moon.

The old doctor of Bologna pries
For simples with impassive eyes,
And mutters o'er a magic rune.

The while his daughter, scarce half-dressed,
Glides slyly 'neath the trees, in quest
Of her bold pirate lover's sail;

Her pirate from the Spanish main,
Whose passion thrills her in the pain
Of the loud languorous nightingale.

XII. CYTHÈRE

By favourable breezes fanned,
A trellised harbour is at hand
To shield us from the summer airs;

The scent of roses, fainting sweet,
Afloat upon the summer heat,
Blends with the perfume that she wears.

True to the promise her eyes gave,
She ventures all, and her mouth rains
A dainty fever through my veins;

And, Love fulfilling all things, save
Hunger, we 'scape, with sweets and ices,
The folly of Love's sacrifices.

XIII.   EN BATEAU

The shepherd's star with trembling glint
Drops in black water; at the hint
The pilot fumbles for his flint.

Now is the time or never, sirs.
No hand that wanders wisely errs:
I touch a hand, and is it hers?

The knightly Atys strikes the strings,
And to the faithless Chloris flings
A look that speaks of many things.

The abbé has absolved again
Eglé, the viscount all in vain
Has given his hasty heart the rein.

Meanwhile the moon is up and streams
Upon the skiff that flies and seems
To float upon a tide of dreams.

XIV.   LE FAUNE

An aged faun of old red clay
Laughs from the grassy bowling-green,
Foretelling doubtless some decay
Of mortal moments so serene

That lead us lightly on our way
(Love's piteous pilgrims have we been!)
To this last hour that runs away
Dancing to the tambourine.

XV. MANDOLINE

The singers of serenades
Whisper their faded vows
Unto fair listening maids
Under the singing boughs.

Tircis, Aminte, are there,
Clitandre has waited long,
And Damis for many a fair
Tyrant makes many a song.

Their short vests, silken and bright,
Their long pale silken trains,
Their elegance of delight,
Twine soft blue silken chains.

And the mandolines and they,
Faintlier breathing, swoon
Into the rose and grey
Ecstasy of the moon.

XVI.   A CLYMÈNE

Mystical strains unheard,
A song without a word,
Dearest, because thine eyes,
Pale as the skies,

Because thy voice, remote
As the far clouds that float
Veiling for me the whole
Heaven of the soul,

Because the stately scent
Of thy swan's whiteness, blent
With the white lily's bloom
Of thy perfume,

Ah! because thy dear love,
The music breathed above
By angels halo-crowned,
Odour and sound,

Hath, in my subtle heart,
With some mysterious art
Transposed thy harmony,
So let it be!

XVII. LETTRE

Far from your sight removed by thankless cares
(The gods are witness when a lover swears)
I languish and I die, Madame, as still
My use is, which I punctually fulfil,
And go, through heavy-hearted woes conveyed,
Attended ever by your lovely shade,
By day in thought, by night in dreams of hell,
And day and night, Madame, adorable!
So that at length my dwindling body lost
In very soul, I too become a ghost,
I too, and in the lamentable stress
Of vain desires remembering happiness,
Remembered kisses, now, alas, unfelt,
My shadow shall into your shadow melt.

Meanwhile, dearest, your most obedient slave.

How does the sweet society behave,
Thy cat, thy dog, thy parrot? and is she
Still, as of old, the black-eyed Silvanie
(I had loved black eyes if thine had not been
    blue)
Who ogled me at moments, palsambleu!

Thy tender friend and thy sweet confidant?
One dream there is, Madame, long wont to
    haunt
This too impatient heart: to pour the earth
And all its treasures (of how little worth!)
Before your feet as tokens of a love
Equal to the most famous flames that move
The hearts of men to conquer all but death.
Cleopatra was less loved, yes, on my faith,
By Antony or Caesar than you are,
Madame, by me, who truly would by far
Out-do the deeds of Caesar for a smile,
O Cleopatra, queen of word and wile,
Or, for a kiss, take flight with Antony

With this, farewell, dear, and no more from me;
How can the time it takes to read it, quite
Be worth the trouble that it took to write?

XVIII.   LES INDOLENTS

Bah! spite of Fate, that says us nay,
Suppose we die together, eh?
—A rare conclusion you discover

—What's rare is good.   Let us die so,
Like lovers in Boccaccio.
—Ha! ha! ha! you fantastic lover!

—Nay, not fantastic.   If you will,
Fond, surely irreproachable.
Suppose, then, that we die together?

—Good sir, your jests are fitlier told
Than when you speak of love or gold.
Why speak at all, in this glad weather?

Whereat, behold them once again,
Tircis beside his Dorimène,
Not far from two blithe rustic rovers,

For some caprice of idle breath
Deferring a delicious death.
Ha! ha! ha! what fantastic lovers!

XX. L'AMOUR PAR TERRE

The other night a sudden wind laid low
The Love, shooting an arrow at a mark,
In the mysterious corner of the park,
Whose smile disquieted us long ago.

The wind has overthrown him, and above
His scattered dust, how sad it is to spell
The artist's name still faintly visible
Upon the pedestal without its Love,

How sad it is to see the pedestal
Still standing! as in dream I seem to hear
Prophetic voices whisper in my ear
The lonely and despairing end of all.

How sad it is!   Why, even you have found
A tear for it, although your frivolous eye
Laughs at the gold and purple butterfly
Poised on the piteous litter on the ground.

XXI. EN SOURDINE

Calm where twilight leaves have stilled
With their shadow light and sound,
Let our silent love be filled
With a silence as profound.

Let our ravished senses blend
Heart and spirit, thine and mine,
With vague languors that descend
From the branches of the pine.

Close thine eyes against the day,
Fold thine arms across thy breast,
And for ever turn away
All desire of all but rest.

Let the lulling breaths that pass
In soft wrinkles at thy feet,
Tossing all the tawny grass,
This and only this repeat.

And when solemn evening
Dims the forest's dusky air,
Then the nightingale shall sing
The delight of our despair.

XXII. COLLOQUE SENTIMENTAL

In the old park, solitary and vast,
Over the frozen ground two forms once passed.

Their lips were languid and their eyes were
    dead,
And hardly could be heard the words they said.

In the old park, solitary and vast,
Two ghosts once met to summon up the past.

—Do you remember our old ecstasy?
—Why would you bring it back again to me?

—Do you still dream as you dreamed long ago?
Does your heart beat to my heart's beating?
    —No.

—Ah, those old days, what joys have those
    days seen
When your lips met my lips!—It may have
    been.

—How blue the sky was, and our hope how
    light!
—Hope has flown helpless back into the night.

They walked through weeds withered and
    grasses dead,
And only the night heard the words they said.

From Poèmes Saturniens

I.   SOLEILS COUCHANTS

Pale dawn delicately
Over earth has spun
The sad melancholy
Of the setting sun.
Sad melancholy
Brings oblivion
In sad songs to me
With the setting sun.
And the strangest dreams,
Dreams like suns that set
On the banks of the streams,
Ghost and glory met,
To my sense it seems,
Pass, and without let,
Like great suns that set
On the banks of streams.

II. CHANSON D'AUTOMNE

When a sighing begins
In the violins
Of the autumn-song,
My heart is drowned
In the slow sound
Languorous and long.

Pale as with pain,
Breath fails me when
The hour tolls deep.
My thoughts recover
The days that are over,
And I weep.

And I go
Where the winds know,
Broken and brief,
To and fro,
As the winds blow
A dead leaf.

III. FEMME ET CHATTE

They were at play, she and her cat,
And it was marvellous to mark
The white paw and the white hand pat
Each other in the deepening dark.

The stealthy little lady hid
Under her mittens' silken sheath
Her deadly agate nails that thrid
The silk-like dagger-points of death.

The cat purred primly and drew in
Her claws that were of steel filed thin:
The devil was in it all the same.

And in the boudoir, while a shout
Of laughter in the air rang out,
Four sparks of phosphor shone like flame.

From La Bonne Chanson

I

The white moon sits
And seems to brood
Where a swift voice flits
From each branch in the wood
That the tree-tops cover. . . .

O lover, my lover!

The pool in the meadows
Like a looking-glass
Casts back the shadows
That over it pass
Of the willow-bower. . . .

Let us dream: 'tis the hour. . . .

A tender and vast
Lull of content
Like a cloud is cast
From the firmament
Where one planet is bright. . . .

'Tis the hour of delight.

II

The fireside, the lamp's little narrow light;
The dream with head on hand, and the delight
Of eyes that lose themselves in loving looks;
The hour of steaming tea and of shut books;
The solace to know evening almost gone;
The dainty weariness of waiting on
The nuptial shadow and night's softest bliss;
Ah, it is this that without respite, this
That without stay, my tender fancy seeks,
Mad with the months and furious with the
    weeks.

From Romances sans Paroles

I

'Tis the ecstasy of repose,
'Tis love when tired lids close,
'Tis the wood's long shuddering
In the embrace of the wind,
'Tis, where grey boughs are thinned,
Little voices that sing.

O fresh and frail is the sound
That twitters above, around,
Like the sweet tiny sigh
That lies in the shaken grass;
Or the sound when waters pass
And the pebbles shrink and cry.

What soul is this that complains
Over the sleeping plains,
And what is it that it saith?
Is it mine, is it thine,
This lowly hymn I divine
In the warm night, low as a breath?

II

I divine, through the veil of a murmuring,
The subtle contour of voices gone,
And I see, in the glimmering lights that sing,
The promise, pale love, of a future dawn.

And my soul and my heart in trouble
What are they but an eye that sees,
As through a mist an eye sees double,
Airs forgotten of songs like these?

O to die of no other dying,
Love, than this that computes the showers
Of old hours and of new hours flying:
O to die of the swing of the hours'

III

Tears in my heart that weeps,
Like the rain upon the town.
What drowsy languor steeps
In tears my heart that weeps?

O sweet sound of the rain
On earth and on the roofs!
For a heart's weary pain
O the song of the rain!

Vain tears, vain tears, my heart!
What, none hath done thee wrong?
Tears without reason start
From my disheartened heart.

This is the weariest woe,
O heart, of love and hate
Too weary, not to know
Why thou hast all this woe.

IV

A frail hand in the rose-grey evening
Kisses the shining keys that hardly stir,
While, with the light, small flutter of a wing,
And old song, like an old tired wanderer,
Goes very softly, as if trembling,
About the room long redolent of Her.

What lullaby is this that comes again
To dandle my poor being with its breath?
What wouldst thou have of me, gay laughing
    strain?
What hadst thou, desultory faint refrain
That now into the garden to thy death
Floatest through the half-opened window-pane?

V

O sad, sad was my soul, alas!
For a woman, a woman's sake it was.

I have had no comfort since that day,
Although my heart went its way,

Although my heart and my soul went
From the woman into banishment.

I have had no comfort since that day,
Although my heart went its way.

And my heart, being sore in me,
Said to my soul: How can this be,

How can this be or have been thus,
This proud, sad banishment of us?

My soul said to my heart: Do I
Know what snare we are tangled by,

Seeing that, banished, we know not whether
We are divided or together?

VI

Wearily the plain's
Endless length expands;
The snow shines like grains
Of the shifting sands.

Light of day is none,
Brazen is the sky;
Overhead the moon
Seems to live and die.

Where the woods are seen,
Grey the oak-trees lift
Through the vaporous screen
Like the clouds that drift.

Light of day is none,
Brazen is the sky;
Overhead the moon
Seems to live and die.

Broken-winded crow,
And you, lean wolves, when
The sharp north-winds blow,
What do you do then?

Wearily the plain's
Endless length expands;
The snow shines like grains
Of the shifting sands.

VII

There's a flight of green and red
In the hurry of hills and rails,
Through the shadowy twilight shed
By the lamps as daylight pales.

Dim gold light flushes to blood
In humble hollows far down;
Birds sing low from a wood
Of barren trees without crown.

Scarcely more to be felt
Than that autumn is gone;
Languors, lulled in me, melt
In the still air's monotone.

VIII.   SPLEEN

The roses were all red,
The ivy was all black:
Dear, if you turn your head,
All my despairs come back.

The sky was too blue, too kind,
The sea too green, and the air
Too calm: and I know in my mind
I shall wake and not find you there.

I am tired of the box-tree's shine
And the holly's, that never will pass,
And the plain's unending line,
And of all but you, alas!

IX.   STREETS

Dance the jig!

I loved best her pretty eyes
Clearer than stars in any skies,
I loved her eyes for their dear lies.

Dance the jig!

And ah! the ways, the ways she had
Of driving a poor lover mad:
It made a man's heart sad and glad.

Dance the jig!

But now I find the old kisses shed
From her flower-mouth a rarer red
Now that her heart to mine is dead.

Dance the jig!

And I recall, now I recall
Old days and hours, and ever shall,
And that is best, and best of all.

Dance the jig!

From Jadis et Naguère

I. ART POÉTIQUE

Music first and foremost of all!
Choose your measure of odd not even,
Let it melt in the air of heaven,
Pose not, poise not, but rise and fall.

Choose your words, but think not whether
Each to other of old belong:
What so dear as the dim grey song
Where clear and vague are joined together?

'Tis veils of beauty for beautiful eyes,
'Tis the trembling light of the naked noon,
'Tis a medley of blue and gold, the moon
And stars in the cool of autumn skies.

Let every shape of its shade be born;
Colour, away! come to me, shade!
Only of shade can the marriage be made
Of dream with dream and of flute with horn.

Shun the Point, lest death with it come,
Unholy laughter and cruel wit
(For the eyes of the angels weep at it)
And all the garbage of scullery-scum.

Take Eloquence, and wring the neck of him!
You had better, by force, from time to time,
Put a little sense in the head of Rhyme:
If you watch him not, you will be at the beck
    of him.

O, who shall tell us the wrongs of Rhyme?
What witless savage or what deaf boy
Has made for us this twopenny toy
Whose bells ring hollow and out of time?

Music always and music still!
Let your verse be the wandering thing
That flutters in flight from a soul on the wing
Towards other skies at a new whim's will.

Let your verse be the luck of the lure
Afloat on the winds that at morning hint
Of the odours of thyme and the savour of
    mint . . .
And all the rest is literature.

II. MEZZETIN CHANTANT

Go, and with never a care
But the care to keep happiness!
Crumple a silken dress
And snatch a song in the air.

Hear the moral of all the wise
In a world where happy folly
Is wiser than melancholy:
Forget the hour as it flies!

The one thing needful on earth, it
Is not to be whimpering.
Is life after all a thing
Real enough to be worth it?

From Sagesse

I

The little hands that once were mine,
The hands I loved, the lovely hands,
After the roadways and the strands,
And realms and kingdoms once divine,

And mortal loss of all that seems
Lost with the old sad pagan things,
Royal as in the days of kings
The dear hands open to me dreams.

Hands of dream, hands of holy flame
Upon my soul in blessing laid,
What is it that these hands have said
That my soul hears and swoons to them?

Is it a phantom, this pure sight
Of mother's love made tenderer,
Of spirit with spirit linked to share
The mutual kinship of delight?

Good sorrow, dear remorse, and ye,
Blest dreams, O hands ordained of heaven
To tell me if I am forgiven,
Make but the sign that pardons me!

II

O my God, thou hast wounded me with love,
Behold the wound, that is still vibrating,
O my God, thou hast wounded me with love.

O my God, thy fear hath fallen upon me,
Behold the burn is there, and it throbs aloud,
O my God, thy fear hath fallen upon me.

O my God, I have known that all is vile
And that thy glory hath stationed itself in me,
O my God, I have known that all is vile.

Drown my soul in floods, floods of thy wine,
Mingle my life with the body of thy bread,
Drown my soul in floods, floods of thy wine.

Take my blood, that I have not poured out,
Take my flesh, unworthy of suffering,
Take my blood, that I have not poured out.

Take my brow, that has only learned to blush,
To be the footstool of thine adorable feet,
Take my brow, that has only learned to blush.

Take my hands, because they have laboured
    not
For coals of fire and for rare frankincense,
Take my hands, because they have laboured
    not.

Take my heart, that has beaten for vain things,
To throb under the thorns of Calvary,
Take my heart that has beaten for vain things.

Take my feet, frivolous travellers,
That they may run to the crying of thy grace,
Take my feet, frivolous travellers.

Take my voice, a harsh and a lying noise,
For the reproaches of thy Penitence,
Take my voice, a harsh and a lying noise

Take mine eyes, luminaries of deceit,
That they may be extinguished in the tears of
    prayer,
Take mine eyes, luminaries of deceit.

Alas, thou, God of pardon and promises,
What is the pit of mine ingratitude,
Alas, thou, God of pardon and promises.

God of terror and God of holiness,
Alas, my sinfulness is a black abyss,
God of terror and God of holiness.

Thou, God of peace, of joy and delight,
All my tears, all my ignorances,
Thou, God of peace, of joy and delight.

Thou, O God, knowest all this, all this,
How poor I am, poorer than any man,
Thou, O God, knowest all this, all this.

And what I have, my God, I give to thee.

III

Slumber dark and deep
Falls across my life;
I will put to sleep
Hope, desire, and strife.

All things pass away,
Good and evil seem
To my soul to-day
Nothing but a dream;

I a cradle laid
In a hollow cave,
By a great hand swayed:
Silence, like the grave.

IV

The body's sadness and the languor thereof
Melt and bow me with pity till I could weep,
Ah! when the dark hours break it down in sleep
And the bedclothes score the skin and the hot
    hands move;
Alert for a little with the fever of day,
Damp still with the heavy sweat of the night
    that has thinned,
Like a bird that trembles on a roof in the wind:
And the feet that are sorrowful because of the
    way,

And the breast that a hand has scarred with a
    double blow,
And the mouth that as an open wound is red,
And the flesh that shivers and is a painted
    show,
And the eyes, poor eyes so lovely with tears
    unshed
For the sorrow of seeing this also over and done:
Sad body, how weak and how punished under
    the sun!

V

Fairer is the sea
Than the minster high,
Faithful nurse is she,
And last lullaby,
And the Virgin prays
Over the sea's ways.

Gifts of grief and guerdons
From her bounty come,
And I hear her pardons
Chide her angers home;
Nothing in her is
Unforgivingness.

She is piteous,
She the perilous!
Friendly things to us
The wave sings to us:
You whose hope is past,
Here is peace at last.

And beneath the skies,
Brighter-hued than they,
She has azure dyes,
Rose and green and grey.
Better is the sea
Than all fair things or we.

From Parallèlement:

IMPRESSION FAUSSE

Little lady mouse,
Black upon the grey of light;
Little lady mouse,
Grey upon the night.

Now they ring the bell,
All good prisoners slumber deep;
Now they ring the bell,
Nothing now but sleep.

Only pleasant dreams,
Love's enough for thinking of;
Only pleasant dreams,
Long live love!

Moonlight over all,
Someone snoring heavily;
Moonlight over all
In reality.

Now there comes a cloud,
It is dark as midnight here;
Now there comes a cloud,
Dawn begins to peer.

Little lady mouse,
Rosy in a ray of blue,
Little lady mouse:
Up now, all of you!

From Chansons pour Elle

You believe that there may be
Luck in strangers in the tea:
I believe only in your eyes.

You believe in fairy-tales,
Days one wins and days one fails:
I believe only in your lies.

You believe in heavenly powers,
In some saint to whom one prays
Or in some Ave that one says.

I believe only in the hours,
Coloured with the rosy lights
You rain for me on sleepless nights.

And so firmly I receive
These for truth, that I believe
That only for your sake I live.

From Epigrammes

When we go together, if I may see her again,
Into the dark wood and the rain;

When we are drunken with air and the sun's
    delight
At the brink of the river of light;

When we are homeless at last, for a moment's
    space
Without city or abiding-place;

And if the slow good-will of the world still seem
To cradle us in a dream;

Then, let us sleep the last sleep with no leave-
    taking,
And God will see to the waking.

Redwood Library

SELECTIONS FROM THE RULES

1. Three volumes may be taken at a time and only three on one share. Two unbound numbers of a monthly and three numbers of a weekly publication are counted as a volume.

2. Books other than 7-day and 14-day ones may be kept out 28 days. **Books cannot be renewed or transferred.**

3. Books overdue are subject to a fine of one cent a day for fourteen days, **and five cents a day for each day thereafter.**

4. Neglect to pay the fine will debar from the use of the Library.

5. No book is to be lent out of the house of the person to whom it is charged.

6. Any person who shall soil (deface) or damage or lose a book belonging to the Library shall be liable to such fine as the Directors may impose; or shall pay the value of the book or of the set, if it be a part of a set, as the Directors may elect. All scribbling or any marking or writing whatever, folding or turning down the leaves, as well as cutting or tearing any matter from a book belonging to the Library, will be considered defacement and damage.